I0028820

ENTERPRISE TRANSFORMATION TO ARTIFICIAL INTELLIGENCE AND THE METAVERSE

LICENSE, DISCLAIMER OF LIABILITY, AND LIMITED WARRANTY

By purchasing or using this book and its companion files (the "Work"), you agree that this license grants permission to use the contents contained herein, but does not give you the right of ownership to any of the textual content in the book or ownership to any of the information, files, or products contained in it. *This license does not permit uploading of the Work onto the Internet or on a network (of any kind) without the written consent of the Publisher.* Duplication or dissemination of any text, code, simulations, images, etc. contained herein is limited to and subject to licensing terms for the respective products, and permission must be obtained from the Publisher or the owner of the content, etc., in order to reproduce or network any portion of the textual material (in any media) that is contained in the Work.

MERCURY LEARNING AND INFORMATION ("MLI" or "the Publisher") and anyone involved in the creation, writing, production, accompanying algorithms, code, or computer programs ("the software"), and any accompanying Web site or software of the Work, cannot and do not warrant the performance or results that might be obtained by using the contents of the Work. The author, developers, and the Publisher have used their best efforts to ensure the accuracy and functionality of the textual material and/or programs contained in this package; we, however, make no warranty of any kind, express or implied, regarding the performance of these contents or programs. The Work is sold "as is" without warranty (except for defective materials used in manufacturing the book or due to faulty workmanship).

The author, developers, and the publisher of any accompanying content, and anyone involved in the composition, production, and manufacturing of this work will not be liable for damages of any kind arising out of the use of (or the inability to use) the algorithms, source code, computer programs, or textual material contained in this publication. This includes, but is not limited to, loss of revenue or profit, or other incidental, physical, or consequential damages arising out of the use of this Work.

The sole remedy in the event of a claim of any kind is expressly limited to replacement of the book and only at the discretion of the Publisher. The use of "implied warranty" and certain "exclusions" vary from state to state, and might not apply to the purchaser of this product.

ENTERPRISE TRANSFORMATION TO ARTIFICIAL INTELLIGENCE AND THE METAVERSE

Strategies for the Technology Revolution

William Kimmerly

MERCURY LEARNING AND INFORMATION

Boston, Massachusetts

Copyright ©2024 by MERCURY LEARNING AND INFORMATION. An Imprint of DeGruyter, Inc. All rights reserved.

This publication, portions of it, or any accompanying software may not be reproduced in any way, stored in a retrieval system of any type, or transmitted by any means, media, electronic display or mechanical display, including, but not limited to, photocopy, recording, Internet postings, or scanning, without prior permission in writing from the publisher.

Publisher: David Pallai
MERCURY LEARNING AND INFORMATION
121 High Street, 3rd Floor
Boston, MA 02110
info@merclearning.com
www.merclearning.com
800-232-0223

W.Kimmerly. *Enterprise Transformation to Artificial Intelligence and the Metaverse.*
ISBN 978-1-50152-190-4

The publisher recognizes and respects all marks used by companies, manufacturers, and developers as a means to distinguish their products. All brand names and product names mentioned in this book are trademarks or service marks of their respective companies. Any omission or misuse (of any kind) of service marks or trademarks, etc. is not an attempt to infringe on the property of others.

Library of Congress Control Number: 2023944139

232425321   Printed on acid-free paper in the United States of America.

Our titles are available for adoption, license, or bulk purchase by institutions, corporations, etc. For additional information, please contact the Customer Service Dept. at 800-232-0223(toll free).

All of our titles are available for sale in digital format at *academiccourseware.com* and other digital vendors. The sole obligation of MERCURY LEARNING AND INFORMATION to the purchaser is to replace the book, based on defective materials or faulty workmanship, but not based on the operation or functionality of the product.

To Susan,
My love, my world, my inspiration

Contents

Preface

This book provides guidance on how organizations can respond effectively to a rapidly converging collection of advanced technologies, methods, and models often referred to as "the metaverse." The arrival of the metaverse will likely lead to one of the most disruptive eras in modern history. We will see our personal, social, professional, and business lives change just as dramatically as we experienced with the arrival of the Internet, smart phone, and personal computer.

Metaverse technologies are emerging much more rapidly than most of us expected. Organizations around the world are being caught by surprise and are not sure how to react. We can see this clearly when we look at just one component of the metaverse, artificial intelligence (AI). The explosive emergence in 2022 of generative AI capabilities, like ChatGPT, provides a stark preview of what lies ahead for organizations. AI could, within a decade, transform most processes used within companies, as well as the products and services they provide. Most workers, from executive management to the learned professional ranks, to the shop floor, will be affected.

There's more. Quantum computing is another rapidly emerging metaverse technology that could be just as disruptive as AI, if not more so. The combination of AI and quantum computing is awesome to contemplate and will have to be seen to be believed.

The challenge for all organizations is becoming clear: Adapt or perish. Inaction is not a viable option.

History has shown that some of the most challenging periods faced by organizational leaders have arisen during the hectic and confusing intervals between the maturing and stabilizing of one technological era and the emergence of the next. Many organizations are slow to react to these new disruptions. They struggle to find solid footing in the changing competitive landscapes caused by these disruptions. Some don't survive the transition. This historical pattern is likely to be repeated as the metaverse era evolves.

However, history has also shown that a few leaders are able to detect early on the general nature of such a disruption, and they develop a quick appreciation for the potential opportunities. This allows them to move swiftly and boldly to embrace the disruption and profit from it. (Consider, for example, Jeff Bezos's response to the Internet's disruption.) These kinds of leaders realize the major shifts taking place in the technological landscape are making their current business models, which were designed for the prior era, outdated. So they adjust.

The critical challenge for today's leaders, therefore, is how to lead their organizations through a timely and successful transformation to the metaverse so they can benefit from and not be sidelined by this latest technology revolution. They should be asking questions such as, "What enterprise qualities or attributes do we need to develop to survive and prosper in this new era? How quickly do we need to act? What are the most important initial actions?"

Among the critical attributes required for organizational success in the metaverse are enhanced agility, adaptability, and speed; a more streamlined, flatter, and networked structure and business model; and deep expertise in metaverse technologies and methods. To transition effectively into the metaverse and develop these attributes, there are three specific areas that should be addressed early on. These actions, which are discussed in detail in this book, should be taken before any large-scale attempt is made to incorporate specific metaverse-era technologies and methods into existing business models and technology strategies. All three actions are interdependent and must be addressed collectively and simultaneously. These actions include the following:

- *Ensure the organization has a cohesive, technology-savvy, open-minded, and nimble enterprise governance structure in place.* This includes the board of directors and the organization's executive-level structure. Complex challenges, as well as compelling new opportunities, will soon be coming at these leaders in rapid succession. They need to be able to sense the opportunities and threats, and perform as a well-prepared, fast-acting, and unified team.

- *Ensure that the organization has an updated approach to developing and using one of the most important tools for effective enterprise governance and strategic planning, a new-era "enterprise architecture" (EA).* A new-era EA is one built on advanced metaverse technologies, such as AI and machine learning. This makes the EA more user friendly (more conversational), more relevant to more employees, and more easily managed and updated. Without access to such a comprehensive and robust central information repository and decision support tool, the complexity of the transformation challenge and the speed of change will likely overwhelm any transformation effort. For many organizations, the development of such an EA will be an overlooked focus area. They will ultimately have to pay the price.

- *In parallel with other transformation actions, ensure that the organization has begun the transformation of the central IT services organization into a structure better suited to a highly agile, networked organizational model.* In the metaverse era, central IT will require a new structure, new skills, and a new way of providing services. Therefore, it should begin its transformation in concert with overall enterprise transformation.

In addition to discussing these three action areas in detail, this book also discusses some of the most important metaverse technologies, concepts, and methods organizational leaders need to understand as they begin to map out their metaverse transformation plans. These discussions are followed by detailed chapters on the main elements of an effective enterprise transformation initiative, concluding with a detailed hypothetical case study that describes how such a transformation can be accomplished.

In summary, helping executives and other professionals chart an effective course to the metaverse is the central purpose of this book. The guidance provided by this book reflects over 45 years of professional and senior executive experience by the author in areas such as enterprise architectures, enterprise strategic plans, information technology roadmaps, enterprise transformations, technology gatekeeping, technology adoption and assimilation, and systems analysis and development.

ACKNOWLEDGMENTS

I want to thank Kat Regala for discovering me and for providing invaluable editing support. I also want to thank my editor, Jim Walsh, for encouraging me to write this book and for being so accommodating throughout the process.

W. Kimmerly
October 2023

PART 1

BOOK OVERVIEW AND KEY CONCEPTS

CHAPTER 1

INTRODUCTION

1.1   THE METAVERSE IS CLOSER THAN WE MIGHT THINK

In late 2022 and early 2023, the release of the AI-based generative bot, ChatGPT, became an instant international phenomenon. It was followed quickly by the release of many similar products by companies such as Meta and Salesforce. Early users were amazed by what this technology was able to do. To many, it seemed almost human in its capabilities, and in some respects, such as speed and breadth of information, it was vastly superior to humans. The range of applications to which this technology was applied was extensive, touching all major industries within a short period of time.

But as impressive as these bots were (and are), flaws in the initial models soon became apparent. For example, sometimes they would cite references, such as legal precedents, that they had simply made up. These lapses were called "hallucinations."

The awesome power of this technology soon began to concern many, including government officials, influential industry observers, sociologists, and technology experts. For example, there was concern over the possibility that artificial intelligence (AI) could transform entire industries, maybe even economies, and cause millions of people to lose their jobs, all before anyone was even remotely prepared for these kinds of consequences.

There was also concern about the use of AI for dangerous and nefarious purposes, such as fake podcasts, videos, and new stories presenting famous people in compromising, humiliating, or damaging situations. Even though these fake uses were contrived and completely false, many observers considered them to be absolutely real. Could this technology make it almost impossible to separate fact from fiction in the future, and if so, what could be the consequences?

These concerns led many governments and renowned business and technology luminaries to call for a moratorium of six months to a year on the development and use of AI technology. This time was needed, they said, for the tech industry to get a better handle on the technology and establish safeguards to prevent its misuse.

However, even in light of all of these issues, ChatGPT remained one of the most important tech stories of 2023 and an endless source of fascination for millions, including thousands of organizations that have already put this technology to productive use. As has been true for many other tech innovations, the expectation is that this technology will continue to improve over time, adding new capabilities and resolving early issues and limitations.

AI is not new, of course. The concept of AI has been researched and discussed for decades. In fact, the basic technology was already in use in applications for years (Siri, for example) before ChatGPT appeared. Until then, most of us had underestimated how developed technologies such as AI and machine learning were, how rapidly they were evolving, and how deeply disruptive they would be.

More to Come

As important as it is, AI is only one component of a much larger collection of rapidly converging technologies that many are calling the *metaverse* (see Figure 1.1). Just as people were surprised by ChatGPT, organizations run a high risk of being blindsided by the speed and impact of the collection of metaverse technologies now bearing down on them. Unfortunately, organizations will not be able to demand a twelve-month "metaverse moratorium" to allow them to study the metaverse and get better prepared for such a major disruption. Therefore, the time to prepare for the metaverse is now. The purpose of this book is to provide guidance on how this can be done.

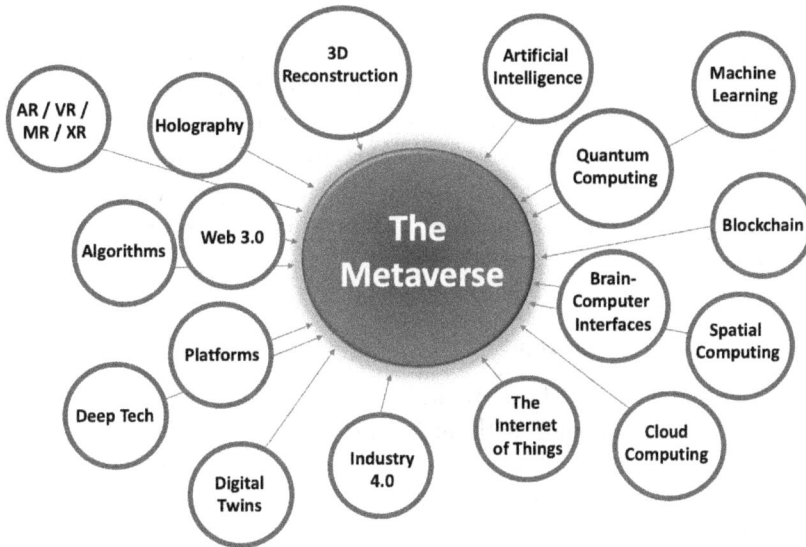

FIGURE 1.1 Converging technologies are driving the metaverse.

1.2 THE METAVERSE: AN OVERVIEW

Research by leading industry analysis firms has revealed a growing global business interest in the metaverse and the expectation that by the middle of the 2020s metaverse technologies will have significant influence of the daily lives of people around the world. [Accenture23]

No Consensus Definition

There is no widely accepted or sanctioned definition of the term "metaverse," although there are numerous suggested definitions and descriptions. A typical description goes something like this: The metaverse is a converging collection of technological innovations that are providing highly immersive 3D experiences and blockchain-based solutions to users via a next generation Internet. For the purposes of this book, the term *metaverse* is meant to convey a broader reality. For example, many have suggested the metaverse is already establishing the basis for Industrial Revolution 4.0. If that is true, and to some extent it probably is, the metaverse is not only about immersive technologies. The concept also includes the business and societal advances these technologies are enabling, such as new business models, new technology-based solutions, new forms of social interactions, a new era of scientific breakthroughs, new industries, and even new economies, much like the Internet economy that was formed with the advent of the Internet. These sweeping changes *in their totality* is the real reason almost all organizations should be planning now to transform to the metaverse.

Two Important Attributes

Much of the focus of the metaverse centers on the central theme of replacing today's "flat" Internet, with its 2D text, video, and other images, with one that is 3D in nature, highly decentralized, and deeply immersive. This new version of the Internet is often referred to as *Web 3.0*. Experts are confident Web 3.0 will be as disruptive when it arrives as were the emergence of Web 1.0 and Web 2.0.

Another essential feature of the metaverse will be the further blending of our digital and physical worlds. This means we will see users interacting increasingly with technology from inside an application rather than from the outside looking in. As a result, the technologies and methods that comprise the metaverse will transform, in fundamental ways, how we experience and interact with our environments, both business and personal. Many of the constraints now imposed by physical locations will be lifted as 3D reconstructions of objects, including humans, can be located or co-located with other physical objects almost anywhere. It follows that these changes will have a significant impact on the way companies design and conduct their business operations.

Current Status of the Metaverse

Just as there is no generally accepted definition of the metaverse, there are a variety of perspectives concerning when the era began, where it is presently positioned on its evolutionary path, and how long it will remain relevant before being displaced by the next technology wave.

One of the more widely-cited timelines of metaverse evolution is offered by Gartner Inc., which hypothesizes a three-phase evolutionary path. (See, for example, the May 11, 2022 article by Shawn Johnson titled *How the Metaverse Will Evolve,* which breaks down the Gartner timeline. [Johnson22]) As the metaverse evolves through these various phases, consistent with the historical seven to eight-year life cycles of other major technological innovations, the next technological era (perhaps "The Quantumverse"), will most likely have begun.

Overall, the general consensus is the metaverse era is well underway in certain critical areas, like AI, machine learning, and augmented reality, and will probably establish its position in industry as a bona fide new era by 2026. It could maintain that position for a decade or more, which is a relatively long period for any dominant technology era to prevail. If the metaverse era has already begun, organizations need to pay close attention to it now. Many organizations are already playing catch up.

The converging technologies that are defining the metaverse, as well as current-era technologies, such as AI, the cloud, mobile, and the Internet of Things, are already being assembled into platforms having the power, speed, and intelligence to solve problems that were previously considered too difficult to tackle. Technological innovations like quantum computing and AI enable tests and experiments to be conducted in a fraction of the time required using older technologies and methods. This can shorten some research projects by years. In addition, these newer technologies and algorithms are able to process vast quantities of structured and unstructured data quickly, leading to more lifelike and realistic experiments.

The scope of metaverse applications already in production use is impressive. A few categories include oil and gas exploration and extraction, healthcare, medical training, games, working environments, tourism, real estate, education, fashion, shopping, and social networks/entertainment. In addition, as the convergence process continues, especially as quantum computing continues to mature, organizations will be able to take on some of the grand challenges of our time in such areas as medicine, climate change, rising sea levels, energy, fresh water scarcity, and agriculture.

Therefore, even without an accepted, formal definition of the metaverse, we can already see its major contours. We can foresee an era wherein converging technologies, such as AI, machine learning, virtual reality, augmented reality, edge computing, and quantum computing are being used to better integrate our physical and digital (or quantum) worlds. We can see this, for example, in 3-D virtual and augmented reality environments. These environments can be used for entertainment, business, engineering, and scientific purposes. In this new environment, we will soon be able to conduct business, visit remote locations, and access educational opportunities in environments mediated by technological advances in new and immersive ways.

Not Without Its Challenges

As is true for all new technological eras, some negatives always accompany the positives. For example, as each major new era begins to exert its influence, jobs can be eliminated, businesses and even entire industries can become obsolete, people can experience psychological problems, new forms of crime often emerge, and societal behaviors change. The metaverse is not likely to avoid these kinds of issues. Already, even before the metaverse and all of its vivid and immersive reality fully arrives, there are large numbers of people addicted to computer games, cell phones, and social media, sometimes to the detriment of their physical and mental health. Much has been written about the correlation, even causation, between social media and rising mental health problems among teenagers. Some people lose the need for any real social interactions at all because real ones no longer seem as interesting, exciting, or rewarding as the virtual ones. We can only imagine the potential risks segments of society will face as these virtual experiences become even richer and more vibrant and lifelike.

We can also envision the metaverse increasing the digital divide that already exists. No one has a clear picture of the costs that might be entailed in gearing up to take advantage of the capabilities offered by the metaverse. Even with the steadily improving price-performance curve for digital technology, the cost to participate in the metaverse might prove prohibitively expensive for many in society, which would in turn raise serious ethical and fairness concerns for some governments. For example, what if certain segments of society are able to obtain far superior healthcare and live longer lives through the use of advanced metaverse technologies, while other segments cannot afford the use of these methods? This same condition might be an issue for education as well. Numerous serious public policy issues could arise, and probably will, in a variety of areas.

As is true with all technological advances, thieves, hackers, and other lawbreakers will very quickly find ways to leverage these advances for their own purposes. There are likely going to be unpredictable holes in the technology where personal privacy can be breached. We have to be mindful of the degree to which the daily life of individuals might become available to overzealous organizations (marketeers, solicitors, pollsters, and retailers) in the metaverse.

This goes far beyond the simple shopping profiles and cookie-tracking issues of today, and might easily get into the more esoteric areas of illicitly capturing brain waves, body movements, and eye movements in response to, for example, viewing certain online ads.

History of Changing User Relationships to Technology: From Remote to Immersive

As noted earlier, one of the more important aspects of the metaverse phenomenon relates to how users have interacted with technology during different eras over the past several decades and how they will interact with it in the future.

For example, as shown in Figure 1.2, we can begin by going back to the early days of computing technology, say the 1950s through the 1960s. This was an era when mainframes were the primary types of computers available, aside from mechanical tabulating machines. In those days, the direct beneficiaries (or "users") of the computing power of mainframes were completely remote, both physically and conceptually, from the actual computing action. All of the computing process steps and related people and equipment were typically housed away from the general public.

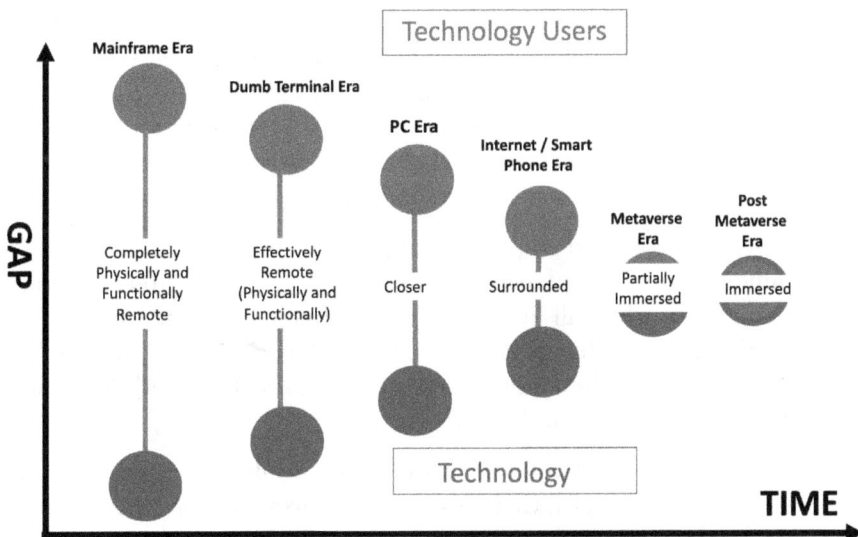

FIGURE 1.2 The gap between users and technology continues to narrow.

Figure 1.2 shows that, after a transitional period of rudimentary networking of "dumb" terminals in the 1970s, the 1980s brought us the personal computer (PC) revolution. At that time, users were beginning to have more direct interactions with computing technology. PCs were typically placed on users' desks or on tables at work or at home. There was associated with this form of technology an immediate, tactile connection between the user and the technology via a mouse, keyboard, or by touching the PC's screen. Not long afterwards, laptops and tablets arrived, so users could carry the computing technology wherever they went.

Even with the increased availability and usage of PCs and laptops, users were still conceptually distant from technology. Basically, the doors to the mainframe rooms had been opened partially, and users had more direct access to, and control over, computing assets. However, there was still a functional distance to be closed. Users were not yet *immersed* in technology. That was about to change.

Technological advances in the 1990s and early 2000s, most notably the Internet, smartphones, and social media, changed major industries, most businesses, and the daily lives of billions of people. The combination of these technological advances began the process of surrounding people with technology, often on a 24x7 basis, both in their work lives and their social lives. Today, countless people live good portions of their daily lives encapsulated by Facebook, Twitter (recently rebranded as "X"), texts, email, and other social media, including being attached to their smartphones as if they have become bodily appendages. A substantial portion of consumer commerce has been increasingly carried out over the Internet, via Amazon for example. To live in the industrialized world in the early 21st century was to be surrounded by, and to some degree immersed in, technology.

Now, another disruptive change is coming, one that will be even more immersive for users of technology. This includes both direct users and indirect users (those who will be affected by technology, despite no direct action on their part). That change is, of course, what is now being called the metaverse. In this new era, the kinds of connections users have with technology will be even more personal and immersive.

For example, assume you have always wanted to visit the Louvre in Paris, but could never make that happen. Of course, you can visit the museum in a 2D way via books and images on a computer screen. However, that is a limited experience. In the metaverse, the expectation is that the Louvre experience can be *brought to you* in 3D imagery so vivid it is almost like being there. You will be able to walk around and explore the exhibits just like any other visitor. You will have left your physical world and entered a virtual world. You will have become fully immersed in this technology-based environment and yet be completely oblivious to the technology. In this example, all you will see is the museum and its contents. You will also be able to hear realistic background sounds, just as if you are actually there. You can easily imagine how this one metaverse solution model could affect industries such as travel, hospitality, museums, electronics, and real estate.

Medical training serves as another metaverse immersion example. Medical students typically obtain 2D information from books, computer screens, class-room presentation images on larger screens, and even chalkboards and white boards. However, to fully understand how the body functions, medical students have traditionally been assigned cadavers to work on. While cadavers do provide an immersive experience for medical students, this practice is expensive and cumbersome for hospitals and medical schools. In the future, cadavers will most likely take the form of 3D reconstructions of real human bodies that can be used over and over endlessly without suffering any damage. For medical students, this will be an engaging experience, not only because the 3D reconstruction provides vivid imagery but because it also allows students to experience, or "feel," physical sensations through advanced haptic technology. As students become fully immersed in working on these digital reconstructions, there will be no real sense of working with technology at all, but one of working with a real body. In a true sense, their physical and digital worlds will have been blended. Several universities and some major hospitals are already doing work in this area.

Staying within the medical realm for another example, consider what it might be like to have a 3D reconstructed avatar or hologram of your own body. Then consider having that avatar populated with your own medical data, vital readings, and medications. Working closely with your physician, either in a medical facility or from home, you would be able to diagnose problems, in an AI-aided way, and observe the effects of various treatment options. There are already countless professionally-refereed medical and scientific papers on the general topic of 3D reconstruction applications in medicine, such as *Detailed 3D human body reconstruction from multi-view images combining voxel super-resolution and learned implicit representation* [Li et al.22].

1.3 THE POWER OF TECHNOLOGICAL CONVERGENCE AND SYNTHESIS

When the major technologies in widespread use today (e.g., the Internet, mobile, and cloud computing) first emerged, they soon converged with each other and with older technologies in highly synergistic ways. As this happened, we were able to see the pace of change quickening, with the intervals between "a new normal" becoming shorter. This pattern is expected to continue as we move into the metaverse. This means many organizations, especially those that are less nimble and resilient, could soon find themselves attempting to compete in an environment for which their existing business models were not designed.

The powerful impact of the technology convergence process cannot be overstated. Consider the game-changing innovations that have already emerged from the technological convergence phenomenon. For example, the smartphone was basically the result of converging into one platform other well-established technologies at the time, such as software algorithms, a mobile phone, an MP3 player, a camera, and an Internet connection capability. The resulting converged product changed the way most of the world communicated, took photographs, accessed the Internet, and listened to music. It also provided a new opportunity for entrepreneurs around the world. Some have used the smartphone to start new businesses or upgrade and extend or enhance their existing lines of business. New livelihoods were created for countless app developers. There is a strong likelihood the converging technological innovations driving the metaverse will have similar impacts on the world.

1.4 AN IMPORTANT NEW PHASE OF THE DIGITAL AGE

Many of the highly disruptive technological innovations we take for granted today were once poorly understood and often dismissed initially as passing fads. These groundbreaking innovations have evolved over the last several decades through a series of fairly distinct eras or phases (e.g., "the PC era"). As each new phase emerged, a corresponding "zone of disruption" also emerged. These disruptive zones overlapped the intersections between older, more established technology eras and the new phases (see Figure 1.3).

1950s – 60s	1970s – 80s	1980s – 90s	1990s – 2024	2024 - 2034
Mainframes / Dumb Terminals	Minicomputers / Ethernet / Client-Server	Personal Computers / Internet /	Cloud / Smart Phones / Social Media	The Metaverse / Quantum Computing

Information Technology Zones of Disruption

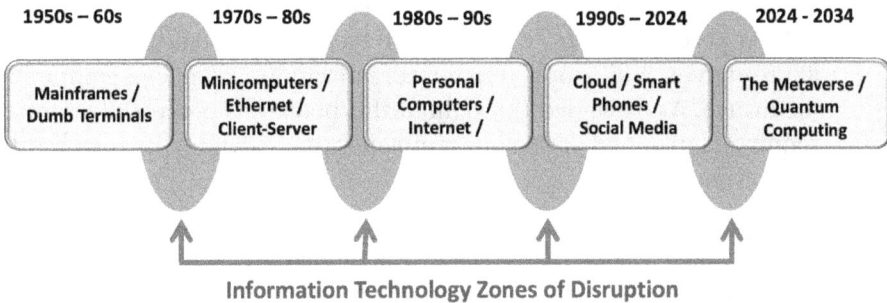

FIGURE 1.3 Major technological eras create zones of disruption.

During these periods of disruption, the leaders of organizations face numerous important questions, most of which at the time have no clear-cut answers. Examples include the following:

· Is this new technology real or just another buzzword?
· Will it affect us, and if so, how?
· How do we bridge the gap between what we already have in place and these new products and technologies?
· How fast should we move, if at all, and in which directions?
· Who can we trust to advise us?
· How will this affect our employees? What are the training implications? Do we need to hire new people with new skills? How many? Which skills? When?

As we examine the timeline in Figure 1.3, we can see how most organizations have been operating in what has been called the "digital age" for at least four decades (dating back to the 1980s, when the term first gained popularity). In fact, many organizations today say, often with justifiable pride, they have achieved "digital maturity." In other words, they have caught up with the latest digital technology advances and have mastered their use. However, the digital age is an ever-evolving and steadily accelerating phenomenon. Therefore, digital maturity achieved in the past, even the recent past, might mean little going forward, especially as we enter the latest zone of disruption, the metaverse.

As organizations work their way through this next disruptive phase of technological evolution, most will find the nature, scope, and velocity of the changes they encounter will disrupt their current business models. We are already seeing that in the sudden emergence of the AI component of the metaverse. This means the leaders of most organizations will require changes in their perceptions about how best to blend technologies (old and new), capital resources, and people into new organizations capable of competing in the metaverse. As explained throughout this book, this process of adaptation will require a much higher level of nimbleness and adaptability than most organizations now possess.

For example, as this newest wave of converging technologies is adopted by organizations, many work functions now performed by humans will become either substantially or fully automated. For many organizations, this will mean displacing human workers. This process will work its way gradually up the organizational structure from mundane functions and tasks to increasingly sophisticated job roles, affecting the realm of professionals and white collar workers. Enterprise governance must understand how these advances will be viewed in different ways depending on the organizational level of the viewer. Executive managers could be enthusiastic about taking advantage of them, while front-line workers could understandably be much more concerned and apprehensive.

Companies will not be deploying metaverse technologies simply to save money. They will apply technologies, such as AI, to design and operate businesses in fundamentally new, nimbler, and adaptive ways. From a business strategy perspective, the more functions that can be automated, either partially or completely, the easier it will be to link organizational functions into truly wired organizations that possess the nimbleness, speed, responsiveness, and autonomous operational capabilities necessary to compete in the metaverse and beyond.

Therefore, the timing and scope of the approaching metaverse zone of disruption elevates the enterprise digital transformation challenge to a new level of urgency. Individuals and organizations that want to become productive participants in this new era need to be preparing now.

SIDE NOTE: *The terms "digital" and "digital technology" are used throughout this book, although it is possible, maybe even likely, that the "digital era" will end sometime during the next decade. Why? A classical digital computer calculates via transistors, which can represent either a zero or a one, and only a zero or a one. This is the "binary digit" that gave rise to the term "digital." However, an immensely faster and more powerful quantum computer calculates with qubits ("quantum bits"), which can represent a zero or a one or both a zero and a one or anything in between. In addition, quantum computers can execute multiple* *commands in parallel, whereas digital computers process instructions in sequence, one at a time, making quantum computers vastly more powerful. We do not know what identifying term will arise after the digital era ends and some new calculating technology, whether quantum or something else, will become the public face of the next revolution. For now, the term "digital" is used in this book.*

1.5 ENTERPRISE TRANSFORMATIONS IN THE METAVERSE ERA

The path forward for organizations seeking to transform to a metaverse state of readiness consists of two major phases which must, for the most part, be performed in sequence.

Phase 1 entails all of the actions necessary to elevate an organization's nimbleness, responsiveness, quickness, and capacity for innovation. These capabilities must be raised to levels compatible with the velocity of change and the kinds of competitive forces we are likely to see in the decade of the 2020s, such as we saw in the sudden AI phenomenon. A substantial portion of this book is focused on how to achieve these agility goals.

Phase 2 involves the disciplined selection and adoption of specific metaverse technologies and methods based on the unique business needs of the enterprise. Some organizations will have to move faster than others in this regard. In general, this phase consists of the logical steps of (1) assessing carefully where any of the various metaverse technologies might be of strategic or tactical business use in the organization, and (2) conducting pilot projects, performing benchmarks, and taking other simple initial actions to ease prudently into metaverse technology assimilation.

Therefore, as the metaverse era continues to emerge, organizations that want to embrace its possibilities must take a fresh look at their strategic and operational decision-making processes and business models as the first order of business. The three most critical, high-leverage places to start are

- the organization's existing enterprise governance structure and methods, including its corresponding business model and organizational structure. If the leadership of an enterprise is not highly nimble, fast, and innovative, the organization as a whole cannot sustain these attributes.

- the current state of an organization's enterprise architecture planning framework (if it has one). This is the central planning and orchestrating heart of an enterprise where AI and other advanced technologies are applied in ways that allow the organization to function in fast, nimble, and accurate ways.
- the organization's current central information technology (IT) services model. This critical function must be redesigned and repopulated with the skills critical to maintaining a metaverse-capable enterprise.

Addressing these three areas effectively is basically the price of competing in the metaverse. These steps will not in themselves get an organization there, but they will give it a chance to get there. Each step is discussed in detail in this book.

What will need to change through an enterprise transformation process for a traditional organization to become better prepared to compete in the metaverse? Table 1.1 summarizes some of the most important changes.

TABLE 1.1 Key change factors for metaverse readiness

Change Factor	Traditional Company	Metaverse-Capable Company
Operating Philosophy	Excel ethically in delivering exceptional products and services in today's digital era using today's digital technologies	Excel ethically in delivering exceptional products and services in the metaverse era using newer metaverse technologies and methods
Governance	Governed from the top by the senior executive suite	Empowered governance with delegated decision authority
Structure	Predominantly a vertical, hierarchical structure with a large middle layer	Predominately a networked structure with a smaller middle
Business Model	Designed for success in today's markets and related competitive dynamics	Designed for success in metaverse markets and related competitive dynamics
Offerings	Based on current technologies and consumer attributes and preferences	Based on metaverse technologies and expected changes in consumer attributes and preferences

(*Continued*)

TABLE 1.1 (*Continued*)

Change Factor	Traditional Company	Metaverse-Capable Company
Skill Sets	Traditional focus, with a more specialized skill set per employee	Metaverse focus, with a more diversified set of skills per employee (a more adaptable workforce)
Culture	"Change is our enemy."	"Change is our friend."
Alliances	Limited and traditional	Extensive and innovative
IT Services	Centralized and staffed with current digital technology skills	Networked, distributed, and staffed with metaverse skills
Enterprise Architecture	Limited and plays ancillary role	Robust and plays vital central role

Enterprise Digital Transformations Have a Poor Record of Success

Over the past decade, most senior executives have understood the need for their organizations to embrace digital technologies in ways that increased their nimbleness, overall performance, and innovative capacity. Formalized responses to this challenge have often been referred to as "digital transformation" initiatives, with the goal being a state often described as "digital maturity." However, research by leading management consulting firms has found that only a small percentage of these efforts ever prove to be successful. [Robinson19].

These persistent transformation failures have left countless organizations stranded between suddenly unsustainable business models of the past and the more innovative and nimble models needed going forward. There are many reasons for this lack of digital transformation success, in addition to the inherent difficulties faced in any significant organizational change effort. These reasons include the following:

- The absence of sustained executive level interest, participation, consensus, and leadership in digital transformation efforts
- Viewing a digital transformation as a project that can simply be layered onto an existing enterprise (where it must compete for resources and priorities), rather than a commitment to infusing true transformational changes and nimbleness granularly throughout the enterprise

- Insufficient staff expertise in key emerging digital technology areas, such as – relative to the metaverse disruption, for example – AI, augmented reality, machine learning, quantum computing, edge computing, and blockchain
- Stubborn resistance to change embedded deeply in most organizational cultures
- Failure of enterprise governance to delegate important decisions and actions to lower-level executives, thereby slowing transformation progress and giving oxygen to negative forces seeking to stall the effort
- Continued executive focus on short-term cost savings rather than longer-term strategic gains
- Negative commentary from a few influential resident gurus whose expertise and prestige are grounded in the current technological era, not the emerging one (akin to the "not invented here" syndrome)
- Lack of a well-articulated, enterprise-wide representation of the expected real-world benefits of the envisioned new business model (i.e., failing to communicate effectively and systematically how the projected changes will clearly make things better for specific stakeholders in specific situations)

For organizations seeking to transition effectively into the metaverse, these issues must be overcome in a timely way. Modest and slow incremental changes at the margins of an enterprise, a common approach to so many current digital transformation efforts, will not suffice. Events are moving too quickly and are too profound for leisurely and narrowly focused transformation actions. To meet the challenges inherent in this new disruption, a level of commitment to transformation not commonly seen among today's organizations will be required.

The kinds of changes companies will be required to make in a metaverse transformation could alter the core foundation of the enterprise, perhaps requiring a reset in its governing philosophy and operational strategy. This is because all companies today are to a substantial degree software companies. [Gnanasambandam et al.22]. That is, they are built on and driven by a structured collection of algorithms and supporting technologies. For most organizations these software systems are based on today's digital technologies. However, the trend is moving steadily toward the use of metaverse-era technologies. Innovative technologies and new capabilities will require new ways of thinking about software-intensive organizational models and revised approaches to software development and use.

Timing is Vital

The question of whether such phenomena as AI, quantum computing, virtual reality, and augmented reality will disrupt conventional business models is not a matter of "if" but "when." As slower organizations continue to struggle with their existing, traditional digital transformation efforts, new digital and quantum innovations continue to advance and converge all around them in powerfully synergistic ways. This means many companies are actually losing ground despite having, at least nominally, digital transformation efforts underway. In other words, too many organizations are still busy fighting the last war (e.g., still wrestling with cloud adoption strategies, while paying less attention to such technologies as AI, augmented reality, machine learning, blockchain, and quantum computing).

In the metaverse, change cycles will be shorter than today. Periods of intense turbulence are likely to increase. Competitive environments will be reshaped repeatedly. Consumers will be more demanding, better informed, and often fickle. Unexpected and unpredictable events, like the COVID pandemic, wars, or the collapse of financial markets, will continue to occur.

What all of this means is that most organizations in most industries are going to have to become much nimbler in responding to fast-changing conditions if they want to be successful in the coming decade.

Therefore, the overriding strategic choice for most companies is simple. Will they investigate and adopt (in a timely way) the appropriate metaverse-era technologies and concepts that can help them remain competitive? Or will they be sidelined by them? If companies do choose a timelier and more proactive metaverse technology assimilation and transformation strategy, how fast do they need to move, in which directions, and via what mechanisms? This book seeks to help organizations answer these questions.

1.6 INCREASED NIMBLENESS AT ALL ORGANIZATIONAL LEVELS

Throughout this book, an important watchword is "nimble." This is one of the key organizational attributes required for success in what promises to be a dynamic and challenging, yet opportunistic, metaverse world. Organizational nimbleness suggests a structure, business model, and culture where the following attitudes and attributes prevail:

- Quick and decisive rather than slow and halting
- Bold rather than hesitant
- Smaller rather than larger
- Decentralized and empowered rather than centralized and tightly controlled
- Flatter rather than steeper
- Networked rather than hierarchical
- Continuous learning rather than episodic
- Lean rather than bloated
- Open rather than closed (to facilitate alliances, for example)
- Change embraced rather than avoided
- Open minds rather than closed ones

The challenge organizations now face is how to take advantage of converging technological innovations to infuse the kinds of attributes listed above throughout the organization. As discussed in Chapter 19, the infusion of nimbleness into the enterprise should be done at all levels, from the most senior executives to the lowest-level company functions. There are abundant opportunities at all levels to make various organizational processes, workflows, business rules, value streams, functions, information flows, teams, and individuals nimbler and more efficient. The technologies that are now defining the metaverse era will certainly open up a multitude of additional opportunities for enhanced nimbleness.

1.7 THE PIVOTAL ROLE OF A NEW-ERA ENTERPRISE ARCHITECTURE

As organizational leaders consider ways to make their organizations more streamlined and nimbler, they will find opportunities to do so within organizational functions at all levels. The number of opportunities will grow quickly as an organization launches the sustained analytical processes associated with transforming an organization from its current state to a metaverse-ready state. The challenge will be how to capture, organize, and blend this continuing stream of ideas and proposed solutions, both strategic and tactical, into a cohesive, prioritized, well-sequenced, and easily accessible transformational game plan. To meet this challenge, the governance structure must commit to the development and use of a modern, technology-enabled, enterprise-wide planning framework and knowledge repository. Otherwise, the challenge will become overwhelmingly complex. This framework is typically referred to as an *enterprise architecture* (EA). The general structure of a representative EA is discussed in Chapter 18.

1.8 HOW THIS BOOK CAN HELP

This book provides a high-level conceptual plan for transforming a contemporary organization into one that can perform effectively in the metaverse. A detailed case study showing how a hypothetical organization might achieve this goal is provided in Chapter 22.

The general steps required are simple in theory, although quite challenging in execution. They include the following:

- Ensure you have a unified, fast-reaction board and C-suite committed to staying the course and navigating the twists and turns associated with a complex digital transformation.
- The governance structure is supremely well prepared to lead such a transformation by being well informed about the transformation process and the key attributes of the new environment they will be transitioning into, the metaverse.
- Senior executives and other managers throughout the enterprise understand what a challenging, even frightening time this will be for employees, and they take actions to help them deal with these fears.
- C-suite executives maintain at least conversational awareness of the major technological innovations driving the metaverse, especially those discussed throughout this book (such as virtual reality and quantum computing).
- Senior executives understand the need to make their governance model an empowered, delegated one wherein subordinate leaders and managers are granted authority for some of the governance workload to help improve the speed and flexibility of the entire organization.
- The governance structure understands the importance of a modernized enterprise architecture, supports the deployment of one, and owns it.
- A "Chief Architect" (a consensus-building enabler, not a dictator) is placed in charge of the overall, day-to-day EA functions.

- The framework upon which the EA operates is constructed using the latest technology innovations (e.g., AI, augmented reality, data science, and modular platforms) to optimize its development, implementation, use, ongoing synchronization of changes, and evolution.
- The central IT function is transformed to make it a distributed, networked function populated with a blend of permanent and on-demand staff having the required mix and levels of metaverse-era skills.

If these steps are taken, and if the commitment of the board and the C-suite holds firm, the odds of success will be much higher than if they are not taken.

1.9   KEY TAKEAWAYS

- To succeed in the metaverse, most organizations will have to modify their current IT governance playbooks, structures, skill profiles, and business models.
- These functions will have to be redesigned around the central objective of achieving greatly enhanced strategic and operational nimbleness – being both quick and accurate in thought and action under turbulent conditions.
- A new kind of advanced technology-enabled enterprise architecture is essential.
- Now is the time to act.

REFERENCES

[Accenture23] *Growing Consumer and Business Interest in the Metaverse Expected to Fuel Trillion Dollar Opportunity for Commerce*, Accenture Press Release, January 4, 2023 *https://newsroom.accenture.com/news/growing-consumer-and-business-interest-in-the-metaverse-expected-to-fuel-trillion-dollar-opportunity-for-commerce-accenture-finds.htm*

[Gnanasambandam, et al.22] *Every company is a software company: Six "must dos" to succeed*, Chandra Gnanasambandam, Janaki Palaniappan, and Jeremy Schneider, McKinsey Quarterly, December 13, 2022 *https://www.mckinsey.com/capabilities/mckinsey-digital/our-insights/every-company-is-a-software-company-six-must-dos-to-succeed*

[Johnson22] Shawn Johnson, *How the Metaverse Will Evolve,* Business News, May 11, 2022 *https://biz.crast.net/heres-how-the-metaverse-will-evolve/*

[Li et al.22] Li, Z., Oskarsson, M. & Heyden, A. *Detailed 3D human body reconstruction from multi-view images combining voxel super-resolution and learned implicit representation.* Appl Intell 52, 6739–6759 (2022) *https://link.springer.com/article/10.1007/s10489-021-02783-8*

[Robinson19] *Why do most transformations fail? A conversation with Harry Robinson,* Harry Robinson, The McKinsey Quarterly, July 10, 2019 *https://www.mckinsey.com/capabilities/transformation/our-insights/why-do-most-transformations-fail-a-conversation-with-harry-robinson*

2

STRUCTURE OF THE BOOK AND KEY DEFINITIONS

This book is designed to help organizations develop and maintain the agility and quickness necessary to compete effectively in a new technological and competitive era, one that is defined by the metaverse. For most organizations, this will require a significant transformation. To achieve the required levels of enterprise agility and quickness, a metaverse-competitive organization must have in place a swift reacting and unified governance structure. This structure must use an advanced form of enterprise architecture-based planning to help develop and implement its official transformational roadmap. Finally, because many of the metaverse skills required for success in the metaverse will be provided by a central IT organization, enterprise leaders need to have some understanding of how best to reorganize central IT services.

To establish a sound context and rationale for initiating these transformational actions, organizational leaders need to have sufficient information about the most important technologies, concepts, and models driving the metaverse. To help organizational leaders develop a good understanding of these developments and be better prepared to achieve their strategic transformational goals, this book is organized into four parts.

Setting the Stage. Part 1 sets the stage by explaining what the book seeks to accomplish, how it is structured, why organizational nimbleness in the metaverse era is an important issue, and how the book will benefit the reader. Part 1 also defines key concepts referenced throughout the book.

Important Historical Context. Part 2 provides important historical information about enterprise IT management strategies and digital transformation efforts. Understanding what has worked well in the past and what has not worked helps frame the transformation challenges for the metaverse in a way conducive for analysis and action. This historical context allows managers and leaders to develop more effective metaverse adaptation strategies for their organizations by avoiding the mistakes of the past. Part 2 also discusses why, historically, organizations have been slow to adapt to major technological waves of change, such as the Internet and cloud computing. Most organizations cannot afford this kind of adaptation lag as we move into the metaverse era. Part 2 offers advice on how to avoid this lag. Finally, Part 2 offers a glimpse into nimbleness in the animal kingdom and discusses important lessons organizations can learn from some highly nimble species. The animal kingdom analogy is used throughout the book.

Important Metaverse Innovations. Part 3 examines nine of the more important technological innovations helping propel the metaverse era. These innovations are deep tech, blockchain, platforms, algorithms, edge computing, quantum computing, immersive technologies (especially virtual reality and augmented reality), holographic technologies, and artificial intelligence and machine learning. Part 3 also provides one chapter of summary information for additional metaverse-related technologies and methods not covered in the other chapters.

Bringing It All Together. Part 4 ties everything together by describing how to achieve improved organizational nimbleness through (1) a more engaged, unified, metaverse-savvy, and nimble governance structure, (2) a much-improved approach to building and using an enterprise architecture, and (3) a strategy for modernizing an organization's central IT function to make it more relevant in the metaverse era. Chapter 22 provides a comprehensive case study showing how one hypothetical company pulled together everything outlined in this book to complete a successful metaverse transformation.

2.1   IMPORTANT DEFINITIONS AND CONCEPTS

A central theme emphasized throughout this book is the strategic importance of three attributes possessed by nimble organizations capable of competing successfully in the metaverse. As shown in Figure 2.1, the term "Nimble Governance" encompasses the overall enterprise governance function, including both the board of directors and C-suite executives. This includes a process of empowered governance wherein executive management delegates certain governance decisions and actions to subordinate management levels.

This frees more time for the C-suite to run a complex organization operating in a dynamic competitive environment. This form of empowerment also enables faster decisions and actions across the enterprise and is a central feature of networked organizations.

The "Nimble Enterprise Architecture" circle shown in Figure 2.1 refers to the critical blueprint for transformation success and supporting central information repository used across the enterprise, not only during enterprise transformation but in ongoing operations thereafter.

The effective functioning of an enterprise governance structure and the systematic use of a sound enterprise architecture go together. Consider a simple analogy: a building contractor performs a construction function by relying heavily on architectural drawings or blueprints as essential tools in the execution of that function. Similarly, the CEO and executive staff perform an enterprise governance function, relying heavily on an enterprise architecture as an essential tool for the exercise of that function. Governance entities or building contractors who choose to operate without the guidance provided by quality blueprints risk a bad result.

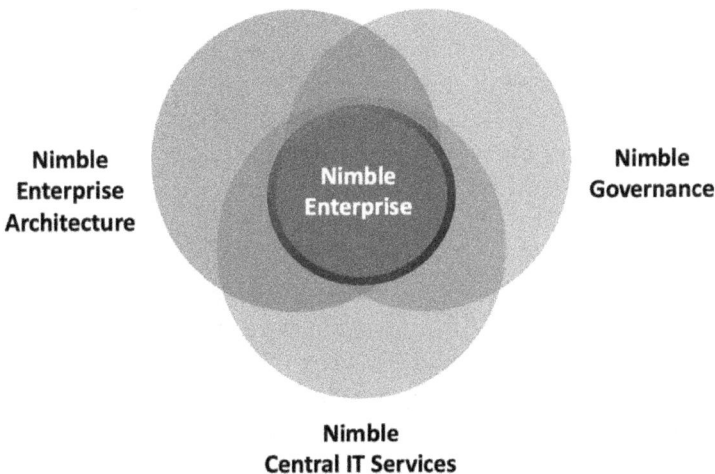

Nimble
Enterprise
Architecture

Nimble
Enterprise

Nimble
Governance

Nimble
Central IT Services

FIGURE 2.1 There are three essential precursors for metaverse-ready enterprises.

The "Nimble Central IT Services" circle shown in Figure 2.1 refers to a reimagined central IT services function. The central IT function so familiar today will not only require a revamp of its skill mix in the metaverse, its structure will have to be leaner and more dynamically decentralized across the enterprise. The actual structure of the IT organization at any point in time will be a function of the ebb and flow of enterprise-wide needs for technical support.

The following sections define important management and organizational concepts used throughout this book. Most readers will already have a reasonable understanding of these concepts. However, because they play such significant roles in any kind of major organizational transformation, they warrant additional discussion. The concepts discussed below include *board of directors*, *executive management* (or C-suite) teams, *enterprise architecture*, and *nimble enterprise*.

Board of Directors

No company or organization would attempt a major strategic transformation without first obtaining the support of its board of directors. The board of directors sits atop, and is largely independent from, the organization it oversees. Its goals are to ensure there is an effective management team, proper strategic focus, a healthful culture, regulatory compliance, competitive success, a positive corporate image, operational success, and benefits to shareholders.

As the legal governing oversight entity for a company (at least for a public one), the board of directors has special responsibilities. The board typically meets at regularly scheduled intervals to assess current strategy and overall business operations, making necessary adjustments to either area as needed. The board might also assume authority for certain important corporate actions, such as dividends, mergers, hiring or firing of senior executives, and setting executive pay and bonuses. Both the New York Stock Exchange and the NASDAQ require all listed companies to have a majority of their board members come from outside the company. Typically, these directors are elected by shareholders, often having been nominated by special committees within the company, while other members have campaigned openly for the job, sometimes as part of a takeover maneuver. Private companies and nonprofit organizations can have boards if they choose, and many do.

As noted earlier, the central role of the governance function is to provide overall direction and control for an enterprise, with the board of directors being largely independent from senior company executives. For the purposes of this book, however, the governance framework concept includes both the board of directors and top-tier executive management acting as a unified team. In the metaverse era, these entities must adhere to their individual legal charters, of course, but still work together in a relatively seamless fashion if an organization is to remain nimble enough to compete effectively under rapidly changing conditions. Forging this kind of seamless relationship, while still maintaining the independence of the board, is one of the first challenges that must be met in a metaverse-era digital transformation.

Senior executives operating in the metaverse environment must be able to make decisions and act on them effectively in very short timeframes. If executives have to wait on the next scheduled board meeting for important decisions, opportunities will be missed and threats might already have caused harm. Therefore, the board and the C-suite must remain in lock step on strategy formulation and execution.

When the COVID pandemic exploded without warning, most restaurant establishments were suddenly presented with a critical event that required an immediate response. Some of these establishments were nimble enough to change their business models almost overnight and survive. Others were less fortunate. Nimble governance is characterized by the kind of governing flexibility and resilience displayed by the proprietors of surviving dining establishments under conditions of extreme stress and time constraints.

Executive Management or C-Suite

Traditionally, governance at the board level has had more of a guidance and oversight connotation, while executive management (such as CEOs and CXOs) has had more of an execution one, such as planning, implementing, monitoring, and controlling business operations to achieve planned results. Management is responsible for maintaining aspirational but realistic mission and vision definitions for their organizations. In support of these mission and vision expressions, management creates an organizational structure to execute the processes and policies used to manage human, physical, financial, and intangible resources (such as culture, corporate image, and goodwill) to achieve defined objectives. Executive management includes the individuals or groups who have been given the authority to make these decisions, are held accountable for executing them, and are evaluated based on level of success in achieving the desired results.

Enterprise Architecture (EA)

The term "enterprise" can be viewed as another way of saying "organization," but it typically has the connotation of a larger or more complex organization. The term "architecture" relates to a plan (such as a blueprint or schematic) for the construction of some entity, such as a building or other structure, service, tool, or product. When the terms are blended, "enterprise architecture" simply means a plan (or blueprint) for aligning business and technology strategies and operations to establish and maintain an organization that consistently meets currently defined objectives. An EA shares the core functionality and objectives of a wide array of other common architectural concepts, such as those used to design and build buildings, bridges, cars, and airplanes. Each of these architectural models contains the total set of detailed, interdependent depictions necessary to build the object of the architecture. For an EA, the object of the architecture is a well-integrated and effective enterprise.

Within the context of this book, the overriding objective of an enterprise architecture is to establish the level of nimbleness and operational effectiveness across an enterprise necessary to compete and win in the metaverse era. Therefore, organizations will want to build on the sophisticated and sometimes brilliant work done in the past in developing and evolving the EA concept. However, the EA concept must be refined further to create a simple and useful repository of real-time information about the enterprise for use by organizations operating in the metaverse.

In this book, therefore, a *nimble* enterprise architecture refers to an updated and digital technology-enhanced version of conventional enterprise architecture processes and frameworks. Conventional enterprise architectures are often not nimble at all. They might have been around in various static forms for decades, and have been used with varying degrees of success, not because of any weaknesses in the underlying concept but because they lacked the robust technologies we have today.

First, a nimble enterprise architecture is nimble in function – that is, it is nimble in its daily operational use. For employees across the enterprise, each with his or her individual set of circumstances and needs, the enterprise architecture must have some immediate relevancy, be easy to use, and easy to understand. It should be modular in design so it can be easily tailored for specific uses, and should feature ease of updating and synchronization of its components. A nimble architecture is always current, credible, and demonstrably useful.

Second, a nimble architecture is nimble in purpose and end-state goals. It is designed to help organizations become highly nimble and innovative enterprises by keeping new business and technology strategies in alignment under turbulent conditions that can strain this alignment. The official architectural blueprint for a company should be used by the governing structure, including both the board and senior executives, to formulate plans, make decisions, and implement business and organizational strategies under rapidly changing conditions. The enterprise governance structure creates and maintains, primarily through the top layers of the modern enterprise architecture, the rules of the game for groups and individuals across the enterprise.

Nimbleness in the actual development, use, and evolution of an advanced enterprise architecture platform is (or soon will be) achieved through the creative use of various converging technologies widely associated with the metaverse era, such as AI, intelligent algorithms, digital imaging, virtual reality, augmented reality, and machine learning. Building the enterprise architecture platform on these technologies will, for example, allow changes in one part of the architecture to ripple quickly and automatically through to other appropriate parts of the architecture that require corresponding changes. Thus, the architecture is always current and important interdependencies are continuously harmonized.

The inability to maintain this kind of timely synchronization among enterprise architecture components has been one of the major drawbacks to conventional architectural approaches. This is because the complexity of the synchronization challenge has traditionally transcended human capabilities. The perpetuation of synchronization lags inherent in many traditional approaches would unacceptably limit organizational nimbleness in the metaverse era. In other words, many traditional EA's do not measure up to the essential qualities of being always current, credible, and demonstrably useful. Metaverse technologies can help solve these problems.

"Nimble" Enterprise

The nimbleness, or lack thereof, of an organization is not defined by the status of any single dimension or factor, such as time to market. The potential sources for enhanced nimbleness permeate the entire enterprise. Therefore, nimbleness must be infused throughout every layer of an enterprise architecture if the enterprise as a whole is to be nimble. Using an analogy from biology, the goal is to infuse nimbleness across an enterprise much in the same way nimbleness has been infused by nature at the molecular or cellular level in highly nimble living organisms.

The following are just a few examples of some of the more important sources of nimbleness in an enterprise. These are capabilities that will need to be translated into the enterprise transformation blueprint maintained in the enterprise architecture.

Flexibility in Strategy Formulation and Implementation

Robert Burns reminded us (paraphrased) of the basic truth that the best laid plans of mice and men often go astray. This reality leads to important questions. For example, does the management of an enterprise embrace the notion that plans almost always need to be altered, often because of the sudden emergence of unforeseen events, and that this is not a bad thing? Is nimbleness in planning processes and products baked into the architectural framework for that company? Are plans reviewed often enough to keep them effectively aligned with rapidly changing conditions? Do the plans themselves have embedded contingency "trigger events" to enhance their adaptability? (Triggers mean, for example, "If A happens, we must immediately initiate action B.") If organizational leaders can answer "yes" to the above questions, they are well prepared to lead a nimble enterprise.

A Flexible Analytical Mindset

This attribute relates to the way problems, proposals, and opportunities are typically dealt with in an organization. Is there one and only one method of evaluation (like a detailed and lengthy ROI justification analysis), or are there ways to adjust evaluative thinking on a shifting contingency basis? The metaverse will require the latter.

Flexibility in People Mobilization

This attribute relates to how people are assigned to various functions, projects, or teams across the entire enterprise. Is the organization geared to the need to allow people to move around fluidly based on the ebb and flow of opportunities and threats, evolving work preferences, or career development opportunities? Or do most people tend to remain, by corporate design, in one area of the business for very long periods of time, frequently doing the same task? If a company is in the second group, it could be at a disadvantage operating in the metaverse.

Fiscal Flexibility

This attribute relates to the management of financial resources. For example, is the annual or quarterly budget unchanging and inflexible, or is there flexibility in the allocation of money and other resources based on important unfolding events? If an organization does not have fiscal flexibility, elevating its level of nimbleness will be difficult.

If the enterprise is imbued with smart flexibility in every opportunity zone, it can

- react swiftly and effectively to developing opportunities, marshaling resources and expertise more adroitly in opportunity pursuit than less nimble competitors
- successfully counter competitive threats that can often appear with little or no advance warning
- enter into and exit from strategic and tactical alliances and business relationships quickly and effectively
- respond more swiftly and effectively to a constant barrage of new security threats, cyber and otherwise
- shift resources (such as people, facilities, and money) within and across the enterprise as needs arise, and do so more quickly and effectively than less nimble competitors

To summarize, a nimble enterprise is the result of a nimble governance structure systematically using a nimble enterprise architecture to build a company capable of making sound business decisions quickly and effectively under turbulent and often stressful conditions. In other words, organizations operating in the metaverse should be able to reconstitute themselves in an appropriate and timely way to adapt to whatever competitive conditions they might encounter. Most of today's organizations lack this level of nimbleness.

2.2 KEY TAKEAWAYS

- Parts 1 and 2 of this book describe the challenges organizations face as the metaverse era begins to emerge and summarize the structure of the book and its objectives.
- Part 3 describes nine important technological developments organizations must understand as they prepare to compete in the metaverse, and includes summaries of additional technologies and methods not covered elsewhere in the book.
- Part 4 brings everything together and discusses the actions organizations must take to remain competitive in the metaverse. These actions center on the transformation of enterprise governance, an updated enterprise architecture concept, and transformed central IT services. A detailed hypothetical corporate transformation to the metaverse is presented in Chapter 22.

PART 2

BACKGROUND AND CONTEXT

CHAPTER 3

EVOLUTION OF IT GOVERNANCE FRAMEWORKS

3.1 INTRODUCTION

The challenge of managing data, computing, and networking resources in organizations in ways that keep them well coordinated with business directions and priorities has always been difficult. Perhaps the most significant challenge in this regard has been adjusting to the arrival of major new technology "eras" (e.g., the arrival of the Internet era). These transitions have been complicated significantly by organizations being burdened by accumulated and deeply embedded resources from current and prior eras. Because new technologies can often render current technologies obsolete, organizations faced with a technological disruption often find themselves at an impasse. To remain competitive in the near term, they must continue to make effective use of their amassed legacy infrastructures, while simultaneously striving to install more advanced technologies.

Many strategies for controlling enterprise data and technology resources, while maintaining an effective blend of older and newer technologies, have been tried with varying degrees of success. Lessons have been learned, and newer approaches have been implemented. However, the pace of technological change has frequently outpaced the ability of organizations to keep up. For example, from the late 1970s through the 1980s, information technology ownership and management became much more democratized and localized with the arrival of minicomputers, PCs, and mobile technologies. This presented organizations with a new level of complexity in managing enterprise IT resources.

We are now entering yet another major technological area, that of the metaverse. This latest disruption will present challenging new issues for overall enterprise governance strategies, and for IT governance strategies in particular. Therefore, it is highly instructive to look back and learn what has worked well in the past and what has been problematic. A good understanding of this history better informs us on how to manage the latest technology disruption, the metaverse.

The Early Days of Computing

In the late 1940s and early 1950s, government and military organizations, such as the US Department of Defense and the Census Bureau, were instrumental in advancing the use of electronic computing devices.

One iconic early computer that led eventually to the widespread use of mainframe business computers was the vacuum tube-based AN/FSQ-7 computer, the heart of the Department of Defense's massive Semi-Automatic Ground Environment (SAGE) national air defense system. As a young systems analyst and contract compliance officer, this author worked with one of these massive computers, which required one whole story of a large concrete building to house it. In fact, the AN/FSQ-7 computer was the largest computer in the world during the 1950s era. [IBM23]

The SAGE computer did contribute heavily to the rise of "business machines" in the 1950s, as organizations across all industries began to take note. Something new was occurring, and business technology companies, such as IBM and Univac, were becoming household names.

The challenge for organizations in this era was simply to understand this new technological phenomenon and develop some sense of how to take advantage of it. These were pioneering days in terms of IT governance. There were no issues of blending older, accumulated computing technology with the new. It was all new. So were the technology management issues.

In a way, the metaverse presents a similar kind of challenge today. Just as managers in the 1950s struggled to understand the often-bewildering concept of computers in general and how to put them to good business use and manage them well, today's managers must invest in developing an understanding of the array of technological innovations that are driving the metaverse disruption, such as AI and machine learning. They will also have to learn how to put these resources to good business use and manage them well.

As we moved into the 1960s and 70s, what we now think of as digital computers accelerated their penetration into mainstream use in business operations. Data centers were built and large mainframe computers were ensconced behind glass walls where they were patrolled by enigmatic workers regarded by many as having somewhat mystical capabilities. Few people knew what they did at the time. Large numbers of new employees with new skills were being hired as the penetration of computers into business environments continued. New hires included IT directors, data processing operations managers, job schedulers, computer set-up personnel, systems analysts, computer programmers, tape librarians, and card keypunch operators.

The major enterprise IT governance challenge during this period centered on the fact that only the IT experts knew anything about what was going on. This made enterprise-level cost and budget controls by non-technical managers difficult because they had to rely on the expertise of the Director of IT. This was the executive who defined which computing assets to acquire, how large the IT staff should be, and what the software development priorities should be.

In today's world, senior enterprise executives are much more technologically astute and have a much better understanding of current business technology costs and priorities. However, the metaverse is introducing a number of new technology concepts and variables. Executives have much to learn, for example, about the benefits and costs of setting up AI and machine learning technologies and capabilities, establishing holographic capabilities, implementing edge computing solutions, and developing augmented reality solutions.

Since those pioneering days in computing, we have seen wave after wave of technology advances come and go. Each new wave ushered in new generations of analog or digital computing technologies and business models, as well as new skills and job descriptions. With each wave, the enterprise IT management challenge became more difficult as new technologies were emerging faster than existing technologies could be assimilated and managed.

For example, the early mainframes of the 1950s and 1960s led to more distributed computing options (e.g., the DEC PDP/11) enabled by new networking technologies, like Ethernet. Later, advances in microchip technologies led eventually to personal computers, the Internet, smart phones, cloud computing, AI, and the Internet of Things. We can certainly expect to see more disruptive digital technology advances over the next decade, especially as the quantum model begins to displace the digital model for many purposes.

Gaining Control of Computer Proliferation

With the emergence of each new wave of technological changes, economies, professions, business models, consumers, and society in general were affected, often in highly disruptive ways. Today, who can even imagine a business office or scientific lab without one or more desktop computers or tablet computers? Or a teenager without a cell phone?

With each of these technology-driven disruptions, organizations struggled with how to "govern" the assimilation and effective business use of the latest technologies. This led to the emergence of various IT governance and enterprise architecture models. The Chief Information Officer (CIO) position soon came into vogue, as did the Chief Technology Officer (CTO) and similar titles. Like everything else, these positions and associated methods have been buffeted by the winds of change and technology advances that have been in a continuous state of evolution since the late 1950s.

For example, one early advance in IT governance and enterprise planning activities emerged in the late 1970s and early 1980s. It centered on a business technology planning framework developed by IBM called "Business Systems Planning" (BSP). This was a structured methodology designed to bring an enterprise-wide view to bear in analyzing the interdependent business strategies, policies, processes, information flows, data, software applications, and digital technology infrastructure components of the overall enterprise.

Without this comprehensive view, the theory went, enterprise leaders had no useful basis for understanding the IT investments they already had, which ones were needed, what the investment priorities should be, what the total IT budget should be, and whether previously approved investments were achieving their intended results. The ultimate benefit of using this methodology, advocates promised, would be a consensus, well-integrated business and technology blueprint that would effectively sync IT strategies and investments with overall enterprise business strategies and goals.

While the theory behind BSP was reasonable and innovative, in terms of useful results, things did not typically go well, as this author can attest from personal experience. Based on the results of these early BSP efforts, it became clear to many organizational leaders that the enterprise IT planning and management methodologies and tools that existed at the time had important limitations that had to be overcome.

For example, because the focus of earlier enterprise planning initiatives was often on cost savings and operational efficiency rather than strategic advances for the enterprise, responsibility for development and execution of a "Business Systems Plan" tended to be delegated and eventually became of use primarily to accountants and IT technicians. As a result, these initiatives lacked the self-sustaining, business-focused momentum that could have been provided by consistent executive team ownership and involvement.

In addition, most enterprise architecture methods were predicated on larger, vertically integrated organizations populated with rational actors and a committed management team. While the structures of most organizations engaged in enterprise architecture initiatives might have looked logical on paper, unofficial, non-sanctioned groups and coalitions often ran important components of the organization. They did this based on their own perceptions of appropriate strategies, not those formulated by a corporate governance structure too far removed from the real action to have significant influence. Many of these informal interest groups were highly resistant to any form of central control and lobbied against change. As a result, meaningful institutionalization of a true business system plan or enterprise architecture was often problematic, sometimes in the extreme.

Complicating the challenge further, many of the early enterprise architecture deployments were paper-based and difficult for the general employee population to access and use. Plus, many business technology plans were heavily oriented toward use by the IT technical staff, not employees in other business and functional areas. This limited their use and acceptance across the enterprise.

Over time, criticisms by individuals and groups with deeply entrenched interests began to give any kind of centrally managed enterprise architecture planning a bad name. Such plans were considered too bureaucratic, rigid, complicated, unrealistic, aspirational, and limiting for business units that favored departmental autonomy. However, without some kind of integrated enterprise master plan or roadmap to go by, companies often suffered the consequences. When it came to the acquisition, management, and effective use of IT assets across their companies, many senior executives trying to operate without an architectural plan for business technology resources had little relevant information to go on.

The information technology governance issues faced by organizations in the metaverse era will be just as challenging but in a different way. As organizations become even more software intensive, dealing effectively with emerging digital and quantum technologies will become increasingly important strategic issues for organizations. As a result, the management challenges for these newer technologies are becoming markedly different from what we have seen in the past. The challenge, therefore, is how to adapt traditional IT governance, enterprise architecture, and central IT concepts (still theoretically sound) to the competitive realities of the metaverse world.

Existing Enterprise Architecture Frameworks and Tools

There are a number of "standard" frameworks and commercial products available to support enterprise architecture planning, development, and use. One note of caution, however, is that many of these were developed in the distant past, perhaps decades ago, and they might not be using current digital innovations and tools to optimize their effectiveness. Also, many existing frameworks entail extensive, labor-intensive, and time-consuming analysis and documentation of the enterprise's functions, processes, systems, data, and technology components and equipment. While this is critical information to capture and document, some of today's slower documentation and characterization methods might not align well with the needs and attributes of lean, agile, and quick companies competing in the metaverse era. In addition, after these large databases were created in the past, it was virtually impossible to keep them current using available tools and methods. This means more advanced tools and technologies, such as AI, will be required to make these analyses easier to perform. The metaverse will offer these technologies and should be used for this purpose.

If a company does want to select a popular, well-established enterprise architecture framework as a way to get started, two of the most well-known and widely-used frameworks are The Open Group Architecture Framework (TOGAF) [Group23] and the Zachman Framework [Zachman23].

TOGAF is an open framework that first became available in 1995. A global organization called The Open Group maintains standards for this framework, based primarily on feedback from its users. The structural basis for this framework is called the Architecture Development Method (ADM).

The Zachman Framework, which is also well-known to most enterprise architects, is a matrix-based "schema" for planning and analysis. The schema uses "what, how, where, who, when, and why" questions about the entire enterprise. Through various processes, the schema seeks to describe complex relationships and dependencies enterprise-wide in an understandable way, with supporting detail provided the farther you go down into the matrix. The schema attempts to organize data based on different stakeholder views.

Another framework that is often used comes at the enterprise IT management challenge from a different and somewhat broader perspective. This "best practices" framework, which evolved from the world of auditing, is called COBIT, which stands for "Control Objectives for Information and Related Technologies." COBIT advocates say it can used for any kind of company in any industry because it focuses on broad areas that are of universal interest, such as architecture, governance, and risk management.

For each of these areas, COBIT has defined detailed objectives and best practices, which can help an organization better understand where it currently stands and where it needs to be at some point in time. One caution with a framework like COBIT is the fact that it has evolved within the context of a more typical enterprise model, not necessarily the kind of "deep tech," nimble, decentralized, highly networked organization that will thrive in the metaverse. As long as this realization is kept in mind, COBIT can be useful for certain purposes.

Many CIOs, CTOs, architecture developers, and executive managers have found these frameworks useful, but often in modified forms. (See Chapter 18, "Enterprise Architecture," for a case study on how a well-designed EA can be used effectively.) These frameworks can most likely be adapted to the needs of metaverse-era organizations, especially if outfitted with modern tools and technologies. In fact, that is currently the recommended approach.

Similarly, there are numerous enterprise architecture documentation and support tools on the market, and some being used with great success. Many of these existing enterprise planning products can support functions such as diagramming complex information flows, documenting the enterprise applications architecture, capturing data architectures, and much more.

Again, beware: The total collection of artifacts produced and organized by these EA tools does not necessarily result in a complete, viable, or nimble enterprise architecture. To achieve that goal, key components of the architecture must be infused with nimble business thinking (see Chapter 19, "Infusing Nimbleness into the Enterprise Architecture"). The intelligent infusion of strategic thinking across all enterprise architecture components is critical, making the difference between something that slowly sinks into oblivion and something that is so helpful and intuitive it will be used every day to run the company.

Several companies, like Workday, SAP, Oracle, and Salesforce, offer excellent enterprise software products that form their own quasi-enterprise architectures in large-scale deployments. These suites and modules can certainly be used effectively, but they do not, in themselves, constitute a complete enterprise architecture, especially a nimble one. Companies considering the acquisition of such a product must begin with a clear view of the strategic imperatives they are pursuing. Only when these imperatives are understood and agreed to can they begin to pay close attention to vendor products. The goal should be to bend the product to strategic imperatives, not the other way around.

Therefore, enhanced nimbleness of an enterprise is not achieved and maintained primarily by the tools used or the software acquired. It comes from the people who build and use the enterprise architecture – their wisdom, corporate knowledge, industry knowledge, technology trends awareness, knowledge of current business priorities, and understanding of evolving customer expectations. Informed user input is what gives life, character, and usability to an enterprise architecture, thereby providing an essential benefit to the enterprise as a whole.

Suggested Approach to Enterprise Architecture

Any organization seeking to create the kind of enterprise architecture that could improve the nimbleness of the overall organization should consider using the following approach:

- Adopt the TOGAF framework or something similar as a starting point. Distill from this framework the basic skeleton of a structure and methodology tailored to your specific organizational attributes and needs. Do not get lost in the framework's intricate details. Details can be added on a priority basis in later phases of the development effort.
- Assign this framework to a small, select team of systems analysts, software developers, and data experts. Charge this team with exploring the whole realm of converging metaverse-era technologies. Their objective is to develop an integrated set of tools, such as AI or machine learning, that can automate the skeletal framework for the architecture in ways that make it
  - comprehensive in scope
  - easy to access, use, and understand

- easy to augment with features such as application programming interfaces (APIs) and open source add-ons, as needed
- easy for users of the architecture to help maintain by updating it themselves with relevant information for which they have access
- modular in design for flexibility in managing and updating the platform upon which it is populated with information and used
- easy to keep its various components (layers and layer components) synchronized
- With this framework in place, tools and all, launch the effort to create the full architecture (see Chapters 18 and 19)

3.2 KEY TAKEAWAYS

- Gaining control of business and technology resources in an organization, and doing so in a lasting, well-coordinated way, has always been a daunting challenge. Achieving this goal at a time when a new, high-tech era is fast approaching, such as the metaverse era is doing right now, is even more difficult.
- Organizational leaders need to be aware of the limitations of, and lessons learned from, prior IT governance practices.
- Organizational leaders also need to understand the need for, and be committed to, the development and systematic use of an enhanced and comprehensive enterprise architecture as the central repository for the basic blueprint for the organization's path forward, including plans and strategies for enterprise IT resources.

REFERENCES

[Group23] The Open Group, The TOGAF® Standard, 10th Edition, 2023 *https://www.opengroup.org/togaf*

[IBM23] *SAGE, The First National Air Defense Network,* IBM, Icons of Progress *https://www.ibm.com/ibm/history/ibm100/us/en/icons/sage/*

[Zachman23] Zachman International, *The Concise Definition of The Zachman Framework by John A. Zachman, 2023 https://www.zachman.com/about-the-zachman-framework*

CHAPTER 4

SLOW RESPONSES TO DISRUPTIVE TECHNOLOGIES

It cannot happen to us. Or can it? Consider the following list of companies:

- Blockbuster
- Compaq
- Enron
- Toys R Us
- BlackBerry
- Radio Shack
- Kodak
- Borders
- Tower Records
- MySpace
- Digital Equipment Company
- Polaroid
- Wang Laboratories
- Pier 1 Imports
- A&P Supermarket
- Sears
- Pan Am
- Bed, Bath, and Beyond

Where are they now?

History tells us many organizations tend to be slow responders when disruptive technology-driven waves, such as the PC, the Internet, or the cloud, appear. This might be understandable when we consider how often the experts have been wrongly skeptical. See, for example, "7 Tech Predictions That Totally Missed the Mark." [Devaney21]

There are many reasons for this kind of skepticism and foot-dragging in the face of major technological disruptions. One common reason for this hesitancy is the hyperbole often associated with imminent technological disruptions. These bombastic buildups can seem excessively far-fetched to many executives. Another obvious reason for initial negativism is the "not-invented-here" syndrome that has hindered countless organizations. Finally, the speed of past and current technology advances has surpassed the expectations of most of us, not just the experts.

However, the stakes are increasingly high. If an organization's senior executives happen to be wrongly dubious in the face of a major technology-driven disruption like the metaverse, the organization as a whole will also be slow to respond, which could endanger the viability of the company. This acceptance lag often exists even when a new disruption has arrived, has been proven in actual business operations, and is widely acknowledged as a game changer.

These patterns of skeptical perspectives and lagging behavior are likely to remain as the metaverse era continues to evolve, and many companies could ultimately pay the price for not responding in a timelier way. This chapter discusses these tendencies and offers advice on how to overcome them.

4.1 TECH INDUSTRY – A HISTORY DEFINED BY ERAS

Longtime veterans in the general areas of organizational strategies and structures, enterprise governance, strategic planning, and enterprise architecture design and implementation will have seen wave after wave of important technology developments emerge, ultimately take hold with the masses, and then eventually mature and be subsequently superseded by the next wave. When each new wave emerged, it typically disrupted the consensus on how best to govern information technology resources and ensure their effective use in enterprise business processes. Looking back over those decades, some of the most important, pervasive, and massively disruptive technological developments affecting global organizations included

- mainframe computers (1950s and 60s)
- microprocessor / microchip technology (60s and 70s)
- networked departmental computers and the client-server model – e.g., the DEC VAX era (late 70s, 80s)

- personal computers (80s)
- the Internet (90s)
- smart phones (early 2000s)
- cloud computing (2000s)
- AI/machine learning/data science/virtual reality (today)

Over time, it became clear to industry observers that each new wave of change was being greeted by organizational leaders with slow, even dismissive responses. For example, many of the companies adopted cloud computing a full three to four years after the time the cloud model had become a proven, viable game changer. For many of these companies, this was a crucial lapse, and they had to scurry later to catch up. Some are still trying.

The fact that these waves of change have occurred about every seven or eight years over the past six decades means most companies are almost always playing catch up. By the time they had adapted to the previous wave of disruptive technology developments, they would be about three years behind in adapting to the next wave. In effect, they were always "fighting the last war" (see Figure 4.1). This cycle was common then and remains so now.

Last Wave: Shallow Tech

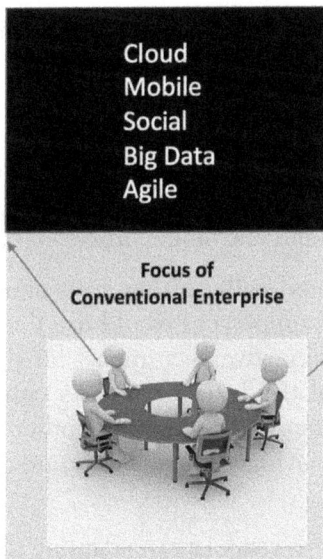

Cloud
Mobile
Social
Big Data
Agile

**Focus of
Conventional Enterprise**

Next Wave: Metaverse / Deep Tech

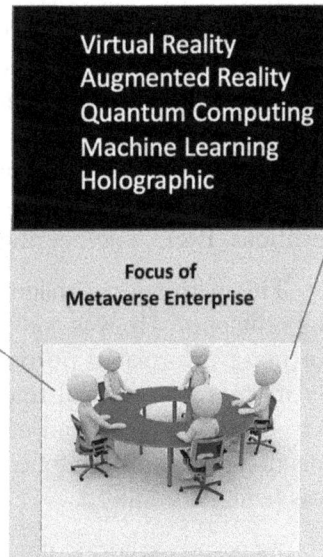

Virtual Reality
Augmented Reality
Quantum Computing
Machine Learning
Holographic

**Focus of
Metaverse Enterprise**

Photo Components Courtesy of Pixabay, Peggy_Marco, developers

FIGURE 4.1 Organizations are typically one wave behind in technology assimilation.

The reasons for this slow-footedness in embracing new technological waves are numerous, but the most important ones include the following:

- Most organizational leaders are risk-averse and, understandably, prefer stability and safety over the adoption of new things. Because statistics show only a small portion of enterprise digital transformation initiatives have been successful, many companies simply will not take the risk. "We don't want to be the tip of the spear," is a common reaction.
- Emerging new technology eras are often denigrated initially by various respected industry experts, while others simultaneously extol them, all of which leads to confusion about their legitimacy. We have seen this schism in reactions to the metaverse.
- Companies often face considerable resistance to new technological developments from entrenched groups and individuals within the enterprise, especially if their expertise is in technologies and methods from the previous or current wave, not the emerging one.
- There is often a lack of meaningful understanding across the company of true business or functional benefits of the new wave.
- Perhaps the most common reason for the slow take-up phenomenon is a blend of simply not knowing what to do and sheer dread of disrupting the status quo until current crises and obligations are resolved.

One example of slow adoption in the late 1990s as witnessed by this author involved the manager of one of the larger business units of a major defense contractor. This manager refused to allow any group or employee within his unit to access the Internet at work. This was well after the Internet had been accepted widely as a profoundly successful and transformational development, not only for B2B uses, but for improved internal and external communications, R&D, engineering, marketing, and customer care.

This particular manager was concerned with cutting costs and improving efficiency. He was convinced that his employees would use the Internet for non-work-related purposes and thereby adversely impact his productivity metrics. His lack of understanding of the Internet and its potential for improved efficiency and cost savings, among its numerous other benefits, meant a potentially beneficial tool for achieving *his most important objectives* was being left unused.

As noted earlier, many companies were years late in adapting their organizations to the cloud computing wave. In addition to the general reasons for technology adoption lags outlined earlier, when it came to cloud computing, these companies were concerned about issues such as

- the security of applications and data processed by or stored within remote cloud resources
- reliability (or even integrity) of cloud vendors and their products and services
- inability to "feel and touch" cloud assets, such as servers, if they were not housed in the local data center (or in a local office, or in a local closet, or under a local desk)
- continuous disparaging and often denigrating commentary by local gurus and wizards whose careers were grounded in what was then current-era expertise (like client-server), not expertise in the new cloud era
- the name "cloud computing," which often invited ridicule

Interestingly, even after the cloud concept had been long established, many of these companies adopted certain cloud-based solutions only after "hybrid" solutions had been developed (i.e., a mix of cloud and on-premise – that is, hands-on – resources).

4.2 DIGGING DEEPER: INNOVATION DIFFUSION AND CHASM CROSSING

For readers who want to understand the theories behind this lagging technology adoption phenomenon, there is plenty of information available. For example, we can begin with a book published in 1962 titled *Diffusion of Innovations*. The book was written by the sociologist Everett Rogers, who based his conclusions on research involving over 500 diffusion studies. [Rogers03] In his book, Rogers categorizes consumers based on their purchasing behavior. Today, the model is widely recognized as the Technology Adoption Life Cycle. [High Tech00] This model provides a basis for analyzing the nature of the adoption or acceptance profiles of a new technological product or innovation. This model is relevant to the rate and extent of acceptance by organizations of the changes brought about by a new technological era like the metaverse.

Fast forwarding to 1991, we have the well-known marketing book by Geoffrey A. Moore titled *Crossing the Chasm*. [Moore14] This book focuses on the specifics of marketing high-tech products during their early start-up period. Moore based his analysis on a classic bell curve distribution. This was his way of helping readers visualize the adoption of a new technology over time, beginning with a few early adopters, followed by the large number of middle market consumers (comprising the vast center section of the bell curve), and ultimately winning over the laggards (positioned on the right tail of the curve).

We can see a similar pattern in how organizations adapt to technological innovations. For example, there are organizations that are inherently technology-savvy. They believe the effective use of advanced technology is one of the most critical success factors they possess. These organizations will, in general, be more likely to thrive in the metaverse. First, they are likely to be ahead of other organizations in their understanding of the metaverse, and will already have multiple metaverse-related initiatives under way, such as pilot projects and benchmarking exercises. Second, they will have a culture and a process framework optimized for the timely and smooth analysis, adoption, and assimilation of technological innovations. Third, they will be populated with an above average number of curious, technologically astute employees continuously on the lookout for the next big thing. For example, as far back as the late 1970s, we could find employees in these tech-savvy companies carrying around bare-boned, clunky, utilitarian-looking Osborne personal computers in brown cases. This was long before most of us had any idea what a personal computer was.

There is a large middle zone of organizations that are less technologically astute but open to new ideas, concepts, and technologies. These might be thought of as close followers, companies that don't want to be the tip of the spear but are alert enough to track technology trends and see clear signals. With some luck, many of these companies will do well in the metaverse. However, many will find this new era very challenging because technology tracking and assimilation will not be among their core competencies. In addition, because they will not have kept their technology infrastructures as current as the tech-savvy organizations, they will have much larger legacy infrastructures to convert to more metaverse-capable infrastructures. This could cost them much in the way of lost time and opportunities.

Finally, we have highly risk-averse organizations, the "if-it-ain't-broke-don't-fix-it" crowd. These organizations tend to adopt new innovations only when motivated by stark competitive realities (e.g., steadily losing customers to more technologically current competitors). The leaders of these organizations will often wait until a technological innovation has become established and widely-used, engaging with it only toward the tail end of its technology life cycle, which means by then they are typically far behind the next technology cycle. Examples are those companies that would only buy "safe" IBM computers during the mainframe era, or "safe" Microsoft-based PCs in the PC era. They much preferred what they considered the to be the "tried and true" over possibly superior technologies, such as early Apple computers. These organizations will tend to struggle early in the metaverse.

A rough approximation is about half of today's organizations fall into the second group, those firms that are conservative and pragmatic but open to new ideas. The other half is divided roughly between the tech-savvy organizations and the highly risk-averse organizations.

> **SIDE NOTE:** *The theoretical framework discussed in this chapter, at least the portion that deals with Geoffrey Moore's* **Crossing the Chasm,** *focuses on consumer behavior. That is, why are some consumers early adopters of technological innovations and others very slow to adapt? The "consumers" who are relative to the thrust of this book are the managers and employees of an enterprise. The fundamental challenge for enterprise governance, therefore, is to motivate enterprise employees to embrace the converging digital innovations driving the metaverse.*

An important consideration relative to the central focus of this book is the "Innovation-Adoption Curve" described in Rogers's *Diffusion of Innovations*. Rather than exploring why individuals change their perspective and eventually decide to adopt a technology, this curve describes change as being caused by the evolution of products and services themselves. In other words, through iterations technologies become a better fit for the needs of individuals and groups. In the *Diffusion of Innovations* theory, it is not people who change, but the innovations themselves.

What causes an individual (or a company) to decide that a particular technological innovation is finally desirable? Rogers and his associates identified five qualities that determine the success and ultimate acceptance of an innovation (or a converged combination of multiple innovations as we are seeing in the metaverse):

- *Relative Advantage.* This relates to the extent to which an idea or product is perceived as being better than the method in current practice. For example, many people ultimately decided the Ford Model T was a superior mode of travel to the horse and buggy. Most business people eventually concluded a smart phone was personally preferable to a BlackBerry. Most likely quantum computing will be perceived by most organizations in the coming decade as being better than digital computing. (However, quantum computing might still fall short in terms of some of the following factors which would slow its adoption.)

- *Compatibility.* Innovations that are consistent with the previous experiences of consumers or adopters are typically preferred. For example, many drivers have preferred the same brand and model of car for decades, even though newer models might offer "better" technology. We can begin to see the kinds of tradeoffs managers face when new technological eras emerge. As managers, we could agree that a new kind of quantum computer might offer a relative advantage over our existing digital infrastructures (see the preceding factor) but still be somewhat too complex for our organizations to adopt right now (see the following factor).

- *Complexity.* Innovations that can be easily understood are, obviously, usually preferred over those that require extensive instruction, new skills, or new habits. For example, some baby boomers still prefer land-line phones in their homes over cell phones. This is because to them, based on their specific needs and preferences, the older models are much simpler and easy to use. To IT people born into the digital era, the quantum computing model could represent a complex hurdle.

- *Trialability.* An innovation that can be "tried on for size" offers better comprehension of the innovation and, therefore, less risk. That is why, of course, many people prefer to drive a vehicle before buying one. In the final chapter of this book (Chapter 22) there is a detailed discussion of how a hypothetical company transformed itself from a traditional company mired in a commoditized, low-margin industry into a metaverse-ready one. Among the priority Phase One actions this hypothetical company took was to create both a Quantum Computing Demonstration Center and a Metaverse Innovations Lab. A central goal underlying the creation of both of these entities involved the trialability factor. The Innovations Lab would be used for experimenting with and trying out in prototypes a broad array of metaverse technologies, while the focus of the Demonstration Center would be solely on quantum computing. In addition to internal use, these facilities would be open, under controlled conditions, for use by existing and potential customers, universities, vendors, and potential alliance partners.

- *Observability.* Being able to see a technology in real situations (not just a demo or prototype) often reduces anxiety and uncertainty. See the above factor.

As we progress through the metaverse era, the governing structures of organizations will first want to consider carefully whether they are, as a whole, largely in the tech-savvy group, the pragmatic but open group, or the highly risk averse group. Typically, of course, this is not a state of being that is decided in advance but a state that happens to have evolved based on other factors that were decided earlier, such as risk tolerance. However, a strong leadership team can address this issue and steer a company in the preferred metaverse adoption direction. However, unless organizations happen to be in especially stable and safe businesses, if they fall into the highly risk-averse group they are likely to find life in the metaverse a difficult challenge.

If a leadership team does decide to try to motivate their employees to become bolder and more tech-savvy and avoid the technology adoption lag mentioned earlier in this chapter, they should study Everett Rogers. This means when selling their employees and customers on the overall metaverse concept and specific technologies, executives should perform a thorough analysis of such issues as relative advantage, compatibility, complexity, trial-ability, and observability.

If these same enterprise governance executives want to infuse into their enterprise the level of nimbleness necessary to function effectively in the metaverse, they need to emphasize the priorities discussed in this book. This begins with a flexible, unified, and open-minded governance structure, the deployment of a leading-edge enterprise architecture, and the modernization of the central IT services organization. Organizations that can effectively factor into their planning and decision-making framework all three of the areas outlined above should have a good head start in preparing to compete in the metaverse.

4.3 FOCUS ON ONE INDUSTRY: HEALTHCARE

To better understand why so many companies lag in technology adoption, we can look at the healthcare industry. We might logically think healthcare professionals and patients would welcome the use of advanced technologies to improve the outcomes of their healthcare encounters. Too often this is not the case. Both patients and care providers have been slow to utilize many advanced technologies.

As for patients, many still prefer face-to-face encounters with trusted human beings when it comes to diagnoses and treatments. They do not want too much technology to get in the way of these close, highly personal healthcare discussions, which are often unnerving to begin with. Many patients, especially the elderly, are not particularly technology literate. For example, they may be uncomfortable trying to set up telemedicine meetings.

As for healthcare practitioners and delivery systems, they tend to prefer, if not demand, methods, tools, and processes that have been well-established and proven over time. The possibility of a technology failure, such as a software glitch or other outage, is too high for many providers to accept. "We are talking life and death here," they will say, and rightfully so. In addition, many healthcare delivery executives and practitioners feel their needs are unique. This means technology-based approaches that might work for others are not appropriate for their own important healthcare functions. This is one of the most common rationales offered by organizations across all industries for avoiding new technologies and solutions ("We're very different, therefore …").

This same line of reasoning can be applied to a multitude of other business, technical, professional, and government environments. When all of this is aggregated into a larger socioeconomic reality, we can see from yet another angle why the adoption of seemingly better technology-based solutions often tends to be halting and slow.

Therefore, as has been true for all technological waves of change, it should not be surprising that there is already some resistance to the accelerating wave of metaverse-based technological developments. The reasons are basically the same as those outlined above, including institutionalized aversion to risks and a basic lack of understanding of what the new wave can offer.

The stakes are high. The companies that succeed in the metaverse era will be the highly nimble ones that understand the potential of these new technologies and how they can enable new business models. This is not a technology-driven wave of change where organizations can afford to wait three or four years to begin to leverage its benefits. If a company is not already somewhat familiar with most of the metaverse-era technologies and trends, it is probably already behind.

4.4 ACCELERATING TECHNOLOGY ACCEPTANCE

Many organizations facing a disruptive technology wave that could alter their competitive environments face a dilemma. To remain competitive in the new environment, these organizations must become nimbler; however, they lack the wherewithal to respond effectively to the disruption. This creates an interesting but dangerous dilemma. The following sections include suggestions to help overcome the inertia in adapting to and exploiting major technology shifts.

Ensure Familiarity with the Incoming Wave

Organizations facing a change wave like the metaverse should seed their staffing with a few talented people who understand what is about to happen in this area (or is already happening). The individuals having these capabilities can be trained within the company, hired, or contracted as temporary resident consultants. This kind of expertise is especially important to have in enterprise planning and decision-making positions. It stands to reason that if something is not understood, it cannot be acted on intelligently.

For example, in the early days of cloud computing, most organizations typically had only a few people who truly understood the cloud phenomenon. Often, these people were not in positions to drive strategy, or worse, even to be heard. Moreover, they tended to be greatly outnumbered by those who at the time often ridiculed the whole cloud concept. Therefore, the cloud phenomenon had early trouble penetrating in a positive way the consciousness of most organizations.

Here is one way to address the positive information penetration challenge. During the early days of cloud computing, the Chief Strategist for a multi-billion dollar business unit of a major defense contractor also served as a key technology gatekeeper for the business. This gave the executive a decent platform from which to speak. In his role as one of the lead technology experts, he prepared a daily news and analysis update that went out to hundreds of employees across the company, including virtually all senior level positions, as well as the leadership of some of the organization's important customers. During the days of cloud infancy, this executive would pepper each daily update with at least one story about cloud computing, along with his commentary on the relevance and importance of the story. As it turned out, through the efforts of this executive and others in the organization, the company became an early leader in cloud awareness and solution models. Later, this became a significant factor in the company winning considerable cloud-related business.

The point of this actual example is this. At least a few people in influential organizational positions, especially acknowledged gatekeepers, must understand as early as possible the implications of an impending change wave. They must then find credible ways to drive home information about these upcoming changes, and then do it over and over in a variety of innovative ways. Often, only through relentless messaging can you get the point across.

No matter how far out a buzzword or new trend might sound initially, executive managers should assign someone (or a small team) to scope it out. Given today's accelerating rate of technological change, executives cannot risk ignorance about a possibly important development. Stress the importance of timeliness. Have the team dig deeply, not just skim a few articles. For areas where they see potential, dig even deeper. Invite in vendors and consultants, being careful to scrutinize what they have to say to filter out their natural bias. Dialogue with peer organizations. Then, if there appears to be something real and significant, communicate the team's findings repeatedly across the enterprise.

Build a Coalition

Assuming there are at least a few executives in the organization who develop a good appreciation for the issues and possibilities inherent in an imminent disruption, the goal should be to build a coalition of dedicated and unbiased information seekers, people having no bias except for true understanding. If this initial respected coalition does find that something substantial and important is on its way, the next step is to expand the coalition. Keep expanding to the point where the organization develops a critical mass of people and groups ready to support, if necessary, an enterprise transformation in response to the particular change wave in question.

Find Attractive Use Cases

Abstractions and buzz phrases are not very good motivators, convincers, or attention grabbers. Assuming there is a coalition committed to persuading an organization to embrace a new technology wave, this group should identify real-life situations where attractive and important benefits can be shown.

Historically speaking, personal computers were not initially popular with most organizations. In fact, they were typically ridiculed as being little more than clunky, boxy, gadgets with fuzzy green screens of interest only to "gearheads" and electronics hobbyists. These first personal computers were seen as distractions from real work.

Then something important happened.

In 1979, Dan Bricklin and Bob Frankston implemented a product called VisiCalc on the Apple II. They launched it on the IBM PC in 1981. The spreadsheet had arrived! The product was an immediate hit and is the perfect example of an attractive use case.

The spreadsheet proved useful across most organizational functions and was fairly intuitive and easy to use. However, you needed a desktop computer to use it. Not surprisingly, personal computer use exploded in organizations in the 1980s. The organizational adoption profile for the PC would probably have looked much different had it not been for that early blockbuster use case.

Similarly, if a company thinks a new technology might be something it can and should exploit, that company should search for one or more use cases where solid, attractive, real-world benefits can demonstrate its potential. Sell it in ways your employees can see as adding actual value to their work lives, ways that can win them over. Do not lose initial employee support by making the initial project take too long. Look for additional good use cases right away. Soon, the initial naysayers will say they have been in full support of the technology the whole time, which is a good thing.

Declare Yourself Competent and Then Become So

Sometimes in life, you simply have to make a leap of faith. We have all seen instances where a company or a division within a company would simply declare itself expert in some area, even though at the time they definitely were not. They might do this, for example, to win a contract that required as a key qualification expertise in the area in question. (This activity is similar to padding your resume.)

One of the more effective ways to do this is to create and hype a showcase of some kind, such as a center of excellence, an innovation lab, or a demonstration center. This was done frequently when the cloud computing phenomenon was emerging.

Let's say, hypothetically, the name of a company is XTech and the technology in question is quantum computing. This company decides to develop such a facility, even though it has no real qualifications in quantum technologies. Let's call the facility "The XTech Quantum Computing Demonstration and Research Center." This glitzy name conveys to the world this company's leadership position in the area of quantum computing. The company then contacts vendors, consultants, academics, and organizations that have real-world expertise and accomplishments in the world of quantum computing and invites them in. Most are delighted to showcase their solutions, products, and accomplishments in this new facility. The company then rides the momentum gained from the first wave of experts to keep a stream of quantum computing-related companies and experts coming in. The center soon takes on a life of its own; it has actually become a valuable quantum computing resource.

What XTech has done is create a "platform" that connects experts in quantum computing with people and organizations who want to learn more about, and possibly adopt, quantum computing. The expert providers of this knowledge and the learners (or "consumers") might even strike deals and form relationships in the center (see Chapter 8, "Platforms"). XTech's only investment has been in the structure that houses the center and a small staff to coordinate various scheduling and support activities.

XTech's benefits would be twofold. First, it will have gained a leadership reputation in quantum computing simply through its ownership of such a showcase center and visible association with true experts. Second, its employees will eventually have learned much about quantum computing. XTech will have done this by having staff members attend the presentations and demonstrations provided by the external entities showcasing their high-tech wares in the showcase center. Through its new relationships and alliances with many of the demonstrating entities, XTech could even credibly claim it now has bona fide expertise in quantum computing.

4.5   KEY TAKEAWAYS

- As the metaverse era continues to take shape, organizations cannot afford the luxury of staying the current course while others, especially competitors, venture more aggressively into this new frontier.
- For example, if you are in the IT services, outsourcing, and consulting business and do not already have a portfolio of metaverse white papers, vetted customer briefing packages, and fledging offering descriptions, you are already lagging in your industry.
- Once organizations get behind in adapting to a disruptive technological innovation, regaining their lost competitive positions will likely be extremely difficult to achieve because change cycles are getting shorter and new waves of change will relentlessly follow.

REFERENCES

[Devaney21] Erik Devaney, 7 Tech Predictions That Totally Missed the Mark, HubSpot, June 10, 2021 *https://blog.hubspot.com/marketing/failed-tech-predictions*

[Rogers03] Everett M. Rogers, Diffusion of Innovations, 5th Edition Paperback – Illustrated, August 16, 2003 *https://www.amazon.com/Diffusion-Innovations-5th-Everett-Rogers/dp/0743222091*

[Moore14] Geoffrey A. Moore, Crossing the Chasm, 3rd Edition: Marketing and Selling Disruptive Products to Mainstream Customers (Collins Business Essentials) Paperback – January 28, 2014 *https://www.amazon.com/gp/product/0062292986/ref=as_li_qf_sp_asin_il_tl?ie=UTF8&camp=1789&creative=9325&creativeASIN=0062292986&linkCode=as2&tag=recovcomed-20*

[High Tech00] *An Overview of the Innovation-Adoption Curve,* High Tech Strategies *https://www.hightechstrategies.com/methods/technology-adoption-lifecycle/innovation-adoption-*

CHAPTER 5

NIMBLENESS IN THE ANIMAL KINGDOM

To better understand the essential attributes of truly nimble organizations, it is instructive to look at what nimbleness means in the animal world and then correlate these attributes with the nimble human enterprise. Nimbleness in the wild is achieved in multiple ways. This chapter looks at two of these ways.

5.1 RAW, PRIMAL, PHYSICAL NIMBLENESS – THE GAZELLE

An ambushed gazelle cannot outrun a cheetah in a short, straight-line burst. Instead, the gazelle relies on its incredible nimbleness to survive. It turns, darts, stops, starts, and feints with extraordinary dexterity, often causing the cheetah to overrun its pursuit path, spinout, and lose closing distance until finally it tires out and gives up. (Muhammad Ali once boxed the same way: light on his feet, nimble, quick, floating like a butterfly, stinging like a bee.)

> *Metaverse Lesson for Organizations: Elevate your levels of nimbleness and quickness.*

Escaping a predator is a commendable maneuver for any gazelle. However, a truly nimble one will avoid getting ambushed in the first place. Equipped with superior sensory perception capabilities and exceedingly responsive nervous and musculoskeletal systems, the gazelle is constantly scanning its environment for the slightest hint of danger. The animal's fast-twitch physiology allows it to bolt into escape mode simultaneously with the first sense of a threat – a slight rustle in the weeds, a subtle change in the sound of birds, a faint whiff of a suspicious smell.

Lesson for Organizations: Substantially elevate your situational aware-
ness and response capabilities.

A final aspect of nimbleness for the gazelle is an intricate cross-communication and mutual protection pact with the rest of the herd. The powerful sensory perception capabilities of one gazelle is amplified by the collective capabilities of the herd – its alliance partners, in effect.

Lesson for Organizations: Elevate your ability to form and evolve protec-
tive, high-leverage, lucrative alliances. Be the leader of such a pack (if
doing so makes strategic sense).

Of course, countless gazelles have had their days ruined by more nimble predators. Or perhaps they were injured, or simply unlucky on those particularly forgettable days. Or maybe they let their guard down for a second too long. These unfortunate gazelles, like countless companies that have lacked sufficient nimbleness, are no longer with us.

In the coming decade, predators in the metaverse business jungle are going to be very nimble and very fast, often running in packs (strategic alliances). In the metaverse era, therefore, organizations will require certain nimble capabilities similar to those of the gazelle:

- They will require superior information processing capabilities, coupled with highly responsive technology infrastructures (analogous to the highly responsive nervous and musculoskeletal systems of the gazelle). These are the attributes that enable faster and more accurate decisions, and thus nimbler responses.
- They will sometimes have to outmaneuver larger and faster competitors to get what they want.
- They will have to respond quickly and effectively to fast-changing conditions, often in unforgiving environments.
- They will have to maintain sophisticated alliances and partnership webs to enhance and extend their own capabilities, often performing as if they are much larger than they actually are.

These capabilities will be provided by an organization's enterprise-wide, well-integrated business and digital technology infrastructure. This kind of nimble business model can best be developed and maintained through the leadership provided by a unified governance structure using an enterprise architecture as the official strategic blueprint and information repository.

5.2 SUBTLE NIMBLENESS – THE CHAMELEON (AND REVERSE CHAMELEON)

In the gazelle example, we focused on pure, primal nimbleness: being faster, quicker, more agile, and more alert than predators or competitors. When we look at the chameleon, however, we can see a different kind of nimbleness, a more subtle and clever one. There will always be organizations that simply lack the wherewithal to be incredibly quick and nimble in a basic, raw, survival-of-the-fittest sense. These organizations will succeed by wile and guile, like the chameleon.

First, let's review why a chameleon does what it does. We might like to think chameleons change their color simply for camouflage, which is what many of us have been taught or assumed. However, chameleons actually change colors for four main reasons. The first reason is to control their temperature. The second is to communicate, much as humans use speech or sign language. The third is to attract mates. The fourth is to intimidate challengers ("Do not tread on me!").

Chameleons can change their colors at will, reconstituting their visible pigmentation and public identity, and they can do so rapidly. That is how many organizations lacking the nimble attributes of an animal like a gazelle will have to compete in the metaverse. They will do this in some combination of three ways. The first is to make themselves blend into the pack for strategic purposes. The second is to stand out from the crowd, also for strategic purposes. The third is to intimidate those who would do them harm, as in a hostile takeover attempt. Let's look in more detail at the first two ways.

Blending In (Less Common)

Most companies like to tout their discriminators (even if they are not real) to try to stand out from the crowd. However, sometimes it is better to blend in quickly and not get unwanted attention.

For example, sometimes an entire industry can get into serious difficulties, like large investment banks did in 2007 and 2008. During that time, many banks desperately wanted to avoid any kind of deep probe from investigators. So, quite understandably, their managers wanted their banks to blend in with other banks, chameleon-like.

The same thing happened for many tobacco companies in the events leading up to the 1998 Tobacco Master Settlement Agreement. This agreement was originally between the four largest US tobacco companies and the attorneys general of 46 states. These states eventually settled their Medicaid lawsuits against the tobacco industry. The goal of the lawsuits was recovery of tobacco-related health-care costs. The four large tobacco companies agreed to curtail or cease certain tobacco marketing practices, as well as to pay, in perpetuity, various annual payments to the states to compensate them for some of the medical costs of caring for persons with smoking-related illnesses. During these events, all tobacco companies wanted to maintain a much lower profile and to blend into the marketplace to avoid getting additional negative interest.

While not a common reaction, organizations do sometimes like to emulate the chameleon's quick blend-in capabilities.

Reverse Chameleon Effect (More Common)

Now, for the second example, which involves changing the business's "colors" swiftly to stand out from the crowd (the reverse chameleon effect).

Let's say your company is an IT consulting and outsourcing services business. Your business is similar to that of all of your competitors. Your company has cloud services, offers cybersecurity services, can take over a customer's service desk in an outsourcing move, and can manage data centers, just like your competitors. Since your company is in a commodity business, you are increasingly competing only on one dimension: the lowest cost.

Assume that, as the new CEO of Allied IT Information Services (AIIS), you want the company to stand out, and you want to do it as quickly as you can. You assemble your brain trust and lay out some new goals and competitive principles:

- *Within six months, you want a complete revamp of your marketing image.* You are changing your company's public image. Using the analogy of a chameleon, you want your marketing image to be as different from before as what occurs when a chameleon changes its color. You want to stand out from your competitors in your new marketing image. When people think of AIIS over the next three years and beyond, you want them to think of robust capabilities in areas such as virtual reality, augmented reality, quantum computing, and edge computing. You want to be associated with breakout-from-the-pack capabilities and non-commoditized core competencies.

This will begin to shift public sentiment and draw increased interest in your company. Simultaneously, you must actually develop the very products and services you say you will be marketing. Some might tell you, quite understandably, "This kind of change takes much longer than six months." Your calm but firm response is, "This is all the time we have. We are in the metaverse era now and operating at a different speed."

- *Next, you say to your team that within three months, you want to change the organizational "skin color" in another way, a way that makes your company look extremely attractive to alliance partners.* You know there is no way you can internally develop a professional-level blend of skills and offerings in such areas as virtual or augmented reality in a six-month time frame. Your business will have to accomplish this goal through a tight network of qualified alliance partners, consultants, and new hires. This means a company-wide effort is needed to create a business and organizational infrastructure that can attract and manage such a network of partners and new staff. Then, you have to go out and actually find and persuade the organizations and individuals you need to join up with you. Of course, highly paid management consultants will tell you this kind of challenge will take you much longer than three months. However, you smile pleasantly and explain that you have no real choice. You note that, "The metaverse slows down for no one. We are running out of time."

- *Next – or more or less simultaneously – you and your AIIS team are going to have to begin a difficult, and to some degree harsh, internal transformation of your strategies for staffing, structures, policies, processes, and procedures.* You are going to be offering new products involving new skills. This means you are going to have to decide, based on your prevailing enterprise philosophy (see Chapter 16, "Organizational Structure for the Metaverse Era"), whether you are going to replace existing people, retrain them, or reassign them. You are also going to have to decide how best to close out existing contracts and proposals that no longer align with your new business strategy. Other similar issues will abound. The only way to deal with these challenges in a useful timeframe is to make transformation a strategic priority of the highest order. Otherwise, your whole strategy could fail.

With a business/digital technology infrastructure in place that emulates in many ways the kind of nimbleness found in the wild kingdom, organizations will be able to

- sense threats and opportunities faster than less nimble competitors
- respond in highly nimble ways to changing markets, customer tastes and needs, economic conditions, and technological innovations and disruptions

- substantially reconstitute itself quickly, as situations dictate
- embrace ongoing innovation as an essential organizational capability
- maintain effective cyber and other security capabilities
- enter into and exit from strategic and tactical business alliances flexibly and quickly as opportunities and threats arise
- maintain a competitive edge in an era when change cycles are getting shorter and shorter, and when frequent periods of turbulence are the new normal
- maintain an environment where workers are the true stars of the company and can achieve their full potential

5.3 KEY TAKEAWAYS

- There are important parallels between the attributes of highly nimble life forms in the wild and the attributes required for organizations that want to operate in nimble ways in the "competitive wild" we are likely to see in the metaverse.
- One example is sheer physical nimbleness and quickness, like we see in a gazelle.
- Another example is a more subtle form of nimbleness achieved through subterfuge and craftiness, as we see in a chameleon.
- Competitive nimbleness in the metaverse requires an exceptional ability to read and react to changing events, a strong, well-integrated, and capable business-technology infrastructure, and an exceptional ability to form, participate in, and detach from strategic and operational alliances.

Key Technologies That Will Enable Organizational Nimbleness in the Metaverse Era

PRELUDE TO PART 3

Part 3 of this book discusses nine technologies or new business models that are already playing important roles in the evolution of the metaverse. These will become increasingly important over the next decade. They include the following:

- Chapter 6: Artificial Intelligence and Machine Learning
- Chapter 7: Blockchain
- Chapter 8: Platforms
- Chapter 9: Algorithms
- Chapter 10: Edge Computing
- Chapter 11: Quantum Computing
- Chapter 12: Immersive Technologies
- Chapter 13: Holographic Technologies
- Chapter 14: Deep Tech

Part 3 also includes one chapter (Chapter 15) containing summary discussions of other important metaverse technologies, including Robotics, Digital Twins, Industry 4.0 / Industrial Revolution 4.0, Internet of Things (IoT), Brain-Computer Interfaces, 3D Modeling and Reconstruction, Spatial Computing, and Web 3.0.

These are technologies and solution methods that organizations will want to track closely and adopt, as appropriate, based on their mission, markets, culture, competitive position, and timeline for becoming metaverse-ready.

However, as emphasized in earlier chapters, before organizations attempt the large scale adoption of any of these technologies, they should have made substantial progress in enhancing their nimbleness, quickness, and capacity for metaverse technology adoption and innovation. This means progress in the three critical areas of (1) responsive and informed governance, (2) advanced enterprise architecture capabilities, and (3) central IT modernization.

The process for tracking, evaluating, and adopting these technologies should be accomplished within the overall governance framework discussed throughout this book. The key components of this governance framework include the senior-level enterprise governance structure, a Chief Technology Officer (CTO) or Chief Architect, a technology evaluation / gatekeeping team, the enterprise architecture itself, and the central IT services organization. The general flow of the process is shown in Figure P.1.

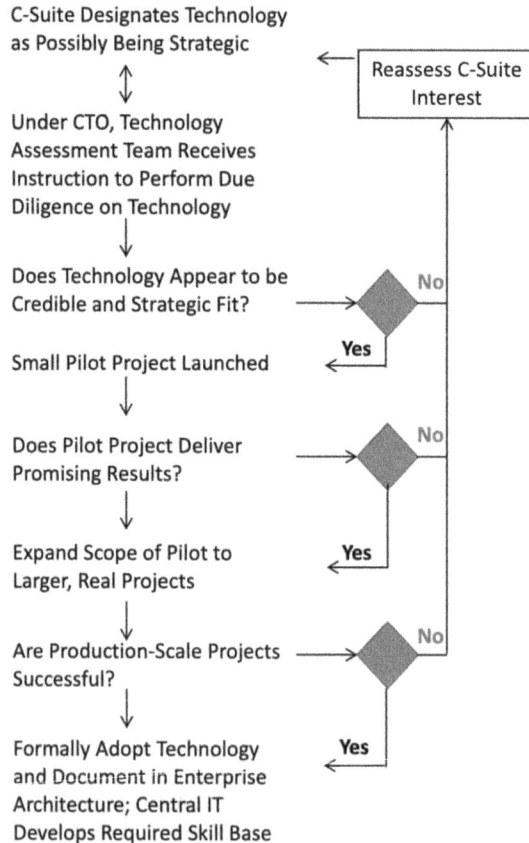

FIGURE P.1 Technology evaluation and adoption process

The formal initiation of the process shown in Figure P.1 to evaluate and possibly adopt a major technological innovation begins with the governance structure, working in close collaboration with CTO or equivalent position, to assess a potential new area of interest and decide whether to pursue it further.

As part of the decision-making process by the governing structure, a small team is assigned gatekeeping and analysis accountability for the entire enterprise, working closely with the Chief Architect. This team, whether formal or informal, might be comprised of one or two permanent staff, but most of the staffing will be temporary staff matrixed in from other organizations. The specific team mix will depend on the technology being evaluated and the area, or areas, of the organization where the technology would be used initially, if adopted. The gatekeeping and analysis team should perform the following actions:

- Monitor industry developments (via published works, conferences, consultants, vendors, competitor websites, and universities)
- Brainstorm possible use cases within the organization
- Conduct benchmarking visits with other organizations
- Develop internal white papers or position papers on the subject
- Conduct small, hands-on pilot projects, assuming access to the technology in question can be arranged
- Expand successful pilots to larger-scale solutions
- Provide regular briefings to executive management, along with appropriate recommendations
- Adopt the technology if the larger-scale production demonstration is successful

Based on input coordinated and provided by the gatekeeping unit, executive-level management takes the actions highlighted in Figure P.1.

Under the direction of the CTO, CIO, or Chief Architect, as appropriate, begin to assimilate gatekeeper input into an initial strategy for the adoption of the technology being evaluated, such as quantum computing. Begin to outline a strategy, even if at this stage you have no reliable timeline of when the technology will be production-ready.

As more is known, the executive team should work with the gatekeeping team, and others as appropriate, to develop contingency or situational "triggers" that will, when activated, accelerate or intensify strategy development. These trigger events might take the form of a highly publicized breakthrough in the availability of the technology, possible news about how the technology has helped cure a major disease or solved some other major societal issue, or a major action by a competitor to embrace the technology and feature it as a key service or product offering.

As action is launched in response to one of the trigger events being activated, the company should shift into the standard sequence of actions described throughout this book. Here are the key elements:

- *Declare Formal Adoption.* Enterprise governance announces formal embrace of the technology as a strategic focus area and outlines the high-level adoption strategy. This executive declaration is captured in Level One of the enterprise architecture.
- *Develop Accountability Breakout.* The executive-level strategy is then broken down into its various implementation and operational components (who, what, where, when, and how), which are also captured in the enterprise architecture. This process is coordinated by the CTO, Chief Architect, the gatekeeping team, and others as appropriate.
- *Establish Supporting Infrastructure.* Central IT then begins the process of training staff or acquiring skilled personnel to support any and all initiatives involving the new technology. These support needs might arise anywhere across the enterprise. Therefore, central IT must have a structure and operating model that is nimble and fast. Another major challenge for central IT will be to integrate, as appropriate, any new technology acquisitions and deployments with legacy IT computing architectures and assets.

Note: The technology evaluation process described in this section will not be repeated for each of the nine technology areas discussed in this book. This Prelude and Figure P.1 will be referenced in the "Key Takeaways" of each chapter in Part 3.

CHAPTER 6

ARTIFICIAL INTELLIGENCE AND MACHINE LEARNING

6.1 INTRODUCTION

In 1981, this author was employed by the Computer Sciences Division at the Oak Ridge National Laboratory (ORNL) in Oak Ridge, Tennessee. One of my colleagues at the time was the first woman to have received a PhD in Computer Science from the University of Tennessee. The subject of her thesis was artificial intelligence, or AI. She was featured in a Spring 1981 article in the *ORNL Review*. The title of the article was *Artificial Intelligence is Coming – Applications at ORNL*. [Johnson81]

This 1981 article is cited here to remind readers that AI, suddenly the hottest topic in the world of technology, has a long history of pioneering work performed in numerous organizations around the world similar to the Computer Sciences Division at the Oak Ridge National Laboratory. The AI concept has had to endure a lot of ridicule along the way, but it has an extensive and sound research and development legacy. Because of advances in technology, AI's time has come finally and it is here to stay, at least until the next major disruptive era.

6.2 THE GROWING IMPORTANCE OF AI IN BUSINESS

To function as an agile enterprise capable of competing in the fast-paced metaverse, coordinated decisions have to be made quickly and effectively across a networked, empowered enterprise. Business actions, such as investment decisions or new alliance agreements, often have to be made under stringent time constraints. Responses to customer questions have to be prompt, relevant, and accurate. Processes need to be streamlined and optimized through the use of advanced technologies. The ability to form teams quickly to pursue opportunities or counter threats must be enabled by exceptional communications capabilities. Improvements in overall business operations need to be continuous and meaningful.

For successful business operations in the metaverse, these enterprise capabilities will be enhanced significantly through the effective use of AI and machine learning (ML). Therefore, enterprise leaders planning on competing effectively in the metaverse need to understand the implications and potential revolutionary impact AI and ML will have on their organizational business models, structures, and competitive strategies.

ChatGPT as an AI Example

In late 2022 and early 2023, a product from the OpenAI Foundation called ChatGPT (for Generative Pretrained Transformer) provided a vivid example of the kind of capability that can be created using AI. OpenAI is a company that received billions of dollars in alliance and investment money from Microsoft, which was in the process of embedding ChatGPT into its various lines of existing and future business. This included Bing, Microsoft's search engine.

The global response to ChatGPT was effusive. The consensus on ChatGPT among early, credible users was one of surprise and even amazement. This came not only from the impressive things the bot could do, but by how its output was, in many instances, almost indistinguishable from human work, and in some cases superior.

The launch of ChatGPT was quickly followed by countless other examples of the innovative use of this AI use case. For example, Salesforce announced right after the ChatGPT debut that it would build a similar AI capability, Einstein GPT, into its line of products and services.

Besides Microsoft and Salesforce, numerous other companies moved, or were soon forced to move, toward similar AI-based capabilities to remain competitive. This latest incarnation of the AI phenomenon is continuing to gather interest. Companies now face a stark proposition: adapt soon to generative AI and other metaverse technologies or run the very high risk of obsolescence.

The sudden emergence and rapid, widespread adoption of ChatGPT is just another indicator of how rapidly metaverse era technologies can emerge and change business and service line strategies. This in turn demonstrates the importance of organizations being nimble enough to adapt quickly and effectively as these innovations emerge suddenly and are adopted quickly by their competitors.

ChatGPT-Like Tools For Enterprise Architecture?

This book has emphasized throughout the critical need for a much more intelligent and robust enterprise architecture framework if an organization is to have any chance of competing effectively in the metaverse. We can imagine how an AI-based tool like ChatGPT, or something similar, could help immeasurably in developing such an EA. Companies that manage to get such a tool in place first will have a distinct competitive advantage over those that are slower to react.

6.3   WHAT IS ARTIFICIAL INTELLIGENCE?

The term "artificial intelligence" can be a little misleading. After all, there is nothing "artificial" about improving the performance of a function, process, task, or organization by programming computers to perform certain tasks that humans can do, and then observing as these same computers "learn" continuously how to perform these tasks better, faster, and more accurately, sometimes performing them even more effectively than humans.

This is accomplished as the computer programs, or algorithms, performing the tasks ingest additional information as they execute, usually in the form of direct feedback from task execution and typically without human intervention in the process. This feedback provides additional data to the software performing the task, which then modifies itself, often becoming smarter and better at performing the task, and the cycle repeats. As these iterations continue, we have continuous learning, or "machine learning." This "execute-learn-execute-learn …" process might be better described as "steadily compounding knowledge" rather than machine learning, but that is just a matter of semantics. It is the steadily increasing capabilities that are important.

Simply put, therefore, AI (and its subset, machine learning), refers to systems or technologies that can imitate human intelligence in the performance of certain tasks and then iteratively improve their performance based on the information they collect through automated feedback means.

As noted earlier, organizations across most industries and lines of business around the world are turning increasingly to AI to transform and accelerate process execution, augment human performance, and develop the insights necessary for improved overall competitive performance. The core objective of AI is initially to replicate, then ultimately exceed, the way humans perceive and react to various real-world problems.

AI and its subordinate components are fast becoming primary catalysts for innovation. Some organizations have focused their AI initiatives on a few core strategic areas, while others, like oil and gas companies, are making AI a priority across entire broad swaths of the enterprise. When executed successfully, AI programs can help businesses make better decisions faster, lower costs, reduce risks, enable faster time to market, and make the enterprise nimbler and faster in carrying out objectives.

6.4   WHAT IS MACHINE LEARNING?

Machine learning is simply the ability of a computer program, or algorithm, to improve its ability to perform a certain task through repeated execution without having been explicitly programmed to do so.

For example, assume a city wants to create a computer program to predict crime patterns. This will be the program's essential task. City officials then load into a computing device an algorithm, along with data about past crime patterns. They continue to add new crime pattern data as it is collected. If the algorithm can successfully learn from this data and improve on its own at predicting future crime patterns, without having been explicitly reprogrammed or otherwise modified to forecast better, this would be true machine learning. The software is teaching itself.

Machine Learning in History

Machine learning is not a new concept. We can, for example, look back at the work of Arthur Samuel. [Esposito et al.17] Samuel was a computer scientist at IBM and a pioneer in AI. In 1959, Samuel designed a computer program that played checkers. The more games the program played, the more it learned and the better it became at the game. The learning was based on algorithms that could learn from and make predictions based on accumulated experiential data. This computer program was one of the first examples of AI in action. As a discipline, therefore, we knew decades ago that machine learning is based on the analysis and construction of algorithms that can learn from experience.

Over the decades since the pioneering work of Samuel and others, machine learning has proved to be an invaluable asset in certain environments, such as the finance industry, because it can solve certain problems at a speed and scale that human minds cannot begin to emulate.

Machine Learning vs. Deep Learning

Machine learning and deep learning (as well as neural networks) are subclassifications of AI that are often defined in similar ways. However, there are subtle differences. The differences among these models relate to how their algorithms actually "learn."

TechTarget has published an excellent article on deep learning by Ed Burns and Kate Brush. The title is simply "Deep Learning." [Burns, Brush21] The authors point out that traditional machine learning algorithms are linear. On the other hand, deep learning algorithms are based on a stacked hierarchy of levels of abstraction that are increasingly complex and sophisticated. They provide as an example how a toddler learns to distinguish the complex abstraction we all know as a dog from all of the other complex abstractions a toddler encounters. He does this by pointing at different objects and being told repeatedly "that is not a dog" or "that is a dog," as appropriate. Over time, the toddler has stacked enough layers of abstraction to understand very well what is a dog and what is not a dog.

The authors also discuss a number of areas where deep learning is used today. These include customer experience, text generation, aerospace / military, and medical research.

A subset of the machine learning concept, and related to deep learning, is neural networks, sometimes called artificial neural networks (ANNs) or simulated neural networks (SNNs). These networks, which mimic the human brain, provide the basis for deep learning algorithms. They operate by mimicking the way that biological neurons signal to one another.

Deep learning neural networks are used in a variety of ways. Commercial applications often focus on complex signal processing and pattern recognition challenges. Other areas include oil and gas exploration, weather forecasting and analysis, handwriting recognition, and facial recognition applications.

One example of the way neural nets are being used involves the more effective management and use of complex technology infrastructures involving cloud computing. They can help optimize, for example, distributed multiple processors, partitioning out workloads seamlessly and efficiently across diverse processor types and in varying quantities based on a variety of parameters. By taking advantage of the broad array of on-demand resource options now available through various cloud services, organizations can support deep learning models of any size.

6.5 AI AND SOFTWARE DEVELOPMENT IN THE METAVERSE

One of the more impactful uses of AI as we move forward into the metaverse and beyond will be AI-augmented software development. As we have noted, most companies today are basically software companies. Almost every process or function used by a company is to some degree driven by or dependent on software. The algorithms required to keep up with complex and shifting business demands will, without automated assistance, become increasingly time consuming to develop and expensive because they require developers with high skill levels. AI-augmented development can help companies meet this challenge. This could become a game-changing approach to software development, one that employs machine learning to deliver better software much faster. Better software means software that is more effective functionally, efficient, easily modifiable, reliable, and secure.

In the metaverse area, therefore, AI will become one of the most critical focus areas in the world of software development. This capability will be important for all companies, but especially those in the process of transforming to the metaverse. Speedy and effective software development will be a critical factor in accelerating the transformation process, as well as a key capability for sustained business success post-transformation. This is because metaverse-era companies will be forced repeatedly, often on short notice, to modify priorities, processes, product or service line portfolios, web sites, and alliance relationships. All of these actions will require rapid and effective software development, and AI-augmented software development is likely to be the answer to this challenge. Therefore, this capability should become one of the Phase One focus areas when planning a metaverse transformation roadmap.

6.6 AI AND THE SINGULARITY

Perhaps the ultimate expression of the likely impact of the metaverse and beyond has existed for several years in the term, the Singularity. This is a hypothetical point in time when the power of AI-powered technologies surpasses the cognitive powers of humans. This could lead, futurists say, to many unforeseen global, societal, and technological consequences, some good, some bad, and some disastrous on a massive scale. The really bad consequences could happen, according to these foreseers, if technology spins out of control in an irreversible way. It could easily become smart enough to bypass controls and guardrails. We have no way of knowing in advance which directions these AI advances might take, whether they will generally be helpful or harmful, or if we will be able to control them if that should prove necessary.

For a while, we could breathe easily about the coming of the Singularity because one of the first futurists to describe the concept, Vernor Vinge, expressed in 1993 his view that within three decades the technological means to create superhuman intelligence would be available. Alarmingly, however, he also felt that shortly after the ability to create superhuman intelligence becomes available, the human era will end. [Vinge93] Those 30 years have passed and the Singularity has not arrived. Yet.

Similarly, the prominent futurist most notably associated with the Singularity idea is Ray Kurzweil, author of the book *The Singularity is Near*. Kurzweil is aligned with Vinge with respect to the meaning and likely depth of impact of the Singularity concept. However, he believes there is a better chance these changes can be leveraged to help society. He has said in his writings that by the year 2045, we will experience a technological singularity that will completely alter the way we regard ourselves as human beings. [Reedy17] If Kurzweil is even close to being accurate, that would give us a little more time to prepare.

If the Singularity were to occur, it would not be a sudden big event. Many critical changes would already have happened leading up to the Singularity. In fact, they are most likely happening now, as noted throughout this book.

Has movement toward the Singularity accelerated more recently? Bots like ChatGPT have astounded observers in their ability to mimic the human brain. In a January 23, 2023 article by Darren Orf titled, "Humanity May Reach Singularity in Just 7 Years," we find through research being conducted by a leading language translation firm that we could approach the Singularity by 2030, if not sooner.

This author explains how AI researchers have been looking for signs of reaching the Singularity by measuring how AI progress is demonstrating skills and ability levels already comparable to or exceeding those of human being. He offers the example of language translation as being one key, human-like metric for assessing computer versus human capabilities. The evidence tells us computers are very close to closing the gap with humans in this metric. [Orf23]

6.7 AI / ML – COST CONSIDERATIONS AND AIAAS

The rapid emergence and evolution of AI-based chatbots like ChatGPT will affect the cost profiles of AI deployments in organizations, making many advanced AI capabilities available for a reasonable cost. However, this will take some time to sort itself out.

Historically, building a useful AI capability has typically required major investments, including hardware, software, and expensive skills. High-performance hardware computing resources had to be readily available to support data analysts and other professionals. Algorithms had to be developed (or acquired) and then operated and maintained. High-end software developers, analysts, and data scientists had to be hired, contracted, or developed (which often took considerable time). Moreover, there was no guarantee of success. According to Accenture, recent research revealed that only 12% of firms had advanced their AI maturity enough to achieve superior growth and business transformation. [Acenture23]

For many organizations, there another option. That option is for a company to buy just as much AI infrastructure support as it needs (both technology and people) for as long as it needs it. This option is called "AI as a service" or AIaaS.

Nimble organizations operating in the metaverse want to stay relatively small, focused, and streamlined. This can run counter to what is entailed in setting up a production-level AI and machine learning infrastructure. This can be expensive not only for the equipment and software required, but for the talented staff required to operationalize the AI infrastructure.

Therefore, one option is to buy only as much of these resources as you need for a specific initiative for a fixed amount of time. Most companies are familiar with the practice of acquiring various kinds of resources on demand, or "as a service." A common example is software-as-a-service (SaaS). A growing number of technology firms already offer on-demand the data science infrastructure components and skills a company might need for their AI/ML initiatives.

According to the technology adoption methodology described throughout this book (see Prelude to Part 3), what a company should typically do in the early phases of adopting a new technology or capability, including AI, ML, and data science, is conduct a few select pilot efforts to get a good understanding for what the technology can do. Based on the results of these pilots, the company can then decide to scale up, scale out, use the AIaaS model, or not use AI at all (not generally recommended).

If developing and maintaining a robust AI and machine-learning core competency is not central to your company's business plan, and if remaining keenly concentrated on your true core business lines is your goal, AIaaS can help you avoid making a large, distracting, and very risky investment. At the same time, through the AIaaS approach, you can still develop experience and expertise in this domain, reap data analysis benefits in a few narrowly scoped areas, and have a much better basis for deciding on the next phase of your company's AI / machine learning odyssey.

6.8 THE TIME TO ACT IS NOW

Examples of AI-based capabilities are offered in this chapter to demonstrate in real, tangible ways how rapidly the world is moving into a new technological era, especially as technologies such as AI and quantum computing continue to converge and amplify their tremendous potential. Once again, the point to take from all of this is organizations need to be transforming themselves *now* to ensure they have the fundamental attributes required to make the swift strategic, tactical, and operational shifts necessary to adapt to these changes.

For example, to look at just one industry, education, generative chat systems can write a research paper on almost any subject for a student within a day, a paper that would ordinarily have taken a month or more of research by the student. The student's instructor would not know the paper had been written this way. Is that a good thing or bad thing? Is the student simply using advancing technologies to get things done as efficiently as possible, much as society has always done? Or is this something that will "dumb down" society in many ways because we will no longer have to research, think, and labor over concepts or ideas and therefore achieve deep learning ourselves?

What this one AI-based product might do to the education discipline or industry should be serious food for thought by all educators and educational institutions.

6.9   KEY TAKEAWAYS

- AI, machine learning, deep learning, and neural networks are members of a related group of "learning" technologies that are collectively forming the cornerstone of innovation, speed, and nimbleness in organizations worldwide.
- Companies that expect to compete effectively in the metaverse will almost certainly have to improve their capabilities in these areas, especially their AI and machine learning capabilities. Whether they do this by building up these capabilities internally, or whether they follow an on-demand strategy and seek out AI-as-a-Service providers, depends on the needs of each specific company.
- If your organization is not proficient in understanding and use of AI and machine learning, and if your executive management team sees potential benefit in their use, your organization should follow the steps outlined in in the Prelude to Part 3 (see Figure P.1). This will ensure the organization can assess carefully and validate (or not) the benefits of these technologies. If the benefits are deemed real and relevant to the company's mission, and

if these technologies get positive results in pilot initiatives, they can be captured in the enterprise architecture as an adopted technology, and eventually be deployed in ways that improve business performance.

REFERENCES

[Acenture23] *The art of AI maturity*, Accenture *https://www.accenture.com/us-en/insights/artificial-intelligence/ai-maturity-and-transformation?c=acn_glb_aimaturityfrompgoogle_13131823&n=psgs_0622&gclid=CjwKCAiAk--dBhABEiwAchIwkdBFfrsG9t3G8DCg-yzBO7yD1OS6ostG54ubYPE-Lo9Ah5IO4aSHl9BoCLBQQAvD_BwE&gclsrc=aw.ds*

[Burns, Brush21] Ed Burns, Kate Brush, *Deep Learning*, TechTarget, March 2021 *https://www.techtarget.com/searchenterpriseai/definition/deep-learning-deep-neural-network#:~:text=Deep%20learning%20is%20a%20type,includes%20statistics%20and%20predictive%20modeling.*

[Esposito, et al.17] Mark Esposito, Kariappa Bheemaiah, Terence Tse, *What is Machine Learning*, The Conversation, May 3, 2017 *https://theconversation.com/what-is-machine-learning-76759*

[Johnson81] Carroll Johnson, *Artificial Intelligence is Coming – Applications at ORNL*, Oak Ridge National Laboratory Review, Spring 1981 *https://www.ornl.gov/sites/default/files/ORNL%20Review%20v14n2%201981.pdf*

[Orf23] Darren Orf, *Humanity May Reach Singularity Within Just 7 Years, Trend Shows*, Yahoo Finance, January 23, 2023 *https://www.yahoo.com/lifestyle/humanity-may-reach-singularity-within-222900100.html*

[Reedy17] Christianna Reedy, *Kurzweil Claims That the Singularity Will Happen by 2045*, Futurism, October 15, 2017 https://futurism.com/kurzweil-claims-that-the-singularity-will-happen-by-2045

[Vinge93] Vernor Vinge, *Technological Singularity*, Whole Earth Review, December 10, 1993 *http://www.aids-3d.com/technologicalsingularity.pdf*

CHAPTER 7

BLOCKCHAIN

7.1 BLOCKCHAIN AND SMOOTHER ENTERPRISE INFORMATION FLOW

Among the many benefits of blockchain is its ability to facilitate the timely flow of accurate, secure information enterprise-wide. As emphasized throughout this book, the smooth flow of information is the lifeblood of any enterprise. Just as blockages of blood flow in the human body can cause serious problems, blockages of information flows can damage the performance of any enterprise. Conversely, the faster and more smoothly accurate and secure information can flow throughout the enterprise, the better it is likely to perform. This is because prompt access to accurate and secure information leads to better decisions made in more timely ways and more fluid overall operations. This can in turn elevate an organization's overall nimbleness and fluidity. For this and other important reasons, blockchain technology must become an important consideration in any metaverse transformation strategy.

7.2 WHAT IS BLOCKCHAIN?

Blockchain is a special kind of distributed database that exists in the form of a shared, immutable (i.e., unchangeable) ledger. This design expedites the process of recording transactions and tracking assets in a business network.

The blockchain database exists in the form of *blocks*, with each block containing a cryptographic hash of the previous block, a time stamp, and end-to-end transaction data. The assets being tracked can be tangible, such as buildings, or intangible, such as patents. Almost anything that has value can be tracked and traded on a blockchain network. This reduces risks and cuts costs for all stakeholders in the items being tracked.

Blockchain excels in delivering secure information because the information it provides is immediate, can be shared in an open but controlled and secure way, and is fully transparent. Because the information is stored within an immutable ledger that can be accessed only by permissioned network members, a blockchain can track various kinds of highly sensitive information with very strong security. The website CryptoManiacs offers a good overview of what an immutable ledger is in a brief article [Crypto23]. The author points out the fact that if a hacker attempts to change anything in a ledger this changes the hash. This means in turn the hacker would have to then change every block in the blockchain, which is impossible. That is why the blockchain is immutable.

Members of a blockchain share a single view of information. Therefore, users of the information can see all of the details of a transaction from end-to-end, providing greater confidence in the accuracy and reliability of the information received. Because this technology contributes so heavily to improved information flow, the judicious use of blockchain in certain environments can be a boon to organizational nimbleness.

Different Kinds of Blockchains

There are several different kinds of blockchains, and there will be more in the future. For example, a *public blockchain* (e.g., Bitcoin) is a large-scale, distributed network. Anyone can join a public blockchain network whenever they want. Anyone can see the network's ledger at any time and engage in the network's consensus-driven process. A *native token* is the basic token used in a public blockchain. The companies that provide public blockchains say this model offers exceptional security. Because every user on a public blockchain can see the ledger at any time, there is always transparency.

Permissioned blockchains define and regulate (permit) the roles various users can play within the blockchain network. Blockchains that are not governed, such as public blockchains, run the risk of new members joining for nefarious reasons. To prevent this from happening, the permissioned blockchain access model uses a tighter governing structure. Under this structure, users require permission and added scrutiny from the governing body before being allowed to join the blockchain. Like public blockchains, these are large, distributed systems that use a native token.

Private blockchains are usually smaller and do not operate using a token. Membership is tightly regulated. Private blockchains are often used by consortia comprised of trusted members who routinely trade confidential information. This method is more appropriate for enterprises seeking to use blockchain only for internal uses.

Following are examples of leading blockchain platforms for possible use in the enterprise:

- *Ethereum:* This is one of the more established blockchain platforms. Because it is decentralized, it is comparable to the Bitcoin blockchain. Ethereum is a good option for smart contracting because it offers extensive functionality and flexibility. Among its negatives are slow processing times and higher transaction processing costs.
- *Hyperledger:* This platform offers free tools and frameworks, allowing developers to build their own blockchain-based solutions.
- *Quorum:* This platform is regarded as being faster than Bitcoin and Ethereum. Quorum is not open to everyone. It is available only to those who have been approved by a designated authority. Quorum is well suited to situations that require both the ability to deliver high-speed private transactions and high-volume throughput.
- *Corda:* This blockchain is used widely within the finance industry. Transactions are processed in real time. This provides better performance than other types of blockchains.

Traditional Databases versus Blockchain

There are significant differences between a conventional database, like SQL, and a blockchain database. The major difference between the two architectural designs is the degree of centralization of each model. For traditional databases, all records are centralized and secured under a central control function, typically a database administrator. However, in a highly decentralized way, each blockchain user has access to a secured copy of all records and all changes so the user can view the origin and life cycle of the data.

While a traditional database organizes data in the form of tables, blockchain organizes its data into blocks that are linked (or chained) together. The blockchain data structure creates an irreversible timeline of data when deployed in a decentralized design. When one of the blocks is filled, it is locked in place and becomes an integral part of the timeline. Each block in the chain is given a time stamp when added to the chain.

Both blockchain and traditional databases have their pluses and minuses, and each is well suited to specific use cases. For example, traditional databases, being long-established and well understood, are easier to implement and maintain, plus they are extremely fast and offer exceptional scalability. Blockchain databases, while typically more difficult to implement and maintain and somewhat slower in operation, offer the advantages of a distributed ledger, exceptional integrity, full transparency, and strong security.

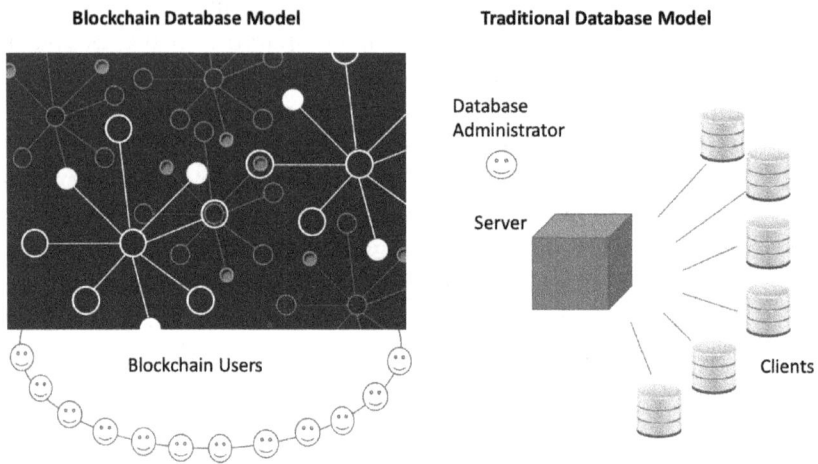

Blockchain Image Courtesy of Pixabay, Geralt

FIGURE 7.1 Traditional databases and blockchain databases have different designs.

As shown in Figure 7.1 and noted earlier, traditional databases are more centralized than blockchain databases. They generally employ a client-server architecture and are under the control of a central authority, the database administrator. Through their database management systems (i.e., controlling software), traditional databases support what is often referred to as *CRUD* functions (create, read, update, and delete). This means, for example, users (as well as hackers) can modify the data stored on a centralized server, as can the database administrator, who can delete data as well. Blockchain databases, however, only support read and write functions. Traditional databases are not fully transparent like blockchain databases because authorization to access or view certain data in a traditional database is granted by the database administrator.

Unlike traditional databases, blockchain databases consist of multiple decentralized nodes, with no centralized management or access control. This means each node or user participates in overall blockchain database administration by, for example, authenticating new additions to the blockchain. Each node is also able to enter data into the database. Full transparency, coupled with a consensus governance approach, ensures the security of the blockchain database. Tampering with or compromising blockchain data is difficult. In addition, blockchain databases are less prone to failure than traditional databases.

In summary, each approach offers great utility depending on the nature of a particular set of requirements. Blockchains would generally be the preferred option if there is a compelling need for a strong, fault-tolerant, and secure way to store critical data in a fully transparent way. Traditional database systems would be more advantageous if speed, performance, and lower costs to create and maintain are the compelling factors. In general, either option would likely be a reasonable choice for most applications, depending on the critical performance objectives that have been defined for a particular application. There are some essential questions to ask when choosing among these options. For example, what are the most important performance parameters for the application in question? Are they speed, lower overall costs, flexibility, and scalability, or are they security, transparency, traceability, decentralization, and immutability? A carefully considered and well-defined mix of critical performance factors for an organization will sway it toward one of the two options.

Other Uses of Blockchain

Blockchain use is still somewhat focused on the recording and storing of transactions for cryptocurrencies such as Bitcoin. However, blockchain technology advocates are already developing and testing other uses for blockchain, including supply chains, payment processing, healthcare (e.g., electronic medical records), managing Internet of Things data, government organizations, and digital IDs.

As organizations develop or implement their plans to transform to the metaverse, smart managers will want to understand blockchain technology and its potential benefits. With this understanding, they can develop their own original concepts for using blockchain to improve their organization's nimbleness, security, efficiency, and capacity for innovation.

One interesting use of digital assets spanning the virtual and blockchain realms is the non-fungible token, or NFT. *Non-fungible* simply means the token cannot be exchanged or replaced because each one has unique properties. Conversely, physical currencies and cryptocurrencies are both *fungible*.

This means they can be traded or exchanged for one another. NFTs are frequently used to authenticate Internet collectibles, including music, games, and especially art. The NFT becomes an authentic, unique, non-tradeable certificate created by blockchain.

As noted, one popular use of NTFs takes place in the world of art. Artists have seen their lives changed because of the sales of art made over the Internet to a new crypto-savvy audience. NFT assures buyers they are getting the genuine article and not a fake. When the NFT is put in a blockchain, the history of the owner's record validates the lineage of the item of art received ensuring the lineage began with the artist chosen by the owner.

Blockchain and Cybersecurity

Because organizational nimbleness depends on the smooth and timely flow of relevant, reliable, and secure information, security is always a concern. If, for example, our daily transmissions over the Internet were not secured through various encryption means, much of what we do would be far too risky, meaning e-commerce would probably never have reached its current robust state. However, contemporary cryptographic management methods and solutions are becoming obsolete. Most are inefficient and increasingly powerless when it comes to staying ahead of the converging technologies described in this book. Current cryptographic methods will become more problematic when confronted with the complex data structures and massive information flows we will see in the metaverse era.

The various forms of cryptography used today generally work well because it takes a tremendous amount of time and effort to crack an encryption key. Experts tell us it would take a supercomputer hundreds of years to break a single public-private code. However, there is the problem. A quantum computer will be capable of doing in minutes what might take a classical digital computer hundreds of years to do. Quantum computing is probably nearer to being production-ready than many of us think (see Chapter 11, "Quantum Computing"). This could present organizations with a serious new level of security challenges.

However, even if the arrival of quantum computing is not imminent, hackers are becoming skilled in the use of other metaverse-era technologies, such as machine learning (see Chapter 6, "Artificial Intelligence and Machine Learning") and cryptanalysis technology. These threats can also pose major problems for today's organizations. For example, if one of today's cryptographic algorithms proves to be vulnerable, it might require years of effort to replace that algorithm with a safer one. This is due in part to dynamic conditions in the evolution of digital technologies, which are contributing to the incompatibility of software and hardware cryptographic solutions. Therefore, governments, organizations, and security experts worldwide are going to have to develop new cybersecurity tools and methods if they want e-commerce as we know it to carry forward into the metaverse.

That is where blockchain comes into play. For example, the full encryption capabilities of blockchain ensures that data can only be accessed by authorized parties while traversing untrusted networks. The immutability and traceability attributes of blockchain ensure data integrity. For every new iteration within a blockchain, the previous state of the system is stored. This feature allows a fully traceable history log. Because blockchains have no single point of failure, denial-of-service attacks are far less likely to be successful. In a blockchain, data remains available via multiple nodes. As a result, full copies of the ledger are accessible at all times. Multiple nodes coupled with distributed operations makes blockchain systems highly resilient.

An Example of Blockchain Use in the Enterprise

One excellent example of how global organizations, both public and private, are using technologies like blockchain and AI to overcome inefficient bureaucracies and their aging infrastructures involves UNICEF and an enterprise called One Smart (OS) City. [OneSmartS23] This blockchain success story is described by Jesús S. Cepeda in an article titled "One Smart: Creating data-driven, verified cities through blockchain and AI." [Cepeda18] The subtitle is "Developing a blockchain and AI software to increase transparency and accountability of government allocations of resources." This article is useful, not only for readers involved in city or municipality planning, but as a way for anyone to get a better feel for the effective use of metaverse technologies in organizations, especially government organizations.

UNICEF Ventures is part of UNICEF's Office of Innovation. This is an organization tasked with exploring emerging technologies with the potential to positively impact children and young people globally. For the past several years, this team has been actively researching and experimenting with blockchain technology. It found this technology can provide efficiency, trust, and security better than any other technology they have explored.

One challenge for this team is that, as cities grow, governments experience an increasing lack of institutional nimbleness, much as we see in many large, conventional organizations. This prevents many of them from respond-ing effectively to citizens' growing demands.

This team was struck by a McKinsey report [Cunningham et al.18] that said inefficiencies in public sector infrastructures are a primary cause for over five trillion dollars in government revenues missing each year. As we have noted throughout this book, for any large bureaucracy, issues such as a large size, the existence of functional silos, frequent leadership changes, and bur-densome legacy systems make it difficult to transition to an improved state. This team was faced with solving that kind of problem. The team began with a focus on one of its portfolio companies called One Smart City (OS City).

The OS City team quickly developed an open source digital certification solution using blockchain to increase transparency, preserve data integrity, and accelerate the use of portable records. According to Cecilia Chapiro, Investment Lead, UNICEF Innovation, OS City currently has similar proj-ects underway or completed in Argentina, Chile, Costa Rica, and Mexico. [Chapiro21] Examples of official records having their use and protection enhanced by this solution include commercial permits, university diplomas, city inspector's badges, fair-trade artisan products, commercial licenses, construction permits, renewable energy purchasing, organic food, and art value. Records show these are providing transparency, security, traceabil-ity, and accountability on public assets, impacting the lives of more than 960,000 citizens.

Obviously, cities around the world are burdened by the same kinds of archaic, unsafe, slow, and often barely functional business and technol-ogy infrastructures discovered by OS City in the cities they investigated. Innovative city officials everywhere, and the technology contractors they use, will certainly want to examine closely the potential of blockchain and AI for creating more responsive, efficient, and effective government operations.

7.3 KEY TAKEAWAYS

- The blockchain concept and its growing collection of use cases pres-ents executives with yet another digital innovation they can leverage for improved overall enterprise performance.
- Blockchain can be used in concert with other digital innovations, like plat-forms and edge computing, to enhance organizational nimbleness, speed, and capacity for sustained innovation.

- Among the key benefits organizations can achieve using the blockchain approach are enhanced agility, time savings, cost savings, increased transparency, and improved security. For example, with respect to impenetrable security, major institutions like Citigroup and the London Stock Exchange have already embraced blockchain technology. They expect to use the technology to improve their ability to protect intellectual property and investment portfolio records.

- If your organization is not up to speed in understanding the blockchain concept and its possible uses in your business model, it should follow the steps outlined in in the Prelude to Part 3 (see Figure P.1). This will ensure your organization can assess and validate (or not) the benefits of blockchain. If the benefits are deemed real and relevant to the company's mission, and if blockchain gets positive results in pilot initiatives, this technology can be captured in the enterprise architecture as an adopted technology, and eventually be supported in ways that improve business performance.

REFERENCES

[Cepeda18] Jesús S. Cepeda, *One Smart: Creating data-driven, verified cities through blockchain and AI,* UNICEF Office of Innovation, December 9, 2018 *https://www.unicef.org/innovation/stories/one-smart-creating-data-driven-verified-cities-through-blockchain-and-ai*

[Chapiro21] Cecilia Chapiro, Investment Lead, UNICEF Innovation, Can Blockchain Increase Agility in the Public Sector? A Case Study of UNICEF Innovation Fund's Portfolio Company, OS City, UNICEF Office of Innovation, July, 2021 *https://www.unicef.org/innovation/stories/can-blockchain-increase-agility-public-sector*

[Crypto23] CryptoManiacs, *Immutable Ledger,* 2023 *https://cryptomaniaks. com/cryptocurrency-glossary/i/immutable-ledger#:~:text=The%20word% 20Immutable%20means%20%E2%80%9Ccannot,record%20that% 20cannot%20be%20changed.*

[Cunningham et. al18] Susan Cunningham, Jonathan Davis, and Thomas Dohrmann, *The trillion-dollar prize: Plugging government revenue leaks with advanced analytics,* The McKinsey Quarterly, January 29, 2018 *https://www. mckinsey.com/industries/public-and-social-sector/our-insights/the-trillion-dollar-prize-plugging-government-revenue-leaks-with-advanced-analytics*

CHAPTER 8

PLATFORMS

8.1 INTRODUCTION

The term "platform" can be used in a variety of contexts, such as a physical platform (e.g., a train platform), political platform, show business platform, or social platform. However, within the context of this book, we are focused on how special kinds of platforms are used heavily in business operations, ways that will have important relevance in the metaverse era.

In a business use context, a platform is not a technology but a business construct that can take multiple forms. A business platform can be an overall business model (e.g., Airbnb), a strategy for organizing resources internally to accomplish certain tasks (a platform team, for example), or a product platform, such as the iPhone. Because the platform concept will play such an important role in the metaverse era organizational strategies and the deployment of metaverse technologies, it deserves discussion in this part of the book.

8.2 DISCUSSION OF BUSINESS PLATFORMS

Consider this business model for a moment: Airbnb has developed a successful business by obtaining rental access and rights to millions of homes around the globe, yet the company owns not a single one of them. This is a prime example of the platform as a business model. This is a model that will be used widely in the metaverse because it is a light-weight business model that is efficient, nimble, and highly adaptable.

A platform as a business construct generates value by facilitating interactions or exchanges between interdependent groups, typically consumers and producers (or buyers and sellers). Examples include Airbnb, Uber, Amazon, and Meta. Business platforms are often integrated with sophisticated business and technology ecosystems that can give it great value.

One important benefit of the platform as a business model is the ability of a platform organization to compete effectively with a reduced investment in costly infrastructure. This benefit can contribute significantly to organizational nimbleness because the organization is not encumbered in its actions by being in a complex linear business or possessing extensive and limiting infrastructure and inventory baggage.

Finally, due to its openness, another major benefit of the platform approach is its extensibility and scalability. This aids an organization in its ability to grow, both functionally (e.g., added product lines) and in terms of scope and size. This is another key attribute that adds to organizational nimbleness and fluidity.

Business-related platforms can also be viewed in two other important ways. For example, there is a product platform, such as the iPhone from which a steady stream of enhanced products has flowed over the years based on the same basic platform. Microsoft Windows is another example. The first Windows platform was released in 1985 in response to growing interest in graphical user interfaces. Since then, the same Windows platform has seen multiple extensions, variations, and refinements. The use of the platform concept in this manner can lead to faster time to markets, quicker reaction to market opportunities and threats, improved operating efficiency and productivity, lower risks by extending a proven product, reduced costs, and higher quality.

There are also internal organizational platforms. These are often used as a way to consolidate and fully empower a collection of organizational resources (people, capital, and supporting services) to accomplish a specific task, and do so with minimal supervisory control.

The remainder of this chapter focuses on the two platform concepts that are the most relevant to an enterprise transformation to the metaverse, the business platform model and the internal organizational platform model.

Platform as a Business Model

The platform as a business concept is not complex, nor is it new. Consider, for example, the village bazaar, a business model used in major parts of the world for centuries. These ancient bazaars had simple physical infrastructures, perhaps just a roof and some tables or shelves, much like today's flea markets and open-air farmers' markets. The core business component of an ultra-simple platform business, like a flea market, is often nothing more than a brief document defining rates for the use of space in the facility and basic procedures for its use.

The platform as a business model is designed to facilitate business exchanges between two or more groups with allied interests, typically consumers and producers. In the simple bazaar example, a "producer" might use the platform to offer a bushel of corn to a "consumer" who would, in turn, offer the producer some form of payment. The owner of the bazaar infrastructure would simply charge producers for space, usually having a higher price for covered space versus uncovered space.

Today, we see examples of business platform models all around us (such as Meta, Uber, Amazon, and eBay). These are massively larger and infinitely more complex platforms than the simple flea market, of course, even though they share the same basic business model concept.

The ability of a good business platform to connect producers and consumers leads to a major benefit of the model – a convenient one-stop facility where businesses and busy consumers can meet, whether physically or digitally, and do business with each other. Think of a local mall or grocery store, each of which connects a large number of diverse suppliers with customers. Standard businesses, such as cloud brokerage providers (that connect cloud providers with companies needing cloud services) or classical systems integrators (that develop solutions or products by integrating resources or components provided by other entities), align well with the platform concept.

Efficiency and Scalability Benefits

In traditional non-platform businesses, scalability and extensibility have been achieved by investing more in internal infrastructure resources. Over time, this has greatly reduced organizational flexibility as companies have become increasingly burdened with their steadily accumulating legacy infrastructures. In today's intricately networked world, scalability and flexibility can be achieved by building highly efficient, light-infrastructure, and well-networked business ecosystems on top of a core business platform. For example, Amazon was able to diversify its initial Internet-based book-selling platform into a completely different line of business, cloud computing services. This strategic move did not require a new platform, but an extended and innovative use of its existing platform.

In the village bazaar example, the owners of these platforms would not have offered bushels of corn or any other products or services. This is because they would not have wanted to be in a supply-chain-based business. They did not want to worry about inventories, spoilage, returned products, or many other infrastructure headaches that producers had to manage.

Under any platform business model, therefore, the core competency for the platform owner is primarily providing the means to connect producers and consumers, although some platform organizations, like Amazon, have built supply chain businesses on top of the platform. Pure platform businesses generally choose not to directly offer the kinds of products and services exchanged by the entities befitting from the platform's connective capability. For example, so far we do not see an Uber branded vehicle or an Airbnb hotel chain. Put more simply, platform businesses provide a means to connect, not a means of production.

Because a platform business typically does not own much in the way of actual product inventories and associated infrastructure and business processes (aside from the platform), they can move much more nimbly and require less capital for strategic moves. This means, product development, research, and marketing budgets can also be smaller and more effectively targeted and redirected as needed.

As mentioned earlier, another important benefit of today's platform business model is the enablement of rapid scalability and accelerated growth. Because of the exceptional scalability and extensibility platform-based business models offer, they are able to make business ecosystem connections on a vast, on-demand, and flexible scale. This leads to intricately connected, synergistic markets and communities of interest where transactions and relationships create their own network effects. Over time, everyone benefits even more.

A good business platform often creates a sophisticated ecosystem of consumers and providers who collaborate with each other, as well as the platform owner, to develop innovations in the products and services being exchanged and methods of exchange. This attracts more participants to the business platform's ever-expanding ecosystem. The beauty of this dynamic is that much of this innovation churn not only benefits consumers and producers, but accrues organically to the business platform itself. Again, think of all the diverse product providers and consumers who are able to meet and exchange goods and services using the Amazon platform.

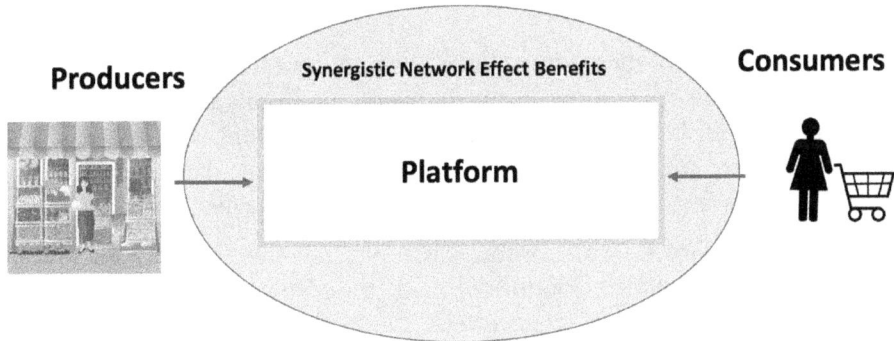

Chart Components Courtesy of Pixbay, Dandelion_Tea and Mohamed_Hassan

FIGURE 8.1 Platforms benefit all participants through network effects.

As shown in Figure 8.1, all participants in a platform business framework benefit from the speed, agility, scale, and reduced costs offered by the platform. The platform model also enables organizations to benefit internally from exogenous innovations, while maintaining levels of scalability and flexibility not possible in conventional business models.

Consider, for example, a classic IT outsourcing company, "Company A." In the purest form of an outsourcing contract, Company A takes over all of the IT resources of another company ("Company B"), people and all. Company A then integrates Company B's IT resources into its much larger overall IT outsourcing business portfolio and infrastructure. The business platform in this instance is the ability of Company A to connect not only users of IT resources in Company B, but users of IT resources from many other companies, to all of the integrated and organized outsourced resources managed by Company A.

Company A can now provide these resources in a number of more efficient ways by, for example, tapping into a variety of partnering resource providers, like cloud service providers, on-demand personnel staffing firms, and various other subcontractors. Users in Company B and all other customer companies do not care about sources and methods as long as contracted IT service level agreements are met. This is an example of a value-added platform model.

Over time, as Company A provides various IT services from its central platform, it will develop valuable expertise in certain attractive areas, say cybersecurity, that it can turn into its own lines of business. In this case, much like Amazon built its cloud computing business on top of its basic business platform, Company A can build a new cybersecurity business on top of its core IT outsourcing platform.

All three of the platform-as-a-business benefits mentioned above – a convenient one-stop source for busy people and organizations, rapid scalability and accelerated growth, and a much more efficient way of doing business – contribute in an important way to enhanced organizational nimbleness, an essential requirement for competing in the metaverse era.

For more information on this topic, see the *Harvard Business Review* article, "Pipelines, Platforms, and the New Rules of Strategy" [Van Alstyne et al.16]. In this article, the authors discuss in more depth the dynamic wherein platform-based businesses facilitate high-value exchanges between producers and consumers leading to competitive advantage. When these results are achieved at sufficient scale, a platform-based enterprise can dominate an industry.

The Internal Organizational Platform Model

Not only is the idea of a pure business platform model not new, neither is the use of "platform thinking" within non-platform-based or more hierarchical organizational models. An increasing number of organizations are evolving their organizational structures to a more networked state by gradually increasing the use of the internal organizational platform model. This model is a method of organizing a structured collection of resources (such as people and capital) and empowering it fully to perform some function or task. For many companies, this results in an interim hybrid organizational model that is still somewhat hierarchical but moving toward a model that is more networked and nimble.

There are numerous variations on the use of the platform concept internally, including models designed for developing or selling products or services, software development, engineering projects, and internal business functions or projects. Any one or all of these might be an appropriate platform candidate for a metaverse-capable organization.

Platform-based internal teams often include people from diverse responsibility areas, all dedicated to a positive team outcome. They have a common charter and are focused on very specific business, functional, or technical outcomes. They typically have full, end-to-end ownership of whatever might be detailed in their charters. One of the most important attributes of this model is the empowerment of these teams to make their own important decisions. This allows them to deliver desired outcomes in a timely manner. A side benefit of this type of platform strategy is the way it can enhance teamwork and collaboration across organizations by sharing corporate knowledge and expertise. As the platform model is used repeatedly over time by multiple teams, employees across the enterprise can discover how to work together more effectively and break down traditional barriers. These benefits can accrue and compound over time as people build up a history of working on multiple platform teams.

We have noted the relative lack of adaptability and flexibility of organizations burdened with excessive bureaucracy and legacy infrastructure. Organizations with these attributes will struggle in the metaverse era, and they are likely already struggling in the current digital economy.

In the metaverse, organizations will be confronted with very narrow windows of opportunity as well as threats that can emerge with little warning. These conditions can only be dealt with successfully by maximizing an organization's nimbleness and adaptability. By adopting the organizational platform model as an organization's central organizing strategy, small, empowered teams can function as agile, entrepreneurial startups across the organization, accountable primarily to their immediate customers. These teams can be formed and disbanded by executive management as needed based on unfolding events. The net effect of this use of empowered teams is a much more resilient and adaptive organization. This allows the organization to assume whatever organizational form is required under the immediate circumstances. They can excel in making the most of whatever opportunities happen to be available at the moment. This level of nimbleness is essential if an organization is to develop and maintain the attributes needed to compete effectively in the metaverse era. By emphasizing a platform-based operational strategy, a firm can

· keep bureaucracy and infrastructure to a minimum
· reduce time to market
· enhance adaptability
· improve critical event response capabilities
· participate effectively in complex and synergistic business ecosystems
· anticipate and react more effectively to competitive threats and opportunities
· enhance teamwork and morale across the enterprise

8.3   PLATFORMS AND DEEP TECH

The platform concept has emerged as a significant consideration, if not the signature design attribute, in the development and operation of deep tech ventures (see Chapter 14, "Deep Tech"). Because deep tech ventures are clearly designed to perform well in a metaverse-like environment, leaders seeking to transform their more conventional organizations to compete well in the metaverse should study these deep tech entities. When they do, they will see the central role being played by platform concepts. Therefore, by adopting the platform model, the leaders of these conventional organizations can more effectively transform their businesses into a metaverse-ready state. They can do this by developing a sound understanding of the management perspectives, platform concepts, and operational strategies of deep tech organizations and ventures. They can learn even more by going beyond studying such companies and establishing strategic business relationships with them.

8.4   SUMMARY

Over the past decade, platform-based business models have grown in importance until they now dominate the global economy. Therefore, the business platform model must figure into the enterprise governance and architecture strategies of all companies that aspire to compete effectively in the metaverse era. For this to happen, organizational leaders, business model developers, and enterprise architects must understand the platform model, how it operates, and how its various enterprise roles and uses can contribute collectively to the generation and sustainability of business value.

Platforms aid in this quest in several important ways. In particular, they help organizations develop new operational and structural strategies. For example, by using the internal platform concept, organizations staff projects and business functions in ways that allow them to function as empowered entrepreneurial startups, with much in the way of delegated decision latitude. One crucial benefit of this approach is decisions can be made quickly at the source of the issue by highly motivated, well-informed, and empowered teams. When executed effectively, this approach can provide a substantial boost to organizational nimbleness.

8.5 KEY TAKEAWAYS

- Use of the business platform model in all of its various forms should become a key strategic focus area for improved organizational nimbleness and business success.
- If your organization is not proficient in the understanding and use of the platform model, and if your executive team sees potential benefit in its use, you should follow the steps outlined in in the Prelude to Part 3 (see Figure P.1). This will ensure your organization can assess and validate (or not) the benefits of the platform concept. If the benefits are deemed real and relevant to the company's mission, and if platforms get positive results in pilot initiatives, this approach can be captured in the enterprise architecture as an adopted methodology, and eventually be deployed in ways that improve business performance.

REFERENCES

[Van Alstyne et al.16] Marshall W. Van Alstyne, Geoffrey G. Parker, and Sangeet Paul Choudary, *Pipelines, Platforms, and the New Rules of Strategy*, Harvard Business Review, April 2016 *https://hbr.org/2016/04/pipelines-platforms-and-the-new-rules-of-strategy*

CHAPTER 9

ALGORITHMS

9.1 INTRODUCTION

Over the past decade, most organizations have become software-intensive entities. See, for example, the recent McKinsey and Company report titled *Every company is a software company: Six "must dos" to succeed.* In this report the authors emphasize the new reality that to compete effectively in the current digital world companies will have to transform themselves into a software company mindset and business model. [Gnanasambandam et al.22]

In this book, we are looking beyond the current digital world to a world that is edging ever closer to becoming a quantum world. Therefore, if companies need to look, think, and act more like software companies today, we can only imagine how important software will become to companies operating in the metaverse and beyond. For the organization of the near future, therefore, when we talk about software we are really talking about algorithms – sophisticated, complex, and often amazing algorithms.

State-of-the-art algorithms and their enabling technologies are no longer confined to laboratories and other advanced scientific and engineering environments. They are used by organizations across multiple industries to improve their business performance and expand their capabilities. This means modern algorithms are swiftly becoming an integral component of organizational strategic planning and business model development. This is especially true for organizations already deploying metaverse-era technologies in support of their core missions.

9.2 AN ESSENTIAL COMPETITIVE REQUIREMENT

Throughout modern history, leaders of organizations have had to make decisions about which investments to make, such as which people to hire, whether to form an alliance with a particular company, whether to create a new product line, and whether to enter or exit a particular market. When their competitors were making these and similar decisions using traditional, labor-intensive methods and tools, these leaders could get by using the same general approach. However, as we move into the metaverse era, more organizations are using advanced technologies, such as AI, and sophisticated, targeted algorithms to make these decisions much more reliably and at unprecedented speed. Organizations that are not using similar tools are operating at a competitive disadvantage. Important factors driving the increased use of sophisticated algorithms include the following:

· Mankind's relentless research into daunting and seemingly intractable global problems can be accelerated substantially through the use of advanced computers driven by cutting-edge algorithms.
· Business connectivity among companies, alliance partners, workers, customers, vendors, and smart devices via ultra-high-speed networks continues to expand and intensify to the point of simply overwhelming human efforts alone to manage it.
· The levels of volatility and unpredictability in markets, industries, and technologies are intensifying at an increasing rate.
· The scale, velocity, and volume of data streams coming from a myriad of sources into businesses continue to surge dramatically, often overpowering the human capacity to cope.

As a result of these accelerating trends, without the aid of more sophisticated software algorithms, enterprise personnel will find it more difficult to perform many business or research functions at a competitive level. The focus of this chapter is on how increasingly sophisticated algorithms are used to create the kinds of lean and nimble organizations capable of competing effectively in the metaverse. Algorithms aid in this quest in several important ways. In particular, they help executives develop nimbler, quicker organizations. Algorithms are used to simplify, streamline, accelerate, or replace many functions and processes now performed manually at all levels of the enterprise, from the executive level to the shop floor (or equivalent).

In addition to enabling internal performance improvements, algorithms are also applied in the solution platforms used by metaverse era organizations when delivering services, solutions, or products to external customers. For example, the website for Mayo Clinic Laboratories provides an extensive catalog of algorithms used to deliver the institution's various healthcare-related services. In this broadly ranging catalog there are 14 algorithms that deal only with topics beginning with the letter "M," such as "Malaria Laboratory Testing Algorithm." [MC23] We can see in this example the duality of how an organization like the Mayo Clinic can have a dominant mission description (delivering premier healthcare services) and beneath that layer actually be a software and algorithm-intensive entity.

9.3 BACKGROUND AND OVERVIEW

Algorithms are not new, of course, nor is the basic concept complex. If you are familiar with computer software, coding, programming, or computers in general, you probably know all about algorithms. They can be defined as logically sequenced sets of instructions, procedures, processes, subroutines, rules, or calculations that are followed in an exact progression to produce a desired output or solve a problem, typically using a computer or other technical device.

The tasks performed by software algorithms can be extremely simple, such as adding up a stream of numbers or searching for an order number. They can also be extremely complex, such as video compression algorithms. The major difference between today's algorithms and those of the past (even the recent past), lies in the vast amounts of data they can process, the myriad data formats they can handle, the dazzling speed by which they can process data, the ability of many algorithms to learn through repeated execution, and the sheer complexity and sophistication of the instruction sets that comprise the algorithms.

The synthesis of continuously evolving digital innovations are enabling algorithms today that function at a scale allowing organizations to leverage the full potential of such tools as AI, machine learning, and 5G. This, in turn, allows organizations to operate both at Internet speed and with the improved accuracy and nimbleness required in the metaverse era.

As an example, Dr. Mark van Rijmenam has written an informative article titled "What is Algorithmic Management?" [van Rijmenam20] The article demonstrates just one of the numerous ways that algorithms are being used in business to automate, fully or partially, managerial and organizational processes. The focus of this particular article is on automating certain aspects of the human resources management function.

Among the examples the author cites is a video interviewing software platform called HireVue that provides a facial analysis capability. This is an AI-based capability that assesses factors such as a candidate's facial expressions, tone of voice, and use of language.

Another example the author describes involves drivers for a food delivery company called Deliveroo. The algorithms used in this example process monthly personalized reports about driver performance, including average time to accept orders, average travel time to restaurants, average travel time to customers, and the number of late and unassigned orders.

Advocates of the algorithmic management of human resources contend that this practice opens new opportunities and efficiencies for companies and employees alike. The potential benefits of algorithmic management include lower costs, improved efficiency, data-driven decisions, and less bias.

Among the disadvantages at this stage in the use of algorithmic HR solutions are worker concerns over being continuously surveilled, lack of employee views and input into what goes into the algorithms, whether the algorithms are fair and accurate, and some feelings among workers of dehumanization.

The current state of this particular algorithmic application presents one of the important challenges in the use of algorithms to manage people, much less replace them. To many, this invokes images of white-shirted efficiency experts – the iconic time-and-motion wizards of the 1950s, wandering around with clipboards and stopwatches striking fear into workers as they intently measure the workers' therbligs (the 18 kinds of elemental motions used by workers). Company executives and algorithm developers will have to involve workers in the development of future algorithms if they are to mitigate these legitimate issues.

Algorithms are Myopic and Literal

Algorithms can be powerful predictive tools, but they are myopic, doing exactly what they are programmed to do and only what they are programmed to do. They do not handle situational nuances very well.

For example, algorithms are used to help banks make decisions about loan applications. They work very well – fast and accurately – when dealing with the more easily quantifiable variables processed by the algorithm (such as credit report data). However, when it comes to more nuanced decision issues, such as bending a bank's loan analysis rules to consider social issues, such as helping disadvantaged businesses, algorithms can be less effective. Of course, with enough development time, resources (such as AI capabilities), and talent, algorithms could be developed that handle these nuanced issues, as well.

Given an algorithm's strict adherence to the instructions it has been given and nothing else, extensive big-picture thinking must be given to the development of an algorithm. If developers have myopia or a blind spot, so will the algorithm. To return to the bank example, to make loan approval algorithms more socially sensitive, developers will have to break all of those additional considerations down into programmable triggers and subroutines. When this kind of extensively-networked, big-picture, trigger-and-subroutine coding is taken to great lengths, you can get very complex algorithms, such as those driving chess-playing computers.

Special Note on Algorithms and Quantum Computing

Chapter 11 discusses quantum computing in detail. That topic is relevant to this chapter because an increasing focus area for quantum computing research is on a special class of algorithms called "quantum algorithms." The context for this class of algorithms is explained in an article produced by NASA's Ames Research Laboratory titled *What is Quantum Computing?* This article explains how quantum computing algorithm development methods can harness certain properties of physics to create revolutionary algorithms that traditional digital computing technologies simply cannot handle. [Tavares22]

As is true for many revolutionary developments that have come from national labs like DARPA or the Ames Research Laboratory, they eventually find their way into the business world. This is likely to happen, probably sooner rather than later, with the quantum computing and advanced algorithm pairing mentioned in the Ames report cited above. Smart leaders should be laying the groundwork now to take advantage of these technologies and methods when they emerge and not be blindsided when this happens, as we saw happen when generative AI emerged suddenly in late 2022 and early 2023.

9.4 DEVELOPING AND MANAGING ALGORITHMS IN THE ENTERPRISE

Many organizations, unlike large companies like Meta or firms heavily into science and engineering, are relatively new to the development of complex, strategic algorithms. To elevate their maturity in this area, these companies can hire people with algorithmic skills or they can form alliances to obtain access to such skills. Some companies are advancing in the development and use of algorithms by creating algorithm labs or centers of excellence.

One way to get useful ideas for developing such a lab or center is to visit the websites of credible universities that have AI and algorithm development centers. For example, the Haas Business School at Cal Berkeley maintains an AI playbook. One section of the playbook is titled, "Play 4. Establish Policies and Practices That Enable Responsible Algorithm Development." This section explains how developers of algorithms must adhere to policies and practices that check for and mitigate against the introduction of any biases into the algorithm development process. One example of an outcome to be avoided in developing algorithms is putting possibly affected communities in disadvantaged positions. The playbook then goes into more depth relative to key participants in the algorithm development process and discusses how they can contribute to the school's responsible algorithm development policies and goals.

This Berkeley playbook provides a good example of the kind of resource a leading-edge organization in the metaverse era will have documented in its enterprise architecture (EA). For example, a team leader or engineer in your company might want information on developing algorithms. He might go to your company's EA Directory and simply type in "algorithms" and immediately get a list of related resources, including an official algorithm playbook like the Berkeley one. Or, more indirectly, he might go to the EA Directory and type in "software," which would show "algorithms" as a sub-category. He would then click on that heading, and then get a subordinate list of options that includes the playbook.

Impact of Algorithms on Structure, Employees, and Staffing

As enterprises transition from traditional organizational and business models to metaverse-era models built around software algorithms, the lives and careers of people at all organizational levels will be affected.

Therefore, organizations operating in the metaverse will be faced with the dual, and sometimes conflicting, challenges of (1) becoming leaner and nimbler if they expect to remain competitive, and (2) acquiring the additional mix of skills across the enterprise necessary to provide important metaverse era services, products, and solutions. So, how do you decrease overall staff levels and add new skills simultaneously?

The largely unavoidable outcome of addressing these two simultaneously opposing forces is some existing people and functions will have to be displaced. This stark reality places a burden on both the organization and individual workers to adapt accordingly. The HR adaptation strategy that an organization will implement in the face of this challenge will be guided by key components of the enterprise governance structure (such as its values and credo), which, of course, should be documented in the enterprise architecture.

For example, some organizations are already inserting algorithm-savvy analysts from large consulting firms, like McKinsey & Company or the Boston Consulting Group, into executive-level organizational positions. This often means displacing traditional, permanent executives with contracted employees operating under agreements to offer particular metaverse-type skills, or in some instances, deliver only precisely-defined products or services. Under this arrangement, we see the oddity of personnel in high-level executive positions being precluded from participating in overall management processes outside the narrow bounds of their contracts. While this approach has certain minuses for the company (e.g., the loss of broad corporate knowledge), it provides the double benefit of increased expertise in a vital, leading-edge technical domain, like AI or algorithms, plus flexibility in executive staffing and manpower planning.

The strategy of displacing certain executives through the use of algorithm-astute contract executives is not limited to the C-suite. This same strategy, or the similar one of replacing people with software, is being used to displace mid-level managers, functional professionals, and production workers. For many organizations, this change is causing ripple-effect displacement disruptions up and down the enterprise.

As a result of these actions, many enterprise structures have a top layer comprised of more operationally-engaged, tech-savvy, algorithm-literate senior executive managers. This is what we would expect to see with more executives now having rich knowledge of, and experience in, the use of algorithms, platforms, and other metaverse era technologies and methods.

In the past, C-suite executives tended to focus much more on strategic issues and overall business performance, always with an eye on Wall Street analysts, while most technical and operational functions and operations were delegated to lower-level managers. Increasingly, senior executives are now using software algorithms to absorb into their own daily activities many of the middle management functions that once existed in typical organizational structures.

The bottom-line impact of these actions is the increased flattening and streamlining of organizational structures, with many middle management positions being displaced (see Figure 9.1).

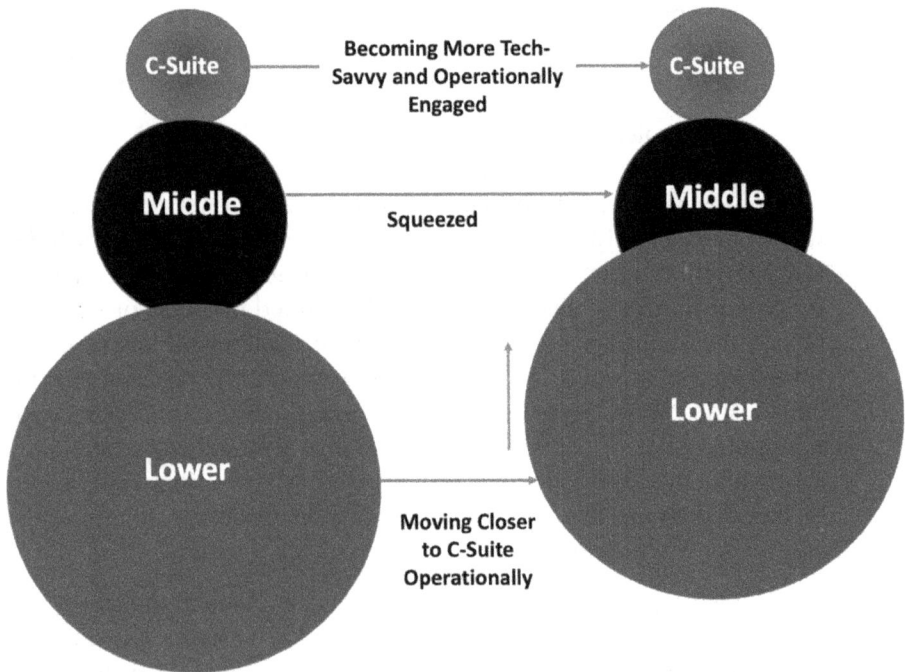

FIGURE 9.1 Streamlining organizations by reducing middle management

The implications of these actions have challenging second-order consequences. For example, because the functions performed by many white-collar workers are now being absorbed by software algorithms, many incumbents are often considered redundant. This is a stark reality that will soon face many highly competent individuals who have spent their careers perfecting their professions and specialties. This will, in turn, present both the displaced employees and their companies' executive management teams with a retraining challenge. Just as many displaced coal miners are being retrained as software coders, some employees with skills in such areas as procurement, legal research, human resources, and finance will either have to find similar work in less digitized companies or be retrained to take on new roles within their digitally-transformed, and soon to be metaverse-transformed, companies.

Transforming the Production Worker

What we once thought of as the "bottom layer" of a pyramid-type enterprise – the realm of blue-collar workers and craftsmen – is also undergoing transformation. The image of this layer as the lowest tier of the pyramid is disappearing as organizations continue to evolve from hierarchical structures of the past to the more horizontal, networked structures expected to dominate in the metaverse era.

This transformation is moving many traditional front-line workers more to the edge of the enterprise, where they are supported by new kinds of functional-area algorithms and technology concepts, such as edge computing (see Chapter 10, "Edge Computing"). They can interact at Internet speed with customers, suppliers, alliance partners, and other operational-level enterprise stakeholders. As these workers move to the customer-facing edge of the enterprise, most will have to be retrained.

This presents a major strategic issue for today's organizational leaders, as well as a profound personal challenge for the employees making this transition. For many workers, the retraining aspect of the transformational challenge will fall upon their own shoulders.

All of the algorithm-related issues mentioned above must be accounted for and reconciled when defining the future-state vision of an enterprise seeking to transform itself to become a viable competitor in the metaverse. Such an organization must have expertise in the use of algorithms to be competitive. At the same time, this strategy could result in the displacement of people and other HR-related issues. There is no easy solution to this problem, but it does require explicit, proactive, and visible treatment in the metaverse transformation strategy. Simply allowing events to uncontrollably happen without regard for the consequences is not an acceptable strategy.

9.5 KEY TAKEAWAYS

- Increasingly, organizations – now basically software entities – are basing the products and services they provide on the capabilities provided by sophisticated algorithms.

- The ability to develop or acquire sophisticated algorithms will become an internal core competency for nimble metaverse-era enterprises.
- The increasing use of algorithms could cause staffing disruptions and challenges throughout the company. Therefore, some the actions taken as a result of this strategy might be harsh for the people impacted unless mitigation strategies are in place.
- Just as organizations as a whole will have to change and adapt to the realities of the metaverse era, so will individual employees. Just as organizations need to be planning now on how best to meet these challenges, so should individuals – and with the same (or greater) sense of urgency.
- Many of today's occupational skills will see less demand in the metaverse era. However, there are numerous new rewarding and high-paying skills that will be required as well. A major challenge for organizations transforming for metaverse readiness is how to reconcile these issues in a proactive, equitable, and visible way.

REFERENCES

[Haas23] *Play 4. Establish Policies and Practices That Enable Responsible Algorithm Development,* AI Model, Haas Business School at Cal Berkeley, 2023 https://haas.berkeley.edu/wp-content/uploads/EGAL_Playbook_Play4_AIModel.pdf

[Gnanasambandam et al.22] Chandra Gnanasambandam, Janaki Palaniappan, and Jeremy Schneider, *Every company is a software company: Six "must dos" to succeed,* McKinsey Quarterly, December 13, 2022 *https://www.mckinsey.com/capabilities/mckinsey-digital/our-insights/every-company-is-a-software-company-six-must-dos-to-succeed*

[MC23] Algorithms, M, Mayor Clinic Laboratories, 2023 *https://www.mayocliniclabs.com/articles/resources/algorithms*

[Tavares22] Frank Tavares, Editor, *What is Quantum Computing?,* NASA Ames Research Laboratory, July 2022 *https://www.nasa.gov/ames/quantum-computing*

[van Rijmenam20] Dr. Mark van Rijmenam, *What is Algorithmic Management?* The Startup, Nov 13, 2020 *https://medium.com/swlh/algorithmic-management-what-is-it-and-whats-next-33ad3429330b*

10

EDGE COMPUTING

10.1 INTRODUCTION

Edge computing is a computing architecture that operates at or near the physical location of the user or the source of the data. This close proximity increases the speed of data capture, management, and transfer, thereby enhancing the nimbleness of organizations. As the metaverse era continues to advance, more and more companies will find edge computing deployments in some form to be useful, if not vital, components of their enterprise architectures.

This trend will accelerate as transformations to the metaverse create decentralized organizations focused on business operations at the "edge" of the enterprise. This is the vibrant activity zone that exists at the interface between an organization and its customers, suppliers, regulators, Internet of Things (IoT) devices, and alliance partners. This activity zone will become even more dynamic in the metaverse, as we will see more IoT-like devices and related data streams converging at the edge. Therefore, organizational leaders and their technical staffs should be preparing now for an upturn in complex connectivity challenges, more complex data management issues, new edge use cases, and increased security challenges at the edge, especially as quantum computing matures and eventually introduces a whole new class of cybersecurity challenges. However, companies that can master these challenges through AI and other means are likely to have a decided competitive advantage.

10.2 WHAT IS EDGE COMPUTING?

As noted earlier, edge computing is designed to bring the capture, storage, processing, analysis, and operational use of data as close to the source of the relevant data stream, or data ecosystem, as is practical. Being close in this context means physically close, as in being located near the devices generating the data, such as sensors, gauges, alarm systems, and various other IoT devices. Faced with this torrent of data, many executives have found they need a better way to extract only the data items essential for accurate and actionable decisions of the moment. A significant component of the answer that has ultimately emerged, at least for many digitally mature companies, is edge computing.

This is important because in many environments, data is being generated on an unprecedented scale and in staggering volumes and velocities. Organizations are finding that the slower speeds, latencies, and costs associated with sending these vast volumes of data back and forth to the cloud or traditional data centers are unacceptable. (*Latency* is the time it takes data to pass from one point on a network to another.) To help facilitate business operations and timely, accurate decisions at the edge, latency must be minimized, which is a benefit of edge computing.

Edge computing has often been used in infrastructure designs where local data center or cloud computing assets are used to process computationally-intensive applications with less stringent timelines, while edge computing processes applications require processing in near real time. However, in agile organizations operating in future metaverse conditions, near real time processing will become increasingly important.

IEEE, in an article titled "Real-Life Use Cases for Edge Computing," provides useful context for readers interested in some of the disadvantages of traditional cloud computing solutions in supporting today's highly networked organizations and the hyperactive activities in play at the edge of the enterprise. Edge computing helps overcome the disadvantages of cloud solutions in these fast paced operational environments. [IEEE22]

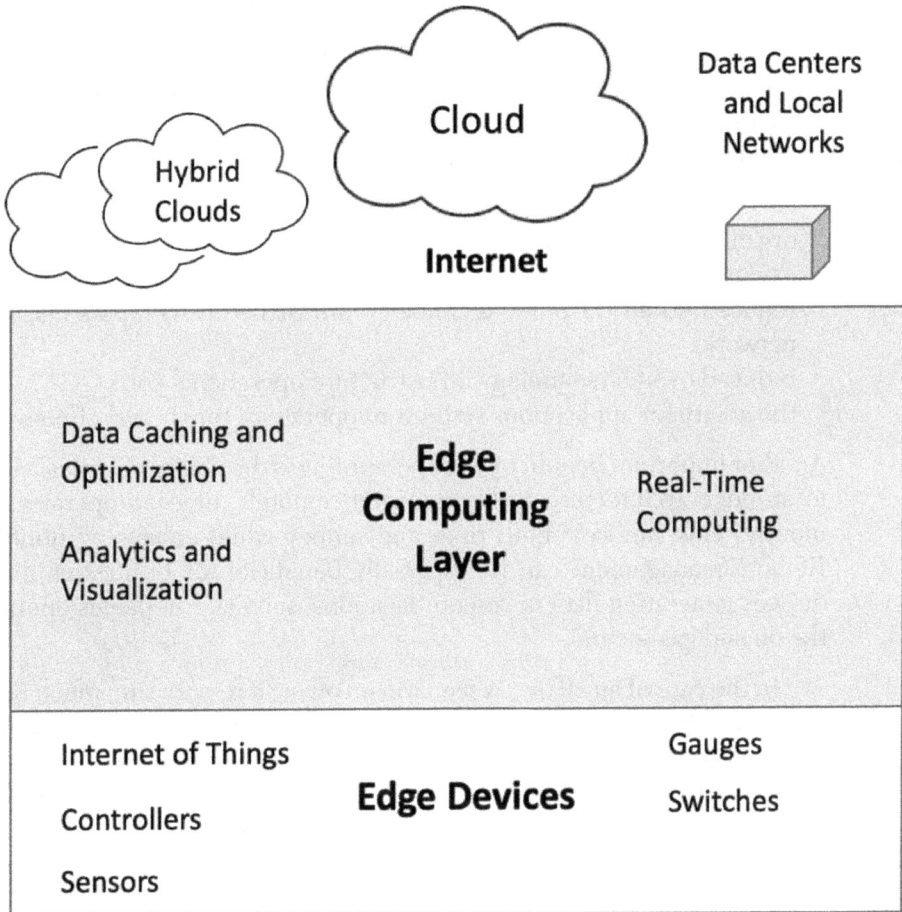

Hybrid Clouds

Cloud

Data Centers and Local Networks

Internet

Data Caching and Optimization

Edge Computing Layer

Real-Time Computing

Analytics and Visualization

Internet of Things

Edge Devices

Gauges

Controllers

Switches

Sensors

FIGURE 10.1 Simple representation of edge computing

By deploying technology resources (such as servers and software) near the point of transmission where employees work, edge capabilities allow organizations to engage more effectively with customers and other stakeholders. Because of the ability of edge technologies to scale, an organization can add capacity or assimilate new technologies without increasing latency or causing network congestion.

Figure 10.1 presents a simplified representation of the edge computing component of a modern technology infrastructure. The edge layer is positioned adjacent to the myriad data streams flowing from IoT devices.

This allows organizations to capture, cache, analyze, visualize, and use data quickly and effectively at the edge to make better decisions faster. With a well-designed edge computing structure in place as a component of a larger overall technology infrastructure deployment, an organization can realize a number of benefits. These include the following:

- an improved basis for timely and effective decision-making and overall organizational performance
- extensive scalability
- reduced strain on other technology infrastructure components, such as networks
- reduced overall technology infrastructure operational costs
- the ability for applications systems to operate in timely and effective ways

Another important benefit of edge computing is the ability of critical elements in an edge architecture to be managed remotely, or even operate autonomously. This can save both time and money while enhancing nimbleness. Remote management can be especially beneficial for businesses that have devices generating data in remote locations, such as companies operating in the oil and gas sector.

In the case of an oil or gas scenario involving a remote site, much time and money can be saved if an edge computing solution can operate autonomously. This can reduce, and in some cases virtually eliminate, the need to dispatch service techs to remote sites. As metaverse-era technologies, such as AI, continue to mature, this kind of edge computing capability will become the norm for many companies.

There are numerous conditions where decisions must be made immediately and where timing is everything. The following are a few more common use cases for edge computing:

- Autonomous vehicles
- Healthcare devices, such as wearable health monitors
- Smart grid
- Manufacturing logistics
- Traffic management
- Security solutions
- Predictive maintenance
- Agriculture
- National defense
- Retail Advertising
- Crime fighting

- Smart homes
- Workplace safety

10.3 SETTING UP AN EDGE COMPUTING SOLUTION

If an organization is new to edge computing and focused primarily on data coming from IoT devices, its leadership should read the TechTarget article by Clive Longbottom titled "How to Implement Edge Computing in Five Steps" [Longbottom20].

Some of the key considerations that should be taken into account when designing an edge solution are summarized in following sections.

Define Edge Computing Objectives

The first step in designing and deploying an edge computing architecture is to understand and agree on the objectives of the deployment. This can be a complicated step, especially if the edge solution must interface with a complex collection of business ecosystem participants. Designers must know, for example, who the key participants are, where they are physically located, key interfacing components of their technology architectures, and customer locations and requirements (e.g., required service delivery speeds). With an effective enterprise architecture in place, the organization deploying the edge solution will already have good information on the existing technology infrastructure (e.g., data centers, cloud deployments, networks, IoT devices, and data architectures). The key is to understand how to deploy an edge solution that makes optimal use of the existing technology infrastructure, while simultaneously meeting the business challenges that cannot be met adequately with legacy technology assets and deployment strategies.

Assess Edge Design and Deployment Options

A key technology option involved in most of today's edge solution design considerations is the current or planned existence of an ecosystem of IoT devices. These devices can be grouped in a number of ways depending on the edge computing deployment objectives discussed earlier. There are tradeoffs involved in these various deployment strategies. For example, IoT devices can be grouped by functionality (and not physical proximity), although this might increase data transfer latency and decrease speed. Or they can be grouped by physical proximity to decrease latency and increase response times. However, this design consideration brings up another consideration. How much intelligence should be built into the IoT devices? One important issue is cost. Intelligent IoT devices are more expensive, but they allow for a less expensive edge platform. The reverse is true. An intelligent edge platform allows less intelligent (and less expensive) IoT devices to be used.

Another central design issue is whether there is a need to define certain readings from IoT devices as critical exceptions that require responsive actions. If so, edge designers must define what these critical exceptions and responses will be and how they will be acted on. Will the responses be automated or will human intervention be required? Once again, this leads to additional cost considerations. Human intervention by highly skilled data analysts can be expensive.

Finally, staying with the deployment of IoT devices as a critical edge computing design consideration, there are several basic physical deployment options that might be used. One example is the hub-and-spoke design. The gist of this approach is the overall architecture of the edge deployment should have the least intelligent devices at the outer edges of the deployment, smarter devices at the next inner level, and the most intelligent device, or devices, at the center, or hub (see Figure 10.2).

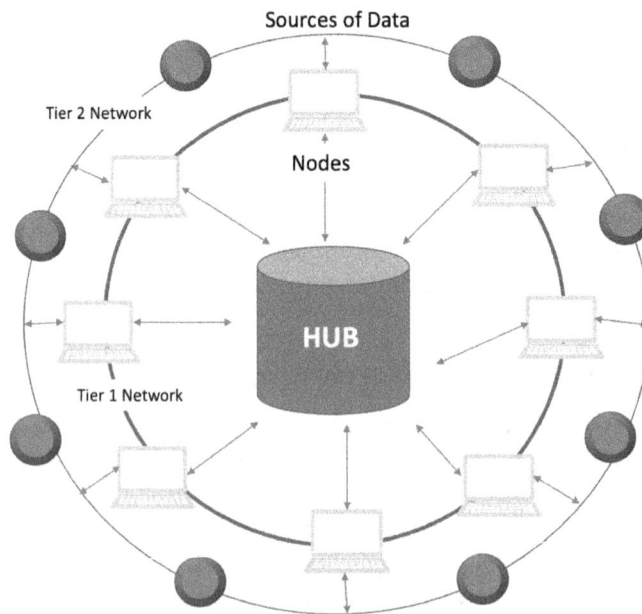

FIGURE 10.2 An example of a Hub-and-Spoke edge computing deployment

As we can see, there is a complex branching tree of edge design and deployment options that designers should take into account. The choice among these various options must be tied back to the edge computing objectives discussed earlier.

10.4 KEY TAKEAWAYS

- As organizations become increasingly networked, as solutions become more sophisticated, and as consumers become increasingly demanding, more products and services will be delivered and consumed at the edge. The longer edge solutions are delayed by an organization, the more time and expense will be involved later in trying to retrofit or overlay edge architectures onto existing cloud, hybrid cloud, and other legacy architectures.
- If your organization is not proficient in the understanding and use of edge computing, and if your executive managers see potential benefit in its use, you should follow the steps outlined in in the Prelude to Part 3 (see Figure P.1). This will ensure your organization can assess and validate (or not) the benefits of edge computing. If the benefits are deemed real and relevant to the company's mission, and if edge computing gets positive results in pilot initiatives, this model can be captured in the enterprise architecture, and be deployed in ways that improve business performance.

REFERENCES

[Longbottom20] Clive Longbottom, *How to Implement Edge Computing in Five Steps*, TechTarget, October 8, 2020 *https://www.techtarget.com/iotagenda/tip/How-to-implement-edge-computing-in-5-steps*

[IEEE22] *Real-Life Use Cases for Edge Computing*, IEEE, November, 2022 *https://innovationatwork.ieee.org/real-life-edge-computing-use-cases/*

CHAPTER 11

QUANTUM COMPUTING

11.1 INTRODUCTION

In 2022, the White House issued a press release titled "President Biden Announces Two Presidential Directives Advancing Quantum Technologies" [White House22] In this press release President Biden discussed the administration's awareness of the enormously important promise of quantum computing and the need for the United States to establish a leadership role, both in advancing the technology and in mitigating any risks the technology might pose to the nation's national and economic security.

The technology analysis firm Verdict has reported on a number of major companies in industries such as defense, finance, and transportation that have already been investing heavily in their quantum infrastructures. They are doing so in the firm belief that the widespread adoption of quantum computing is not far away and they intend to be ahead of the competition as this occurs. [GlobalData22]

As these examples and many other recent developments make clear, any plan to transform an enterprise to the metaverse must include quantum computing as an important transformational focus area.

11.2 IMPORTANCE TO METAVERSE TRANSFORMATION

The central theme of this book is how to infuse sufficient nimbleness into today's companies to be competitive in the metaverse era. An examination of quantum computing is essential in this regard because out of all the technology innovations shaping the metaverse, AI and quantum computing are the ones most likely to be the developments that could be as important in their potential impact as the Internet.

Quantum computing is closer to increased business use than many might think. For example, as far back as 2019, Google proved that a quantum computer can solve a problem in minutes, while it would have taken a classical computer 10,000 years to solve the same problem. In quantum computing, therefore, we are looking at many, many orders of magnitude more capability and speed, with greater efficiency, than can provided by conventional computing technology (i.e., the basic binary digital model).

Even though quantum computing is still in its early stage of emergence as a tool for widespread enterprise business use, its potential impact means all organizations need to be tracking its development closely right now and thinking about how they can best adapt to it when it arrives. Delays could be costly for many organizations. We saw this same phenomenon, although less impactful in terms of potential scale of impact, when cloud computing emerged. Too many companies either ignored the arrival of cloud computing or denigrated it initially instead of performing meaningful testing and experimentation. This allowed competitors to gain competitive ground at their expense.

Organizations should be looking for potential uses of quantum computing now so they can be prepared to help their businesses embrace this technology as soon as it becomes more widely available.

11.3 WHAT IS QUANTUM COMPUTING?

Quantum computing is more than a specific technology or kind of computer. The concept encompasses a diverse collection of disciplines, including aspects of mathematics, physics, and computer science, including new approaches to software development. These disciplines are collaborating to identify better ways to apply quantum mechanics and fundamental physics to computing and calculating mechanisms, both hardware and software. The goal is to develop computing technologies that are able to solve complex problems several orders of magnitude faster and more efficiently than is possible with traditional digital computers.

For a comprehensive general overview of quantum computing, we can turn to the US Department of Energy. In a 2023 report titled *DOE Explains Quantum Computing*, the Department provides an overview of some of the more critical elements of quantum computing, like qubits, and then discusses some of the ways that scientists have demonstrated the incredible speed and power of this technology in such applications as searching massive data bases to facilitate research. For an introduction to quantum computing, this report is a good source of information. [DOE23]

Another good resource that defines quantum computing and offers examples of its current use is offered by NASA. The title of the report is *What is Quantum Computing?* [NASA22] This report gets into more of the fundamental physics concepts that make quantum computing possible, including quantum tunneling and quantum entanglement.

11.4 THE SCIENCE BEHIND QUANTUM COMPUTING

To better understand the technology underlying quantum computing, we need to examine certain relevant quantum physics concepts, especially superposition and entanglement. This is because when we study physics at the level of atomic and subatomic particles, the universe can behave in quirky, unexpected, and counterintuitive ways. These seemingly odd subatomic behaviors are what make quantum computing possible.

Superposition

Superposition is the ability of a quantum system or subatomic particles to be in multiple states at the same time *until measured.*

To simplify this concept (which has intrigued some very smart physicists for decades, including Einstein), consider a coin that has been flipped into the air. While the coin is suspended and spinning, our logical, macroscopic minds can comprehend it as being both heads and tails simultaneously. It is only when the coin lands and one side and is observed (measured) can we conclude with complete certainty that the final state is either heads or tails.

Another way to think about superposition is to consider Erwin Schrödinger's famous cat analogy. His thought experiment has proved useful in explaining this difficult concept, even though the great physicist used it originally to gently ridicule the way some physicists at the time were viewing the superposition principle.

In this experiment, a cat is tightly sealed in a box in a way that makes any observation from outside impossible. Inside the box is an apparatus that includes a vial of deadly poison, a Geiger counter, a hammer, and a vial of radioactive material. One or more of the atoms of the radioactive material might or might not, with equal probability, begin to decay over the course of an hour. If an atom does decay, the Geiger counter will detect the radiation prompting the hammer to break the vial of poison and thus kill the cat. If no atom decays, the cat lives. Schrödinger suggested, somewhat facetiously, that during the hour the cat is in the box, it is simultaneously both dead and alive. It is only when you open the box (i.e., measure the state) does the cat's true status revert to a single state, either dead or alive.

Another view of superposition can be expressed more in computer science terminology than physics terminology. We know the traditional binary computer model is capable of performing amazing things. However, its underlying structure, even in supercomputers, uses a simple sequencing of bits with values of either 0 or 1 to represent two possible states, much like an on-and-off switch. These on-off states are activated by a previously sequenced set of commands (i.e., programs, code, or algorithms) which process data entered into the computer.

Instead of the on-off bits that traditional computers use, a quantum computer uses *qubits*. Consider a globe or a sphere with a bit at either of the two poles. That is the limiting factor of a binary computer. However, a qubit can exist at any point on the globe. In other words, a binary bit can be either a zero or a one, and that is it. A qubit, however, can be a zero or a one, both a zero and a one, or an infinite number of values in between. It can also exist in multiple states at the same time.

Because of these attributes, a computing device designed to process qubits can store and process vast amounts of data, orders of magnitude more than a binary computer, and use less power in the process.

In addition to a quantum computer being able to store multiple states at once, it can also process them simultaneously. Unlike classic computers that work in a serial, one-instruction–at-a-time sequence, quantum computers can work in parallel, performing multiple tasks or calculations simultaneously. A quotation by Seth Loyd expresses this condition in a different and insightful way: "A classical computation is like a solo voice—one line of pure tones succeeding each other. A quantum computation is like a symphony—many lines of tones interfering with one another." [Loyd00]

Entanglement

In general, the term *entanglement* in physics represents a curious and seemingly illogical (to some) condition that explains how two subatomic particles can be intricately and firmly linked to one another. This is true even if the particles are separated by vast distances, as in billions of light-years of space distances. Even in the face of this vast expanse of separation, a change induced in one particle will affect the other. If you find this phenomenon baffling, it has also baffled many great scientists, including Einstein, who called it "a spooky action at a distance." Over time, additional research has validated entanglement using photons and electrons.

As for entanglement in the world of quantum computing, changing the state of an entangled qubit will instantaneously change the state of a paired qubit, thereby accelerating the processing speed of quantum computers. This phenomenon is a key factor in enabling quantum algorithms to offer an exponential increase in speed relative to traditional digital computations.

11.5 IMPLICATIONS FOR ORGANIZATIONS

All of this sounds promising, but consider the implications. If the entire digital computing model is eventually upended by quantum computing, think of all of the other things that will be upended as well. Just within the enterprise IT sphere, this includes existing software (an almost incomprehensible amount of code), software development languages and tools, systems analysis approaches and strategies, computer hardware, and IT skills. However, the actual impact would extend far beyond enterprise IT. In fact, for most of us, it is hard to conceive of what the quantum era world will look like.

However, quantum computers should not be viewed as a full replacement for traditional computers within the next decade. They are evolving as a different kind of computational resource, one that organizations will use to solve complex problems beyond the capabilities of today's computer technology. The initial use will be in solving scientifically or technically challenging problems. Widespread use in traditional business organizations will happen more slowly. Nonetheless, business organizations need to be watching this area closely today because the evolution of quantum computing is not on a predictable timeline and could crash onto the scene as a viable option sooner than expected, just as we saw happen with AI.

Among the existing fields of use for quantum computing are healthcare research, national defense and warfare, drug discovery, finance, intelligence, air traffic management, aerospace modeling and design, utilities, polymer design, weather forecasting, and digital manufacturing.

Some of the companies already heavily engaged in quantum computing include Nokia, HP, Airbus, Booz Allen, Accenture, Northrup Grumman, Alibaba, Lockheed Martin, Raytheon, IBM, Microsoft, Mitsubishi, Biogen, Volkswagen, Google, D-Waves Systems, NEC, AT&T, and SK Telecom.

11.6 DO PRODUCTION QUANTUM COMPUTERS CURRENTLY EXIST?

In a November 9, 2022 article in Forbes titled "IBM Announces New 400+ Qubit Quantum Processor Plus Plans for a Quantum-Centric Supercomputer," author Paul-Smith Goodson offered an update on IBM's latest developments in quantum computing at the time. Among his observations was IBM's assertion that it would take more classical bits than atoms in the universe to represent a state on a new quantum computer produced by IBM. [Goodson22]

An extensive amount of R&D work has gone into quantum computing over the past two or three decades, and now actual success stories are appearing. A recent article, "2022 Preview: Quantum Computers May Finally Become Useful Tools," provides some context on this point. [New Scientist21] The article cites an IBM executive who indicates IBM is working toward a "quantum business advantage" – the point at which a quantum computer can solve genuinely useful problems for researchers or companies significantly faster than classical computers can. As of today, The world's largest quantum computer in terms of qubits is IBM's Osprey, which has 433. Google, Honeywell, Intel, and Microsoft are also considered to be among the leading quantum computer innovators.

A ZDNet article by Daphne Leprince-Ringuet cites an actual use case in quantum computing. [Leprince-Ringuet20] This case involved a grocery chain (Save-On-Foods) that had been using quantum computing to improve the management of in-store logistics. The article notes the company approached D-Wave Systems with a logistics problem that classical computers had been incapable of solving. The D-Wave solution reduced the computing time for some tasks from 25 hours per week down to seconds.

11.7 CURRENT AND POTENTIAL APPLICATIONS OF QUANTUM COMPUTING

Quantum computing has the potential to revolutionize certain professions, industries, disciplines, methods, and products. Here are some examples:

- Data analytics (e.g., NASA will use quantum computing to analyze the enormous amount of data they collect about the universe, as well as research on better and safer methods of space travel)
- Finance
- Healthcare (e.g., DNA gene sequencing, brain tumor detection, and other tests performed in seconds instead of hours or weeks)
- Aviation (e.g., more sophisticated airline modeling capabilities, and improving the routing and scheduling of aircraft)
- Cryptography
- Forecasting (e.g., national weather trends and hurricane predictions)
- Pattern matching (such as finding patterns in data and using these to predict future patterns)
- Self-driving cars
- Medical research

11.8 QUANTUM COMPUTING AND SECURITY ISSUES

As quantum computing continues to evolve, organizations of all sizes, even nations, will be forced to become more familiar with quantum technology because hackers and competitors certainly will. In fact, much of the hotbed of quantum experimentation around the world today is being driven by security issues, both by the defenders and the hackers. For example, many encryption keys commonly used today to enable Web-based commerce are considered effectively unbreakable by digital computers. However, these keys will become easy prey for hackers armed with quantum-based tools unless defense measures based on the same technology are put into place.

Conversely, quantum computing will enable a new generation of cryptographic tools for cyber defense, such as quantum cryptography. This means even though cybersecurity experts will find that some of their existing tools and methods will have become obsolete, they will benefit from powerful new, quantum-based tools.

11.9 KEY TAKEAWAYS

- Even though quantum computing is still relatively new and evolving, it could very well be the next great disruptive event in technology, and thus hold great promise for all of society. It might be closer to more widespread use than many think.
- Organizations that are heavily dependent on computer technology cannot afford to wait until quantum computing is well established and widely used before acting. That will be too late for most technology-dependent organizations.
- Executives must ensure now that a sufficient level of quantum computing literacy exists in their organizations and that senior management is kept informed of new developments. In addition, executives should be developing and updating, as needed, quantum computing contingency strategies. These should identify trigger events that, when activated, will spur the organization into action with respect to quantum computing exploration and adoption.

REFERENCES

[DOE23] *DOE Explains Quantum Computing*, U.S. Department of Energy, Office of Science, 2023 *https://www.energy.gov/science/doe-explainsquantum-computing*

[GlobalData22] GlobalData Thematic Research, *The state of quantum computing in 2023*, Verdict, December 15, 2022 *https://www.verdict.co.uk/quantum-computing-predictions/#:~:text=Tech%20firms%20aim%20to%20commercialize%20quantum%20computing&text=IBM%20is%20on%20track%20to,will%20likely%20begin%20in%202027*

[Goodson22] Paul-Smith Goodson, *IBM Announces New 400+ Qubit Quantum Processor Plus Plans for a Quantum-Centric Supercomputer,* Forbes, November 9, 2022 *https://www.forbes.com/sites/moorinsights/ 2022/11/09/ibm-announces-new-400-qubit-quantum-processor-plus-plans-for-a-quantum-centric-supercomputer/?sh=5b019b95eaa9*

[Leprince-Ringuet20] Daphne Leprince-Ringuet, *Quantum computers are coming. Get ready for them to change everything,* ZDNet, November 2, 2020 *https://www.zdnet.com/article/quantum-computers-are-coming-get-ready-for-them-to-change-everything/*

[NASA22] *What is Quantum Computing?* NASA Ames Laboratory, July 6, 2022 *https://www.nasa.gov/ames/quantum-computing*

[New Scientist21] *2022 Preview: Quantum Computers May Finally Become Useful Tools,* New Scientist, December 29, 2021 *https://www.newscientist. com/article/mg25233661-700-2022-preview-quantum-computers-may-finally-become-useful-tools/#:~:text=2022%20preview%3A%20Quantum% 20computers%20may%20finally%20become%20useful%20tools&text=A% 20POWERFUL%20quantum%20computer%20could,that%20classical% 20machines%20find%20impossible*

[White House22] *President Biden Announces Two Presidential Directives Advancing Quantum Technologies,* White House Press Release, May 4, 2022 *https://www.whitehouse.gov/briefing-room/statements-releases/2022/05/04/ fact-sheet-president-biden-announces-two-presidential-directives-advancing-quantum-technologies/*

CHAPTER

12

IMMERSIVE TECHNOLOGIES (VR, AR, MR, AND XR)

One of the more important areas associated with the metaverse technological innovation convergence process is the field of immersive technologies. This includes virtual reality (VR), augmented reality (AR), mixed reality (MR), and extended reality (XR). Frequently, these technologies are what people think of first when they hear the term "metaverse."

12.1 DEFINITIONS

This chapter discusses a family of related technologies that are in the immersive category. The first two, mixed reality (MR) and extended reality (XR), are discussed for context only. The deeper focus of this chapter is on virtual reality (VR) and augmented reality (AR). These are currently the two most widely-used immersive technologies in business applications.

Augmented Reality

Simply put, *augmented reality* (AR) is a technology that can be used to overlay physical objects with real-time digital qualities or attributes. For example, a technician working on a malfunctioning generator at a remote field site can, through a smart phone or other handheld device, arrange to have a digital schematic or field service manual sheet from the home office overlay the troublesome generator component. This means the physical object (the generator) has been "augmented" by the digital overlay. Therefore, augmented reality exists when computers and algorithms have added virtual attributes (such as images and sounds) to physical objects. In augmented reality, the user is never completely separated from the real, physical world. There are countless practical applications for this approach, which is one reason AR is used so extensively today.

Virtual Reality

The state of being in, or vividly sensing, *virtual reality* (VR) is to be in an artificial, lifelike, 3D environment, removed from the real physical world. These kinds of environments are animated by the combination of computer hardware, modeling or simulation software, and various sensory devices, such as goggles, headsets, body suits, and gloves. The person experiencing virtual reality can partially control what happens in the environment by manipulating these sensory devices. As technology advances, these virtual environments are becoming increasingly lifelike. The goal of virtual reality is to completely isolate the user from the real, physical world for the duration of the virtual experience.

Mixed Reality

Mixed reality (MR) is often viewed as a hybrid or in-between form of reality that entails the blending of real and virtual worlds. The objective is to create environments where physical and digital objects or conditions can co-exist and interact in real time.

Extended Reality

Extended reality (XR) is a relatively new and all-encompassing term for all forms and gradations of immersive technologies. The rationale for the emergence of this term is to eliminate some of the confusion brought on by the increasing overlaps among VR, AR, and MR.

12.2 CONVERGENCE OF IMMERSIVE TECHNOLOGIES

The technology convergence phenomenon driving the metaverse is occurring on both a macro level and micro level. At the macro level, newer technology innovations (such as quantum and edge computing) are converging both among themselves and with existing technologies (such as cloud computing and smart phones) to create powerful new platforms and solutions.

There is also convergence going on at the micro level, such as the convergence taking place within the family of immersive technologies, particularly VR, AR, and MR.

VR and AR are still generally regarded as separate concepts, at least for now. However, there are increasing overlaps in VR/AR definitions, attributes, and typical use cases. This has contributed to the evolution of MR.

What we have, therefore, is a continuum with the "physical world" at one end and the "virtual world" at the other. If we happened to be living in a static world, VR would sit in a fixed position toward the virtual world end of the continuum, while AR would sit in a fixed position toward the physical world end. However, the world in this context is increasingly dynamic. This means AR and VR are constantly shifting along the continuum, sometimes bumping into or partially overlapping each other. This has given rise to what the tech industry calls MR, which contains elements of both AR and VR. For a more detailed discussion of this continuum, please read the article by Khullani M. Abdullahi titled "The Reality-Virtuality Continuum." [Abdullahi16]

However, the convergence process for immersive reality technologies is even more complex than that. As shown in Figure 12.1, there are four concepts currently interacting. In addition to VR, AR, and MR, we have *extended reality* (XR). The XR model has emerged as a way to assimilate all immersive technologies under one unifying concept to reduce overlaps and confusion.

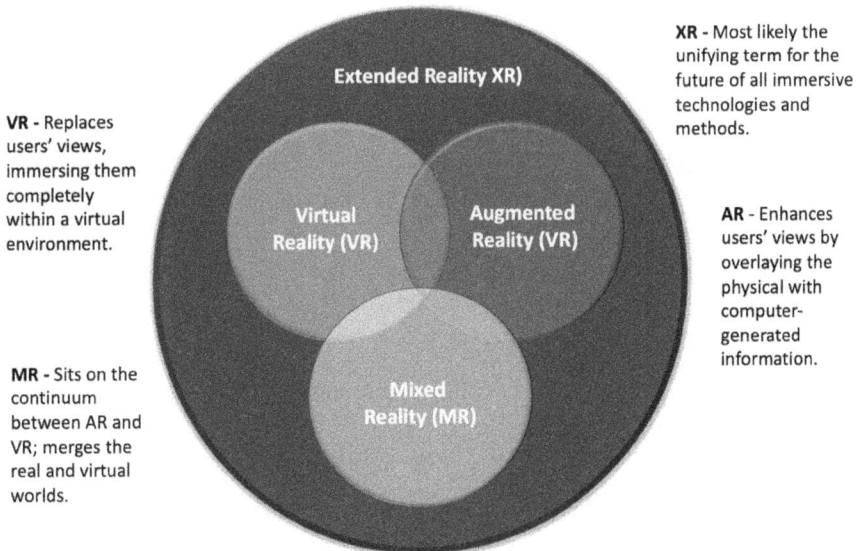

XR - Most likely the unifying term for the future of all immersive technologies and methods.

VR - Replaces users' views, immersing them completely within a virtual environment.

AR - Enhances users' views by overlaying the physical with computer-generated information.

MR - Sits on the continuum between AR and VR; merges the real and virtual worlds.

Extended Reality XR)

Virtual Reality (VR)

Augmented Reality (VR)

Mixed Reality (MR)

FIGURE 12.1 Converging family of immersive technologies

Over the past few years, the central focus of immersive technologies has been on AR, VR, and MR. As the convergence process continues, we will likely hear more about XR.

Focusing on VR and AR

As noted, virtual reality (VR) and augmented reality (AR) are presently the two immersive technologies that are most widely discussed and most routinely associated with the metaverse. Therefore, these are extremely important technologies that must be factored into strategic deliberations for elevating the agility and future competitiveness of organizations, as well as their product and service offerings as they prepare to compete in the metaverse. We focus here on these two immersive technologies, with more of an emphasis on AR.

There are some distinctions between VR and AR. VR seeks to completely insulate the user from the real, physical world and immerse them in a virtual world that the user can manipulate in various ways via wearable VR accessories (such as gloves, googles, and headsets).

AR does not insulate the user from the physical world, but integrates the virtual world with the physical one. AR applications typically center on the use of a smartphone or similar device (e.g., a tablet). The user focuses the phone's camera on the object of interest, say a malfunctioning boom cylinder on an excavator, and produces a live-streaming video of the cylinder on the screen of the viewing device being used. The screen then receives an overlay of digital information in a form like a schematic or diagnostic data.

How VR is Currently Being Used in Business

Even though AR is presently considered by many as being the immersive technology best suited to enterprise business needs, many businesses are using VR as well. Example areas of VR use include training, architecture, and construction (e.g., translating paper blueprints into 3D models, and then into immersive VR simulations), pattern recognition and data visualization, sports, and manufacturing and production.

Companies such as Lockheed, Boeing, and Airbus are heavy users of VR to eliminate the need for expensive, full scale aircraft prototypes. As another example, auto manufacturer Audi is offering a VR experience as an integral component of its marketing strategy.

How AR is Being Used in Business

While VR is currently used most heavily in games and entertainment, the predominant applications for AR are found in business enterprises. Perhaps the best way to understand what AR is and why it is important to businesses is to look at some common use cases.

Training and Development: From training medical specialists, including physicians who upgrade their skills in complex medical procedures, to training employees in new products, to training field staff in maintenance procedures, AR is already establishing a major training presence in organizations across all industries. AR provides an immersive experience allowing those being trained or developed to visualize with incredible clarity and realism concepts, models, processes, products, and methods germane to their lines of work. Moreover, those being trained can repeat lessons to their satisfaction without needing a human trainer involved.

For example, many health delivery systems are working with universities and national labs to allow health education students to use 3D holographic anatomy technology to examine virtual cadavers and explore more deeply (and efficiently) the human body. This method reportedly significantly minimizes the time spent in a traditional cadaver lab, while also improving educational outcomes. The use of this type of approach is expected to spread to all medical education institutions.

Sports: For an example from the sports world, we can look back to an article by Alvin Manalac in *Virtual Reality Marketing* titled, "Dallas Cowboys AR Hype Up." The article discusses how the Dallas Cowboys organization has been using virtual and augmented reality to enable its stadium to be one of the premier sports venues in the world from the perspective of the fan.

Merchandising and Retail: The Internet changed the dynamics of retail selling, causing consumers to become better informed, more demanding, and often fickle. Consequently, retailers and merchandizers became obsessed, and rightly so, about optimizing the shopping and purchasing experience of their customers. However, that challenge is a tough one, considering such issues as inventory management and style changes.

Many consumers begin their shopping on the Internet, a digital experience. Some of them then go to brick and mortar stores to augment their digital impressions with actual physical, tactile contact with the product. (This assumes they can find the same item in a store they first noticed on the Internet.) By being able to approximate this kind of shopping behavior, augmented reality will allow many businesses to bridge the gap between the digital and the physical and introduce new and improved ways for customers to shop. If this new, integrated digital/physical method of shopping becomes popular, as it probably will, brick and mortar shopping establishments will face additional adaptation challenges.

Industrial and Field Services: In the past, engineers and field services personnel, often working in remote locations, had limited access to the expertise required to solve new or unexpected problems. Field manuals, whether a hard copy or accessible via a smart phone or tablet, were typically designed to inform or instruct on normal situations.

AR allows engineers and technicians to access in real time remote, expert support from anywhere in the world to deal with unexpected or unusual situations. The home base expert can superimpose, in real time, digital overlays of schematics, blueprints, diagrams, maps, or whatever else might be needed directly into the worker's field of view. This information might be superimposed clearly on a photo of a broken water pump, machine part, gas line, gauge, sensor, property marking, or piece of heavy equipment. If the field worker has "smart glasses," this will free the worker's hands to work on the problem. These aspects of AR add nimbleness to an important component of the worker's organization.

12.3 HOW TO GET STARTED WITH AR/VR

Similar to how they have already responded proactively to the metaverse in general, many enterprise executives already have their organizations engaged in adopting AR, VR, or both. However, many other executives still dismiss AR and VR as being not ready for serious business use. The same has been true for almost all major technological innovations, at least when these technologies were in their emergent states (see Chapter 4, "Slow Responses to Disruptive Technologies").

Such a dismissive outlook could cause the companies managed by these reluctant executives to miss out on many benefits these technologies could provide. Even worse, dismissing technologies like VR and AR could put the entire enterprise behind the curve in terms of developing the levels of nimbleness and innovative capacity necessary to compete in the metaverse.

Fortunately, getting started with AR, VR, or both does not require a major initial investment. If an organization has one or two good developers, especially if they have gaming experience, the organization can tap these individuals, acquire a good VR headset or two, install some rudimentary AR capabilities, and have the basis for beginning a small AR/VR innovation lab.

As discussed elsewhere in this book (e.g., the role of the spreadsheet in accelerating the adoption of personal computers in organizations in the 1980s) one of the critical initial steps in getting started with AR/VR is to choose compelling initial use cases, especially ones that can be completed in a short amount of time. These should not be novelty solutions that might be interesting to observe but lack clear business relevance. The business relevance and associated potential benefits should be obvious to one or more senior executives. This will allow the AR/VR innovation lab to receive additional funding and be encouraged to come up with larger projects.

One way to help foster executive excitement in the early stages of the innovation lab's operation is to develop initial solutions that can benefit one or more external customers. Nothing pleases executives more than having a major customer compliment the company for having provided it with what they believe is an innovative and helpful solution.

Soon after these successful initial use cases have been completed and demonstrated true business value potential, AR/VR will have taken root in the enterprise at a small initial cost. At that point, additional future investments are likely and larger, more strategic AR/VR initiatives will be launched.

The scenario just discussed assumed a company that wanted get started with AR/VR in a small way with a limited initial investment. This does mean there will not be other companies that want to, or are being forced to, start with a much bigger AR/VR investment. These companies should consider the standard technology adoption and assimilation process used throughout this book. That process is outlined in the Key Takeaways section of this chapter

12.4 KEY TAKEAWAYS

- Virtual reality and augmented reality are converging technologies that are immersive. Strong capabilities in these and other immersive technologies, such as AI, will be essential for many companies operating in the metaverse era.

- Organizations not already making productive use of these technologies will be poorly prepared to compete in the metaverse.
- If your organization is not proficient in the understanding and use of immersive technologies, and if your executive managers see potential benefit in their use, your organization should follow the steps outlined in the Prelude to Part 3 (see Figure P.1). This will ensure the organization can assess and validate (or not) the benefits of immersive technologies. If the benefits are deemed real and relevant to the company's mission, and if immersive technologies get positive results in pilot initiatives, they can be captured in the enterprise architecture and be deployed in ways that improve business performance.

12.5 REFERENCES

[Abdullahi16] Khullani M. Abdullahi, *The Reality-Virtuality Continuum*, Search Medium, April 10, 2016. *https://khullani.medium.com/the-reality-virtuality-continuum-db166a704c01*

[Manalac22] Alvin Manalac, *Dallas Cowboys AR Hype Up*, Virtual Reality Marketing, November 18, 2022 *https://www.virtualrealitymarketing.com/case-studies/dallas-cowboys-ar-hype-up/*

13

HOLOGRAPHIC TECHNOLOGIES

13.1 INTRODUCTION

The use of holographic technology in organizations is not new. For example, Microsoft first announced Mesh in 2021. This was a mixed reality service that allowed people in different places to meet in a virtual reality form and share a digital space as if they were next to one another. When the event was announced, the leader of Microsoft's VR business area appeared on stage as a hologram.

There are many similar instances of holographic technologies being used by major technology companies in their evolving business lines. Therefore, no discussion of the metaverse would be complete without examining the important role of holograms in the overall metaverse equation and in developing metaverse-ready organizations.

13.2 BACKGROUND

Some say the origin of the hologram dates back to 1947 when a Hungarian scientist, Dennis Gabor, discovered what would later become known as a hologram. The discovery came when he was attempting to improve the resolution of electron microscopes. Others say hologram technology began in 1962, when Yuri Denisyuk of the Soviet Union and Emmett Leith and Juris Upatnieks at the University of Michigan developed laser programs that recorded objects in 3D.

While holography was initially used more heavily in gaming, the technology is increasingly being used in a variety of industries to address a broad array of customer use cases. Examples include training applications of all kinds, legal documents (as in living wills in estate planning), entertainment, the arts, virtual meetings, national defense, real estate, and healthcare.

13.3 HOW HOLOGRAPHIC TECHNOLOGIES WORK

Holograms can take many forms, such as a seal on a driver's license or a strip or square on a credit card. A holographic display is generated when light diffraction is used to create a virtual 3D image, or object, in volumetric space. The most popular perception of a 3D hologram is that of realistic, electronically-developed image of a person or object that appears to the viewer to be present but actually is not.

Holograms are intriguing and often satisfying to the viewer because our eyes are accustomed to viewing objects in a volumetric, three-dimensional world. Holography is able to infuse otherwise flat, 2D digital displays with this more natural 3D perspective. Therefore, holographic images can engage the full visual, mental, and emotional faculties of the viewer much in the same way real world physical images do, with substantially the same perceptions of depth, texture, and contours. Holographic objects appear to blend seamlessly into the environment much as physical ones do. Research has shown that holographic representations of people are much more comfortable and engaging to viewers than 2D computer screen-based meetings or videos.

The perception of true eye contact with others is especially important in this regard, leading to more participants in a holographic event paying attention to each other and to the person speaking. Researchers also tell us that depending on the nature of a group meeting, there can be a significant gain in concentration and information retention through person-to-person eye contact.

A Note on Avatars

Presently, cartoonish and sometimes humorously stylized avatars are often used as surrogates for real human beings in immersive virtual space encounters or engagements. These avatars can, to a minor degree, mimic a human being through gestures and expressions. For many kinds of remote engagements, this is good enough. However, there is often an innate desire for increased realism and seriousness for more solemn engagements. In an urgent meeting of top military officials faced with a serious global situation, the use of stylized avatars for remote participants would be out of place, and even 2D screen sessions would be less than desirable. For important officials who could not attend such a meeting in person, the visual fidelity and rich personal connections offered by a well-engineered and effectively presented holographic presence might be the next best thing.

13.4 EXAMPLES OF HOLOGRAM USE CASES

3D holographic displays are already being used in a wide variety of ways. In particular, companies can showcase products and services that uniquely enhance customer interactions. Fashion is a prime example. The following sections include a few other examples.

Communications

Holograms are fast becoming a new focus area for achieving advanced forms of communications, as seen in the evolving family of holographic products from companies like Microsoft and Cisco. Holographic solutions are used to connect individuals and groups in highly realistic, immersive ways. These solutions offer much more in the way of realism, authenticity, natural perspectives, and visceral impact than any other forms of remote face-to-face or group-to-group communications. These solutions offer more than faces simply staring at each other. They are more dynamic, with people standing up and walking around, or entering and leaving the meeting, making it much more like a real in-person meeting.

Museums

Museums use holograms to make treasured art and artifacts available to the public in safe and explorable ways. The British Museum of London made a hologram of a 2,300-year-old mummy available for both researchers and the public. The Science Museum Group and Imperial War Museums recently worked with a company named Perception Codes to create holographic exhibitions to bring 3D museum artifacts into schools and homes.

Military Applications

There are countless good uses for holograms in national defense and war-fare. For example, fully dimensional holographic images are being used for improved reconnaissance in the military. Holographic maps of battle fields allow armed forces personnel to view the terrain in realistic three-dimension, look around corners, check inside buildings, and otherwise train for danger-ous missions. These maps are also useful in evacuation and rescue missions.

Chris Chinnock offers a good perspective on the military's use of hologra-phy in an article titled "Military's Holographic Displays." The author focuses on the concept of battlespace visualization and discusses the role holography can play in providing the next generation 3D displays defense officials and other military personnel desire. [Chinnock22]

Information Storage

Holograms have the potential to store vast amounts of information. Unlike CDs and DVDs, which store their data on the disk's surface, holograms store data in three dimensions and those pages can overlap in the storage space. In a *Discovery Magazine* article titled "Is Holographic Data Storage the Next Big Thing?" author Avery Hurt discusses the fact that holographic storage does not move the media. Instead, a light is routed to where the data is stored. Avoiding this mechanical move operation is a critical innovation that allows much faster data access. Faster data access is just another capability that can contribute to enhanced organization nimbleness, which is a key goal of enter-prise transformation to the metaverse. [Hurt22]

Medical Applications

Many experts say holography is on its way to revolutionizing various aspects of medicine. When using 3D images for training and display, holograms require no viewing devices or glasses. Students and doctors can simply look, unen-cumbered, at the images, which can include incredibly complex body organs and systems, such as the brain, heart, liver, lungs, nerves, and muscles.

Prakash Mehta has written an informative article on this subject titled Medical Applications of Holography. [Mehta23] In this article he discusses 12 different medical use cases for holography. Examples include Holography in Otology, Holography in Orthopedics, Holography in Dentistry, and Holography in Ophthalmology.

Fraud and Security

Holograms are complex, challenging to make, and difficult to forge, which makes them valuable security devices. In an article titled "The Latest Developments in Holograms as a Security Feature," Paul Dunn explains how holography has become a valuable option in helping organizations securing their data, making tampering, alteration, forgery, and other intrusions more difficult. [Dunn22]

Art

Artists all over the world are using holograms in innovative and striking ways. A recent London exhibition presented a show of creative holography among a large number of highly regarded artists using different media. Artists from around the world also contributed recently to an exhibition in New York, while artists from Canada, Italy, the US and UK were chosen for an exhibition using holography and the media arts in Santa Fe, New Mexico.

13.5 3D HOLOGRAMS IN REAL TIME?

Since they were first discovered, holographic technologies have continued to evolve, but the ultimate goal has always been real-time 3D holograms.

One well-known problem with virtual reality headsets is they can make users feel ill. There have been numerous reports of nausea and eye strain when using devices like VR headsets. This can happen because VR creates an 3D image even though the user is viewing a 2D display at a fixed distance. The solution to this problem may be holograms. This is because holograms can provide a changing perspective based on the position of the viewer. This allows the user's eyes to adjust their focal depth when alternately focusing on images in the foreground and the background.

A recent article from MIT indicated that real-time 3D holograms are much closer to becoming a reality. Daniel Ackerman of the MIT News Office wrote the piece "Using artificial intelligence to generate 3D holograms in real time." The article discusses a new method called "tensor holography" that might make it possible to create holograms for virtual reality, 3D printing, medical imaging, and more, while operating on a smart phone. The author suggests 3D holography would benefit such technologies as VR and 3D printing, while immersing VR viewers into much more realistic backgrounds, reducing eye strain, and mitigating other side effects of the extended use of holography. [Ackerman21]

13.6 KEY TAKEAWAYS

- Holograms used to be thought of as "fun house" types of displays, the kind of swirling, dancing ghosts you might find in the Haunted House at Disney World. However, the practical uses of holographic technologies are not limited to entertainment purposes, but are becoming a commonplace in today's industries and businesses. As we get closer to true real-time 3D holograms, we are likely to see significant growth in use cases for these technologies.
- If your organization is not proficient in the understanding and use of holographic technologies, and if your executive managers see potential benefit in their use, your organization should follow the steps outlined in in the Prelude to Part 3 (see Figure P.1). This will ensure the organization can assess carefully and validate (or not) the benefits of holography. If the benefits are deemed real and relevant to the company's mission, and if holography gets positive results in pilot initiatives, this technology can be captured in the enterprise architecture as an adopted technology, and eventually be deployed in ways that improve business performance.

REFERENCES

[Ackerman21] Daniel Ackerman, *Using artificial intelligence to generate 3D holograms in real time*, MIT News Office, March 10, 2021 *https://news.mit. edu/2021/3d-holograms-vr-0310*

[Chinnock22] Chris Chinnock, *Military's Holographic Displays*, Light Field Lab, April 7, 2022 *https://www.lightfieldlab.com/blogposts/military-holographic-diplays*

[Dunn22] Paul Dunn, *The Latest Developments in Holograms as a Security Feature*, Keesing Technologies, 9/05/2022 *https://platform. keesingtechnologies.com/the-latest-developments-in-holograms-as-a-security-feature/#:~:text=The%20new%20holography%20provides%20highly,using%20a%20smartphone%20light%20source.*

[Hurt22] By Avery Hurt, *Is Holographic Data Storage the Next Big Thing?* Discover Magazine, January 17, 2022 *https://www.discovermagazine.com/technology/is-holographic-data-storage-the-next-big-thing*

[Mehta23] Prakash Mehta, *Medical Applications of Holography*, Integraf, 2023 *https://www.integraf.com/resources/articles/a-medical-applications-of-holography*

CHAPTER 14

Deep Tech

14.1 INTRODUCTION

Deep tech describes organizations, often startups or joint ventures, that are focused on developing innovative, high technology-based solutions to meet national or globally important scientific, medical, or engineering challenges. Closely associated with deep tech ventures are the metaverse-era technologies they use, such as AI, machine learning, advanced material sciences, photonics, digital twins, and quantum computing. However, deep tech ventures also make effective use of well-established and largely commoditized technologies and methods, such as cloud computing, especially for the non-differentiating components of their solution models or platforms. In other words, deep tech ventures excel in integrating new technological developments with existing technologies to develop solutions to solve complex and important global problems.

Even though deep tech is not a specific technology, the concept is built around and enabled by various metaverse technologies, depending on the mission of the deep tech venture. Therefore, the deep tech organizational model is an important concept to understand for organizational leaders preparing to transform their companies in the metaverse era.

The complex challenges addressed by deep tech ventures often require lengthy periods of research and development. Due to the research and development-intensive nature of the challenges being addressed, and given the needs of most startups, major capital investments are typically required before any discoveries or solutions can be developed and commercialized.

These investments are typically made by venture capital organizations or commercial business alliance partners who expect to benefit from deep tech venture discoveries or inventions.

For a potential investor, a deep tech venture's risk profile is based largely on the probability the research will eventually result in useful outcomes. If the research does have a useful result, the potential value of the solution is likely to be so great the risks of commercialization failure are likely to be minimal. This is because competition is likely to be limited. In solving a problem or making a discovery, the deep tech venture produces valuable intellectual property no one else is likely to have, at least for a significant period of time.

Today's deep tech-enabled discoveries and innovations are occurring at the intersection of three critically important megatrends (See Figure 14.1):

· The first is the growing threat posed by worldwide developments, including current and future pandemics, climate change, changing demographics, increasing resource scarcity (especially fresh water), terrorism, poverty, diseases, global financial meltdowns, and an aging population.
· The second megatrend involves major advances in basic scientific and engineering capabilities (based substantially on the effective application of today's converging advanced technologies and methods).
· The third megatrend is the metaverse itself.

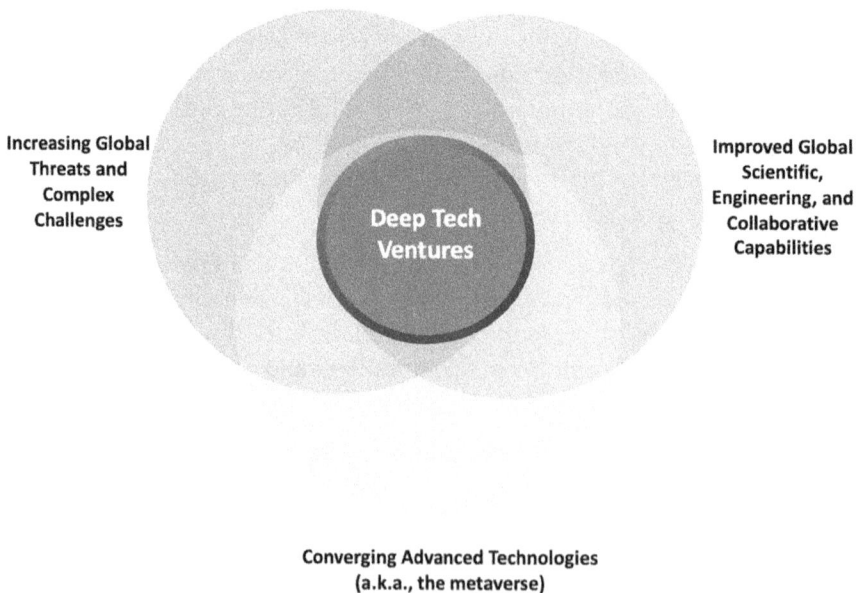

Increasing Global Threats and Complex Challenges

Deep Tech Ventures

Improved Global Scientific, Engineering, and Collaborative Capabilities

Converging Advanced Technologies (a.k.a., the metaverse)

FIGURE 14.1 Deep tech is solving global grand challenges.

Deep tech discoveries are affecting numerous industries, and this trend will continue throughout the 2020s and beyond. Some observers have noted that deep tech is an extremely important development because it has the ability to accelerate the arrival of the next Industrial Revolution, with the potential to change the world in multiple ways.

Many of the attributes associated with deep tech ventures are already being emulated by other successful metaverse-oriented organizations. Much like deep tech entities, these organizations tend to

- emphasize platform-based business models, organizational structures, and solution architectures (see Chapter 8, "Platforms")
- maintain a lean permanent staff and minimal permanent infrastructure to reduce costs and optimize flexibility
- acquire as many resources as possible on an on-demand, as-needed basis
- make extensive use of emerging metaverse-era technologies and methods
- have a high level of comfort participating in and leveraging business alliances and strategic ecosystems

14.2 DEEP TECH OVERVIEW

Not a New Concept

Deep tech ventures are certainly not new. The US Government has been in the deep tech venture business for some time, and examples include federally funded entities such as DARPA, n-Q-Tel, and US National Laboratories (such as the Oak Ridge National Laboratory). Among the globally disruptive, game-changing innovations emerging from these kinds of deep tech ventures was the Internet. Another example was Moderna's effort to develop a vaccine during the onset of the COVID epidemic.

Comparison With "Shallow" Tech Organizations

Deep tech organizations are typically different in many respects from more conventional (*shallow tech*) organizations. Deep tech organizations tend to be sharply focused on solving complex problems of widespread interest and impact, even global challenges. This narrow focus on scientifically challenging problems often requires a longer strategy timeline than those typically used by many other companies. This is because deep tech ventures frequently form multidisciplinary teams (scientists, engineers, and venture capitalists) to deal with complex unknowns for which answers must be found. Often this requires extensive research and trials, both of which take time, sometimes five years or more.

However, even though deep tech ventures can take a longer time to achieve their goals, they can also develop an impenetrable competitive position when they do, in effect rewriting the rules and crowding competitors completely out of the market.

Expertise in the design and use of platforms is especially important for deep tech organizations. Their business models feature empowered, highly motivated platform teams that have internalized the platform's vision as their own and have in-depth knowledge of the platform's products or services, market dynamics, architecture, systems, data sources, and algorithms. These platforms can be powerful competitive weapons, especially against more traditional, less nimble organizations.

Another important way deep tech companies differ from shallow tech organizations, especially those that tend to focus only on incremental refinements at the margins, is their commitment to achieve unassailable differentiation. Most conventional firms that deal in commoditized, "shallow tech" solutions develop repeatable offerings that are not very innovative and can be deployed at scale. These organizations are understandably reluctant to abandon sunk-cost investments in existing products and services, trained product managers, and marketing collateral. Shallow tech organizations are simply more tightly moored to the status quo than deep tech organizations.

However, this reluctance to abandon solutions and materials that have worked in the past and are expensive to reproduce often becomes a problematic strategy for many of these firms. For example, as many commercial IT services firms are now finding, undifferentiated solutions typically lead to the formation of commoditized industries. This leads to crowded market spaces where the only true discriminator among competitors is which company can offer the lowest cost. The customer is saying, in effect, "I will choose the lowest-cost provider, since they all offer the same thing."

Deep tech organizations, as well as other organizations now operating successfully in the early stages of metaverse, avoid this trap by developing groundbreaking solutions to help customers solve challenging problems. This gives these firms dominant, if not exclusive, industry positions for extended periods of time. Because of their expertise in the use of the most recent scientific and engineering advances, they have the ability to function productively at the center of technological innovation convergence, develop cutting-edge solutions that cannot be easily copied by competitors, and shift gears or change directions as needed without losing momentum. Their ability to form powerful alliances makes it possible to tackle extremely difficult challenges and potentially disruptive solutions without having to invest heavily in leading-edge technologies, expensive infrastructure, or resident world-class expertise. These resources can be obtained, at least to some degree, as needed from alliance partners.

Deep Tech Attributes Traditional Firms Should Emulate

As noted previously, many observers have suggested that deep tech is either the most important technological development since the first Industrial Revolution or is the beginning of the next Industrial Revolution. This transformational trend is altering how we view the continuing evolution and blurring the intersection between technology and organizational strategy. This trend has the potential to shape our world in unprecedented ways.

If conventional organizations are to be successful in transforming from their digital-era business models to metaverse-era ones, they will want to emulate many of the attributes and methods of deep tech ventures. As they do this, they will not limit their transformational focus solely to technological issues. Instead, they will understand that their transformations will have to be multidimensional. For example, these organizations will require enhanced collaborative capabilities to enable seamless interactions with business ecosystems partners. They will have to be prepared to utilize, as a normal way of conducting business, AI-based, algorithm-driven systems capable of operating at vastly improved scale and speed. They will have to cultivate a renaissance-like aspect – that is, they must become highly nimble, regenerative, hyperconnected, ever-evolving entities.

To summarize, even though deep tech organizations are different organizationally in many respects from more traditional organizations, their organizational models do contain certain critical attributes that more conventional organizations will need to develop as they transition into the metaverse era. These include

- mastery of converging, advanced metaverse-era technologies, in conjunction with the use of prior era commoditized technologies, to create new solution platforms and innovative ways to deliver value to customers
- a superior ability to form and participate in mutually beneficial alliances and partnership networks
- expertise in the design and use of sophisticated, efficient algorithms
- being highly skilled in the design and use of platform concepts as critical mechanisms for organizing resources and solving problems

- having a heavy reliance on the use of on-demand resources
- flatter, smaller, simpler, and well-networked organizational structures

Of course, simply observing or benchmarking deep tech organizations or ventures is only a start. The leaders of a shallow tech organization seeking to emulate the deep tech model as part of the organization's metaverse transformation strategy must find ways to infuse deep tech attributes formally into its future-state enterprise architecture. This allows these attributes to be validated and recognized organization-wide as integral components of the transformed business model and the associated strategies that will propel the organization successfully into the metaverse.

Transformation Strategy Recommendation: Align With a Deep Tech Organization

One way a conventional organization can accelerate its transformation to a successful metaverse-ready state is to formally align in some way with one or more successful deep tech organizations. This should not be difficult because deep tech ventures often rely on in-kind investments from outside resources, financial and otherwise, to continue operations.

Aligning With a Deep Tech Firm in a Synergistic Relationship

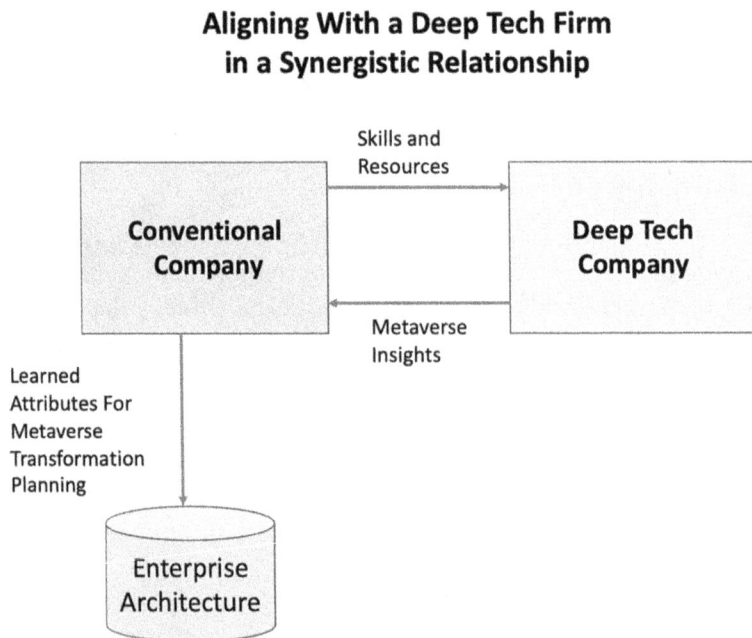

FIGURE 14.2 There are benefits to aligning with a deep tech company.

Typically, organizations such as national labs, universities, and venture capitalists play the most visible roles in supporting the creation, launching, and ongoing operational support of deep-tech startups. However, conventional enterprises can also be highly desirable collaborating partners with deep tech firms because of their ability to provide a complete suite of proven business and management resources and skills. These traditional resources and skills can be used by deep tech firms to help balance the more free-wheeling organizational practices many startups have. In addition, many deep tech firms need to integrate more advanced, metaverse-type technologies with their more conventional, commoditized technologies, such as cloud resources. Traditional companies, with their existing business connections, can help make this happen.

As shown in Figure 14.2, when a conventional or shallow tech organization integrates with a deep tech venture by supplying skills and resources, it can gain metaverse and deep tech insights in return. This new knowledge can be invaluable in formulating its own metaverse transformation strategy. Of course, these learned metaverse insights should be captured, converted to concrete transformation objectives, and stored in the company's enterprise architecture to help guide the transformation process.

However, a conventional firm seeking to align strategically and operationally with a deep tech organization should not plan on providing skills and resources to the metaverse partner "as is," much as it currently uses them itself. The leaders of the conventional firm must understand the mindset of the leaders of the deep tech firm and adapt, to the extent they can, the delivery of the skills and services to the unique attributes of the deep tech firm's vision, strategy, culture, and business model. For example, the conventional organization might be asked by the deep tech firm to help it provide more discipline to how it manages its capital investments. If the conventional organization manages its own capital investments through a detailed stage-gate process with several gates and lengthy review steps, it will want to tailor this more bureaucratic process to the leaner and more streamlined management style of the deep tech firm.

To partner effectively, leaders of conventional organizations have to recognize that their more conventional business model strategies and resources were not developed in the metaverse environment. This means they will most likely have to be modified to some degree to establish physical and logical interfacing compatibility with their deep tech partner. While adapting to the attributes and behaviors of the potential deep tech partner takes effort, the adaptation process itself moves the conventional organization closer to being able to operate as a metaverse-ready organization, which is, of course, the goal.

14.3 KEY TAKEAWAYS

- Companies truly committed to transforming to compete in the metaverse will want to benchmark and profile selected deep tech organizations, ideally those doing business in their own markets or industries.
- Because deep tech organizations (or joint ventures) will already be functioning effectively in a metaverse environment, the insights shallow tech managers can glean from deep tech company profiles can be helpful as they begin to develop or update their own metaverse transformation plans.
- One of the best ways to learn about and begin emulate key aspects of a deep tech business model is to formally associate with such a venture.

OTHER METAVERSE-RELATED TECHNOLOGIES

In addition to the metaverse-era technologies covered in previous chapters, this chapter provides brief summaries of other technologies that are either important now or likely to become more important as the metaverse becomes better established in the business world. Leaders of organizations need to have at least a conversational grip on these technologies, trends, and developments. They include

- robotics
- digital twins
- the Internet of Things (IoT)
- brain-computer interfaces
- 3D modeling and reconstruction
- spatial computing
- Web 3.0
- Industry 4.0 / Industrial Revolution 4.0

Robotics

Imagine that you are feeling bored. You cannot decide between taking an afternoon stroll along the rim of the Grand Canyon or a walking tour of the Augusta National Golf Club – without leaving your easy chair. You are probably living in at a time when the fusion of AI and other metaverse technologies with robotics is at an advanced state. You will guide a robot along a path, experiencing the walk as if it is you taking the steps. This is just one promise of robotics in the metaverse era. There are countless other uses for this technology fusion, especially on factory floors.

When the technologies covered in this book – AI, machine learning, digital twins, holography, edge computing, IoT, algorithms, AR, and VR – are applied to the world of intelligent robots, the potential applications are staggering. This is especially true in such areas as national defense, law enforcement, logistics, healthcare, manufacturing, border patrols, and package delivery.

Metaverse-era robotics are likely to play an outsized role in medicine, and soon. For example, in an article printed in the National Library of Medicine titled "Where Robotic Surgery Meets the Metaverse," authors Fijs W. B. van Leeuwen and Jos A. van der Hage discuss what some call the surgical metaverse, which involves a combination of robotics, augmented reality, and AI. [van Leeuwen et al.22]

The implications are clear. With advanced robots providing the locomotion and physical dexterity and AI providing the brain power, we are going to see some truly amazing robots in the near future.

Digital Twins

A *digital twin* is a computer-enabled, 3D virtual model that accurately reflects the size, shape, and behavior of a physical object, such as a wind farm, a building, a car, a crane, or an entire jet airliner (allowing engineers to test the plane safely under various flight conditions). Researchers, scientists, and engineers have found the use of digital twins to be an excellent way to explore problems that would otherwise be far too expensive, too dangerous, and sometimes too unethical, to explore using the real objects.

Typically, the object being studied is outfitted with special technologies, such as Internet of Things devices, gauges, or electrodes to infuse the digital twin with real-world data. This makes the functioning of the digital twin highly accurate and lifelike. Often, various metaverse-era technologies, such as AI, analytics, and machine learning, are used in this process to enrich the output. The goal is to be able to generate accurate simulations to predict how the real object will perform or operate over a complete life cycle under certain controlled conditions. The digital twin is an essential tool in modern engineering methods and practices.

The devices embedded in or attached to the real, physical object produce data related to performance parameters such as heat generation, centrifugal drag, energy consumption, stability, structural integrity, blockages, and vibrations. This information is then conveyed to linked computing resources and algorithms to create the digital twin of the physical object. After this data is loaded into the computational resources, the virtual model can perform realistic simulations of how the real object would behave under the same conditions being fed into the virtual version. The goal is to learn what kinds of enhancements, remediations, modifications, or other changes need to be made to the physical object to improve its performance.

How is this process different from a simulation? A simulation informs on what *might* happen while a digital twin reveals in real time what is *actually* happening throughout a complete life cycle. Both simulations and digital twins use digital models to replicate a system or object. Because a digital twin is an immersive, virtual environment, it provides richer investigation and analysis opportunities. Another difference is scope. Simulations typically focus on one specific process, whereas a digital twin can be used to simulate any number of processes simultaneously across full life cycles. Another major benefit of digital twins is their ability to generate real-time information that can be fed back and forth between the virtual model and the real object. This allows investigators and researchers to analyze more issues from more perspectives than is possible with simulations.

Readers interested in more information about the differences between digital twins, models, and simulations should read "How to tell the difference between a model and a digital twin" by L. Wright and S. Davidson. [Wright20]

Among the benefits of the digital twins is the ability to develop safe testing spaces. They are also used to discover design problems, structural flaws, inefficiencies, stress points, and other important information that can be used to develop improved designs, correct problems, provide improved maintenance, and otherwise optimize performance. Using this information, engineers, production managers, and equipment operators can make informed action decisions at the first sign of a problem, as reflected in the digital twin, rather than risking a complete equipment breakdown later.

The Internet of Things

The Internet of Things (IoT) is one of the more important technological concepts of the current decade. Even though the IoT is already in widespread use, it will continue to play an important role well into the metaverse era (and perhaps beyond), influencing organizational strategies as enterprises transform into the metaverse era.

The IoT refers to connected networks or ecosystems of interrelated physical entities or devices outfitted with sensors, gauges, software, electrodes, and other technologies. These devices connect with and exchange data with other devices and systems over the Internet or other networks. Importantly, these data exchanges can be done without requiring human-to-human or human-to-computer interaction. The technologies that enable the IoT, such as embedded devices, allow Internet connections among an endless array of objects, including cars, heart monitors, farm animals with biochip transponders, thermostats, and household appliances.

The growth of embedded IoT devices continues to grow. The total number of such devices is difficult to estimate, but most estimates fall into the range of about 17 billion in 2024, increasing to about 30 billion by 2030.

The information emitted from IoT devices is typically routed to an edge computing platform (see Chapter 10, "Edge Computing") or similarly configured technology deployment. The data is then typically sent either to a cloud-based system for analysis or it can be analyzed in local data centers. In most IoT deployments, the embedded devices communicate with one another or with other devices in an IoT ecosystem depending on the levels of intelligence embedded in the devices. Again, much of this takes place without human intervention.

Among the technological developments that have made IoT feasible and effective are cloud computing platforms (which minimize the IT resource management challenges for consumers and businesses), advances in network connectivity speeds and capabilities, AI, machine learning, data analytics, neural networks, and advances in in powerful, cost-effective, and highly reliable sensor technologies.

Brain-Computer Interfaces (BCIs)

Aside from quantum computing, perhaps the technology solution with the longest timeline to widespread use is the *brain-computer interface* (BCI). This solution has much potential in so many areas; as such, it is the focus of intensive research, with thousands of research papers reporting on its possible uses. BCIs are specialized communications links between human brains and computers of various kinds. Basically, BCIs allow humans to control computers and other devices using their thoughts.

Much of the work with BCIs remains experimental. Researchers continue to focus on complex variables, such as the uniqueness of the brain signal attributes of individual people.

One critical area of research for BCIs is helping people with disabilities overcome them. Some BCIs allow people suffering from paralysis to spell words on a computer screen and regain some control of their limbs. Work continues on providing the ability to restore a lost sense of touch. In a completely different field, a BCI might allow a soldier to operate a battlefield drone, hands-free.

Many researchers think BCIs will eventually be able to extend human capabilities by allowing them to control complex automated equipment and machinery using only their thoughts. More generally, however, BCIs simply enhance human-computer interactions, and they might eventually be able to do this in a myriad of use cases.

BCIs connect to the brain in two basic ways: implanted devices or wearable headgear. Implanted BCIs are typically surgically attached directly to brain tissue. Direct implants are believed to be more appropriate for users with severe neuromuscular disorders or physical injuries. For example, a person with paralysis could use an implanted BCI attached to a specific neuron region to regain precise control of a limb. Implanted BCIs measure signals directly from the brain, reducing interference from any other tissue. As with any form of brain surgery, there is always a risk of rejection or infection in this surgical approach, which is the reason for using this approach only in severe cases.

Wearable BCIs typically involve the use of headgear outfitted with conductors. The conductors measure brain activity that can be detected on the scalp. Most wearable options use electroencephalography to measure electrical activity in the brain. There is research underway on BCIs that use portable methods to acquire data. If successful, this would allow patients or subjects outfitted with these conductors to operate devices while moving around without restrictions.

3D Reconstruction

Simply put, *3D reconstruction* is a method that allows an object to be "recreated" within a virtual, 3D space using computing resources. The 3D image produced by the reconstruction process is powerfully vivid both in scale and geometry, which enables an improved technology-environment comprehension. The essential difference between a 3D model and a digital twin, as discussed earlier, is that a 3D reconstruction is used to visualize the design and construction of a product or system, while a digital twin allows designers and developers to interact virtually with the product or system.

The data for the object being recreated can be input into this method in a variety of ways, including photographs or a scan of the actual object. The utility of this method comes after the reconstruction is created. Without using or touching the actual object, which might not be desirable for a number of reasons, the recreated version can be handled or utilized in a variety of ways. Examples include, most notably, medical applications. Other examples include priceless art or history objects, law enforcement, retail sales, and the creation of 3D graphics for the entertainment industry. Some have used the method to capture special events or moments so they can be relived, almost as if they are happening again.

Spatial Computing

Just as deep neural networks can be challenging to understand if you are not already familiar with the technology involved, *spatial computing* is often dismissed as just another buzzword, another bewildering aspect of the emerging world of metaverse technology. However, spatial computing is simply a phrase that relates to the way that we will interact with technology in the metaverse. Generally speaking, the shift will be to interact with technology in an immersed way from *inside* the technology rather than from the *outside looking in,* which is presently the norm.

Spatial computing is difficult to define precisely because it is an overarching concept that includes many of the other technologies covered in this book. These include, for example, AR, VR, IoT, and AI. Spatial computing is a metaverse-era concept that encompasses and describes the methods and technologies used to capture, process, and manipulate or use 3D data. More specifically, spatial computing is the sum total of technologies and capabilities that will lead to users stepping inside the realm of computers, rather than just interacting with that realm from a distance. This is a large transitional shift from how we have interacted with computers in the past.

Web 3.0 uses the converging technologies discussed in this book to conceal various aspects of the technology from users by integrating user interfaces seamlessly into the physical environment. Spatial computing will build on this to make computers a blended part of the environment, thereby leveraging natural human spatial capabilities to make better use of our time and tap our full potential.

Spatial computing will also aid in the automation of the interrelationships among machines, equipment, people, objects, and their respective environments to optimize their interactions. Spatial computing, including all its component technologies and methods, has the potential to transform how companies optimize operations across the entire enterprise. We can only imagine the profound impact this capability would have on future organizational designs and business models, as well as factories and other production environments and facilities.

Examples of spatial computing in use abound, including disease tracking and management, tracking the origin and spread patterns of deadly viruses, tracking and analyzing species possibly facing extinction, modeling water supply problems, enabling driverless modes of transportation, accelerating drug development (e.g., antidotes for exotic venoms), digital phenotyping, and oil and gas exploration.

Web 3.0

The World Wide Web (Web) provides the foundational layer for using the Internet. It provides the means for the creation and use of websites and a myriad of application services. Web 1.0 and Web 2.0 refer to major phases in the evolution of the World Wide Web as the platform evolved through various technologies and formats.

- Web 1.0 refers to the approximate period from 1991 to 2002. During this phase, most websites contained static pages and most users were consumers, not content producers.
- Web 2.0 was characterized by user-produced content uploaded to social media, blogs, and forums. Web 2.0 is the same basic structure used today.

Web 3.0 is generally viewed as the next evolutionary step for the World Wide Web. Many experts in this area contend this next phase could be as disruptive as the first phases of the Web. Among the key attributes often mentioned for Web 3.0 are full openness, increased decentralization, blockchain technologies, token-based economics, and greater user utility.

The goal of Web 3.0 is to move beyond unique Web addresses that store data in multiple fixed locations to become more decentralized. This will involve the ability to find information based on its content, which means it could be stored in multiple locations simultaneously. AI will play a major role in this transformation. This development could impact the business models of companies like Meta and Google.

As noted, Web 3.0 will make extensive use of AI, enhancing the semantic Web capabilities and ubiquitous location possibilities, to provide relevant data to users quickly. This will be done in part by using AI to sift through data to extract the specific information a user is seeking. (Note: This is the kind of capability a nimble enterprise architecture supporting metaverse era organizations should have.)

Industry 4.0 / Industrial Revolution 4.0

The terms Industry 4.0 and Industrial Revolution 4.0 remain controversial. After all, the skeptics say, you can recognize a true revolution only in retrospective, not while it is happening – that is, if one actually is happening. However, it is unwise to ignore the transformational impact of the robust intelligence being built into today's production devices and processes (the realm of AI and machine learning), the growing use of 3D virtual spaces, and the massive data capacity of today's devices and networks and their fast computational speeds. These developments are changing business models, production strategies, and operations globally.

Discussions of Industrial Revolution 4.0 will arise with increasing frequency over the next few years. Organizational leaders need to be familiar with the issues being debated in this area, as new technologies continue to emerge and current technologies continue to evolve.

We should remember that when it comes to industrialization the world has never been, and is not now, in one homogeneous state. Patterns of industrialization differ markedly all over the world, and they have differed markedly since the late 1700s. This is the historical time frame from which most experts date the beginning of the industrial transformation, at least for what was to become the industrialized parts of world.

Historians tend to agree there have been three industrial revolutions since the mid-1700s, although they are not consistent in identifying the specific change agents driving each revolution. There is less agreement that there has been a fourth, although it is included in these overviews of each revolution because there are many who feel it has arrived.

- There is broad agreement that the original Industrial Revolution ("Industrial Revolution 1.0") involved the transition from an agricultural economy to an increasingly industrialized one. This was a time when the labors of both humans and animals were transformed through various kinds of machinery innovations. Among the specific drivers typically cited are the mechanization of processes, the mass extraction of coal, the steam engine, metal forging, smelting, steel, canal travel (rather than the use of mules), looms, steam-driven printing presses, spinning mills, and early factories.

- Industrial Revolution 2.0 began in the 19th century as a number of major inventions and discoveries changed the way items were produced, distributed, and exchanged. Among the key drivers for this revolution were electricity and electrification, mechanized assembly line production, indoor plumbing, the discovery of gas and oil, the combustion engine, rise of chemical industries and their products, telegraph, telephone, airplane, and automobile.

- Industrial Revolution 3.0, which emerged in the early to mid-1950s and continues today, was driven by advances in early electronic calculating devices, chip technology advances, and the transition from analog technology to the digital era. Other signal events of this era included the Internet, nuclear power, interstate highway system, smart phones, satellites, social media, AI, robotics, IoT, machine learning, 3D printing, and a general rise in the standard of living and life expectancies.

- Industrial Revolution 4.0, which began in the 1990s with the Internet, is building on Industrial Revolution 3.0 era digital technologies by infusing them with intelligence and immersive experiences. Much of what defines Industrial Revolution 4.0 – if in fact such a revolution is happening – involves the complete suite of technologies described in this book (e.g., AI, VR, AR, machine learning, quantum computing, advanced algorithms, digital twins, and holograms). The use of these technologies is leading to the creation of intelligent "learning" systems (such as those that enable new kinds of semiautonomous factories). This revolution is supported by advances in disciplines such as data analytics and advanced algorithms, as well new technologies, such as machine learning, 3D reconstruction, and digital twins. This era is also characterized by a shift to renewable energy, such as solar, wind, and geothermal. In countries outside of the US, there has been a significant move toward nuclear energy.

Many believe Industrial Revolution 4.0 will not have arrived fully until additional technology advances, such as quantum computing, Web 3.0, and BCIs converge with many of the metaverse-era technologies already in widespread use, especially emerging AI capabilities like chat bots.

15.1 KEY TAKEAWAYS

- This chapter provided overviews of important metaverse era technologies, methods, or concepts not covered in prior chapters. Some of these technologies (e.g., the IoT and Web 3.0) are already generally well understood, but still warrant discussion. Other technologies covered in this chapter are more conceptual in nature, but are still the subject of much metaverse discussion (e.g., Industrial Revolution 4.0 and spatial computing). Still others are more narrowly focused, but still important (e.g., digital twins and 3D reconstruction), or are still heavily experimental (e.g., BCIs).
- Each organization facing the need to transform to the metaverse will be in its own unique position with respect to mission and industry, level of metaverse maturity and understanding, strategic goals, and required skill levels. Therefore, the degree of relevance and relative priority of any of these technologies will be highly situational.
- Therefore, overviews of major metaverse technologies, such as those covered in this and preceding chapters, can help organizational leaders think about those that have the most potential relevance to their specific situations and plans for the future. They can then work those that are most promising into their individualized, organization-specific transformation plans.

REFERENCES

[van Leeuwen et al.22] Fijs W. B. van Leeuwen and Jos A. van der Hage, *Where Robotic Surgery Meets the Metaverse*, The National Library of Medicine, December 14, 2022 *https://www.ncbi.nlm.nih.gov/pmc/articles/PMC9776294/*

[Wright20] Wright, L., Davidson, S., *How to tell the difference between a model and a digital twin.* Adv. Model. and Simul. in Eng. Sci. 7, 13 (2020) *https://doi.org/10.1186/s40323-020-00147-4*

PART 4

PUTTING IT ALL TOGETHER

16

ORGANIZATIONAL STRUCTURE FOR THE METAVERSE ERA

16.1 INTRODUCTION

In an article by McKinsey and Company titled "Organizing for the future: Nine keys to becoming a future-ready company," the authors offer a number of important insights relative to an organizational structure for the metaverse. [De Smet et al.21]

As these authors note, most of today's organizations emphasize the kinds of traditional hierarchies that can be traced back for centuries. These hierarchies were built with objectives and criteria in mind – top-down leadership, efficiency, control, risk avoidance – that are inconsistent with the demands the metaverse is already placing on many organizations.

Therefore, when facing an impending, technology-driven disruption like the metaverse, one of the most important issues an executive team must address is the current structure of their organization. Can the current organizational model carry them forward successfully in a rapidly changing world? If not, what kinds of changes need to be made? At what scope and speed? Evolve what we have or build something radically new?

This issue is certainly relevant for most organizations today. As the metaverse disruption gains momentum, an immersive, AI-driven, rapidly changing economic environment will have major competitive implications for most organizations. Therefore, the need for adaptive organizational changes is a critical discussion topic for boards of directors and C-suite executives.

If organizational leaders are not already doing so, they should execute the following two-step process right away.

Step 1: Perform a Metaverse "Reality Check" Based on Your Circumstances

Do not take anyone else's word for the overall competitive implications of the metaverse or how it might affect your organization in particular. Each situation is unique. Organizational leaders should perform their own due diligence. Tapping into the best resources available, senior executives must ask and answer these kinds of questions:

- Exactly what is the metaverse disruption? Give us facts.
- How serious is the metaverse disruption? Is all the talk mostly hype or is there a real opportunity? What evidence is there to support the positive metaverse rhetoric, as well as the counter arguments of the naysayers?
- What is the generally accepted timeline for truly significant, game-changing impacts on the economy? Are these timeline estimates believable? What is the evidence?
- What will the disruption look like if it does affect us? How will our markets change? How will the behaviors of our customers change? What would be the most likely critical implications for us? What are the likely very near-term impacts to our organization, if any?
- What are our competitors doing? Have any of them already begun to adapt to the disruption in a major, transformational way? Which ones, if any, should we be tracking or benchmarking?

Obtaining credible answers to these and similar due diligence questions will not be easy because opinions about the metaverse remain diverse, as they were initially for all prior technological disruptions. However, there are many credible sources available to help in answering these questions, including respected, independent industry analysis firms, large management consulting firms, universities, and technology vendors. Or, if you have the talented staff, your organization can do its own research. Therefore, there are many ways to come up with reasonable, balanced answers to solidify your own perspectives, whatever they might turn out to be. Once you are firm in your thinking and conclusions, proceed accordingly.

If, as will be true for the majority of organizations, this "reality check" does indicate the metaverse disruption is real and to some degree already here, and if it appears likely to affect your organization in significant ways, then proceed to step 2. If not, consider yourself lucky, and you can, if so inclined, stand pat with your current structure and business model.

Step 2: Begin to Plan the New Organizational Structure

After performing a credible reality check, most organizations will find themselves recognizing the need to move ahead with transformation actions at some level and scope. Some will haltingly venture into utilizing the metaverse technologies, while others will adopt these technologies more aggressively. The latter will have recognized the high probability that the metaverse disruption is real and already impactful to their organizations. They will have seen this reality, for example, in the massive global interest in AI-based ChatGPT.

If you have decided that your organization is going to have to adjust to these changing events, the next step is to further evaluate the attributes of the metaverse phenomenon. Analyze how these attributes taken as a whole might affect your company. Based on these likely impacts, evaluate alternative organizational structures that can harmonize with these attributes. Settle on the structure most likely to help your company adapt successfully to the key attributes of the metaverse and launch initial transformation actions.

The more important attributes of the metaverse itself were covered in the preceding chapters of this book. An overview of representative organizational structures for operating in the metaverse is provided in the following sections.

16.2 ALTERNATIVE ORGANIZATIONAL STRUCTURES

Having concluded that organizational changes will most likely be necessary, executive leadership is faced with a broad array of possible organizational design options. To settle on the optimal go-forward structural transformation strategy, executives must agree on the most important organizational qualities or characteristics required to be competitive in the metaverse era. This leads to questions such as the following:

- What are the most critical organizational attributes we must develop? Agile? Nimble? Fast? Adaptable?
- Should our organization be bigger, smaller, or about the same size?
- Flatter or steeper?
- Centralized or networked, and to what degree either way?
- Top-down driven or extensively decentralized and empowered?
- Self-contained or alliance and business ecosystem-intensive?
- Private or public?

- Stand-alone or merged with another company?
- Change the skill mix and structure at the senior executive level or stay the same?
- Engage in divesting certain business lines? Adding business lines?

The answers to these and other questions will drive a company toward one side or the other of the organizational structure continuum shown in Figure 16.1.

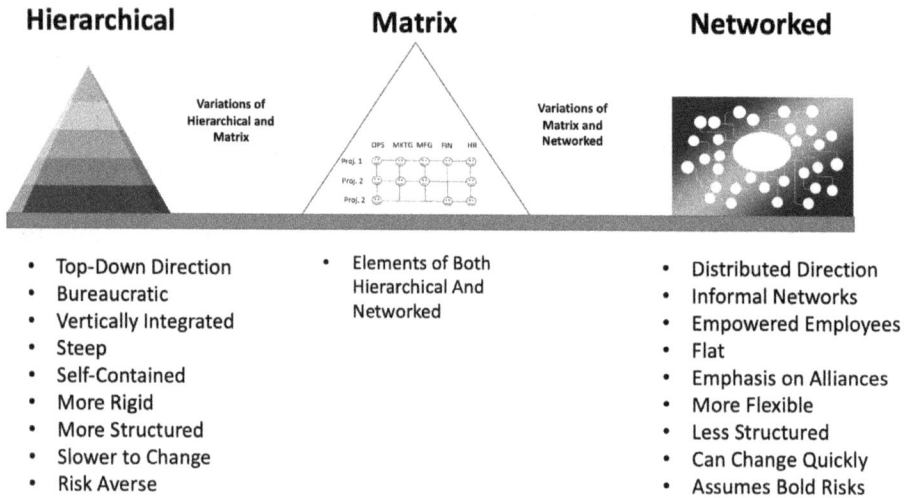

FIGURE 16.1 There is a continuum of organizational structure options.

Certain companies, especially those in more stable industries and markets, could feel less immediate impact from the metaverse. They will most likely have structures that position them toward the left side of Figure 16.1, a position they might have held for decades. Deep tech companies will tend to cluster on the far right side of Figure 16.1. The majority of today's companies will most likely fall left of center, but will be edging slowly to the right as their existing, current-era digital transformation initiatives (not metaverse transformation initiatives) continue to make progress.

For analysis purposes, we can take a deeper dive into the two most extreme positions, the vertically integrated, top-down company on the left in Figure 16.1 and the fully decentralized, networked company on the right. Examining the two extremes can help provide some insights into an appropriate middle ground structure for the typical metaverse era organization.

The Vertically Integrated Model

One organizational option is the classic pyramid structure shown on the far-left side of the chart in Figure 16.1. This is the traditional, vertically integrated, top-down, command-and-control type of structure we have seen in the past. For many, this model might seem a relic of the industrial age of the 1940s and 1950s. However, there are still situations today where this kind of organization can still function effectively. In fact, within some economic and competitive domains the vertically integrated model might even be making a comeback.

For example, we can look back to the COVID epidemic and to the severe disruptions to global supply chains. Some organizations whose supply chains were constrained (or cut off completely) began to utilize their own private sources of supply chain materials, such as electronic chips, previously acquired from outside sources. In other words, at least for now, vertical integration might be finding new life as the result of a global catastrophic event. If it happened once, it could happen again.

So, what exactly is a vertical organization, and will that structure still be effective in the metaverse era?

Vertical organizational structures are managed from the top down through a very clear and well understood chain of command. Everyone knows who the boss is. Only the highest levels of managers make important strategic decisions, and these flow down from the top. Middle managers accept these decisions and directives, including the tasking and performance objectives guidance they carry with them. These mid-level managers, adhering to established and often voluminous policies, procedures, guidelines, rules, and position charters, take on some of the tasking themselves. However, they typically pass most of the tasking instructions and work objectives on to lower-level workers, whom they supervise. Middle managers delegate the work to subordinate units through detailed task assignments, budgets, defined processes, deliverables, and goals. All of this takes place within a well-defined bureaucratic structure with clearly defined lines of communication and well-circumscribed collections of functional responsibilities. Lower-level employees complete the work (or not) and progress reports flow back up through middle management to upper management for approval or remedial actions.

This structure does offer several benefits, such as tight controls, risk mitigation, full compliance with rules and regulations, stability, predictability, and protection from having too many unpredictable outside suppliers.

Among the negative consequences of these layers of rigid structures and communication channels is the slow, tedious flow of information down, across, and then back up the organization. This contributes to the general inability to change enterprise directions in a timely way. For example, steeply vertical organizations found it more difficult to respond in effective ways to the sudden COVID outbreak in late 2019 and 2020. They were simply not designed to make swift, highly strategic decisions and then have them implemented in the kind of time frame this largely unforeseeable situation demanded.

Let us consider a hypothetical carpet and flooring manufacturer in Dalton, Georgia. Perhaps this company began as a family business and traditionally operated under a tightly controlled pyramid structure for decades. As the metaverse becomes more important, the management of this company might choose to reassess its organizational structure. The management team may not feel the urgency of the coming changes in technology. However, to be prudent, the senior staff might inquire if anyone thinks the company needs to do anything differently to remain competitive in this new era they keep hearing about. If so, how and to what extent? The owner/CEO might simply conclude his pyramid structure is still completely satisfactory.

This type of classic organization operating in a relatively stable market can probably get by, at least for a while, without changing much structurally and continue to compete well in the metaverse. However, its marketing and sales functions will certainly want to pay close attention to technologies like virtual reality showrooms. Its manufacturing division will certainly want to stay current with developments in AI-based autonomous factories. Therefore, even though this kind of organization will be affected by the metaverse, the impact might not be to the extent that a change in structure and business model will be called for, at least not in the near term. However, these kinds of organizations are likely to be the exception.

Let us consider another example: NuTech International IT Services (NIIS), a hypothetical purveyor of enterprise IT outsourcing services, remote data center and network management services, cloud brokerage services, and service desks. Let's say NIIS was founded a few decades ago by a brilliant engineer who still runs the company with a top-down iron grip in a steeply vertical organizational structure. In the early stages of the company's growth, when IT infrastructures and related issues were more stable and less complicated, NIIS could develop reusable product and service lines and the related marketing collateral that they could deploy efficiently at scale for years. NIIS could also command premium contract prices because of the company's stellar reputation, world-class engineering expertise, and highly innovative (at least when built over a decade ago) integrated services management centers. However, as we moved into the cloud era with the emergence of more on-demand options for IT products and services, NIIS's markets became increasingly undifferentiated and commoditized. Eventually, it found itself operating in a densely crowded, highly commoditized market space with many competitors. Now, NIIS finds itself stuck in a competitive environment characterized by lowest-cost competitions for IT service contracts.

When any organization's structure, business model, culture, and framework of policies and procedures were established decades ago, as we see with NIIS, changing from that long-solidified model to a new structure is always difficult. This is especially true if the founding regime still has significant influence. Such firms were built with tight controls, stability, and risk management as the most critical operational goals, not necessarily innovation or agility. For many lines of business in certain industries, this kind of organizational strategy will have a difficult time competing effectively in the metaverse era.

For any company in a competitive environment similar to NIIS's where there are many players selling commoditized, undifferentiated products, establishing a more fluid, nimbler organizational structure is vital. Inherent in that revised master organizational strategy is the imperative to create more differentiated products and services, the kinds that will be demanded in the metaverse. All components of the company must become focused on and contribute to the development of this new slate of products, services, and value streams. (See Chapter 22 for a hypothetical case study on how this might be done.) Therefore, NIIS, unlike the north Georgia flooring company, needs to change, and without hesitation and with steely determination.

That brings us to the networked organization.

The Networked Organization

Anyone familiar with the matrix organizational model will already have some understanding of networked organizations (see Figure 16.2). However, matrix organizations were used with varying degrees of success long before we had the kinds of digital technology resources we have today. Today's high-speed, high-volume networking and communications capabilities make it easier to design, implement, and operate a networked organization.

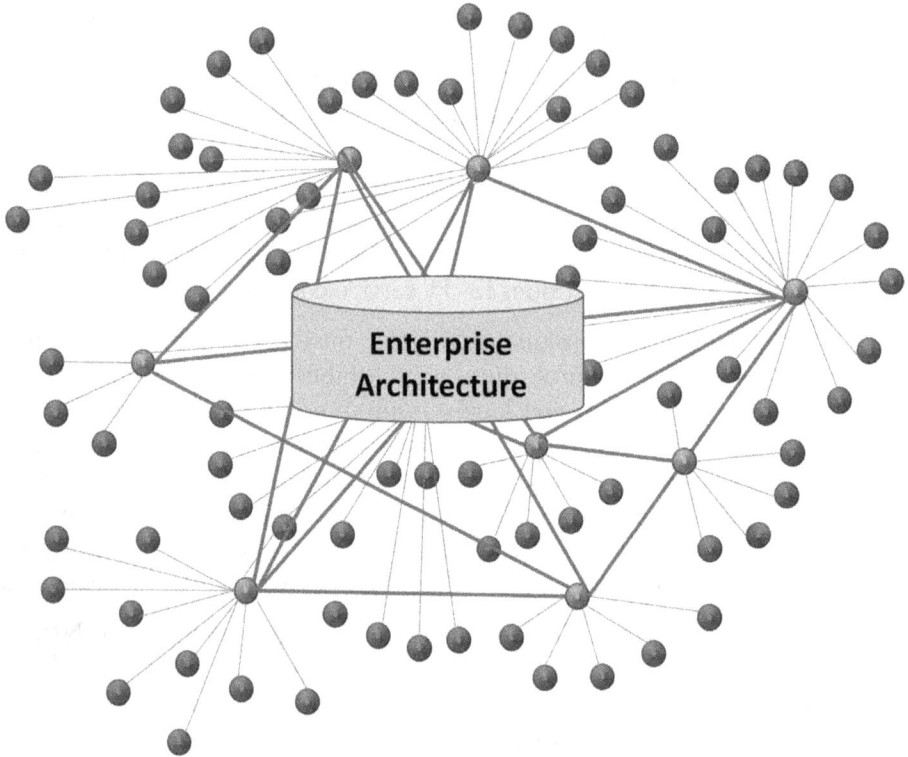

FIGURE 16.2 The decentralized, empowered networked organization

Leading the Networked Organization

Many longtime managers of vertical, hierarchical organizations will look at the organizational chart for a highly networked organization, like the one shown in Figure 16.2, and scratch their heads, partially out of curiosity and partially in amusement. They will wonder how such a bizarre structure can function without clear leadership and control from the top. "Is this nothing more than a mob?" they might reasonably ask themselves.

Maybe they are right. After all, scientists tell us the frontal lobe of the brain is in charge of such critical functions as thinking, planning, organizing, problem solving, scrutinizing, movement, and maintaining short-term memory. Any organization has to have a "frontal lobe," doesn't it? Otherwise, it would by definition be nothing more than a mob, a group of people doing random things without a means for coordinated thinking, reflection, coordination, and impulse control.

The "frontal lobe" in any enterprise is its governance structure, which is the primary source of enterprise-wide thinking, planning, organizing, problem solving, and communicating. Should not this "frontal lobe" sit atop the body of the organization, much as it sits atop the human body?

Not necessarily.

A well-managed networked organization is not a loose collection of autonomous, well-resourced small teams doing whatever they please with no one to guide them. A networked organization is like a living organism, and as such, it requires a "frontal lobe" in some form to provide direction for the overall enterprise. Unlike the vertically integrated organization, where the entire brain sits atop the pyramid, the "frontal lobe" for the networked organization typically resides in the center of the organization, as shown on the left side of Figure 16.3, and manages outward toward the customer. Beyond that, this frontal lobe is also somewhat distributed in a networked and empowered organization, which is more like a unified and centrally coordinated collection of multiple frontal lobes. That is, forward thinking and decision-making powers are shared, making the entire enterprise smarter, faster, and nimbler.

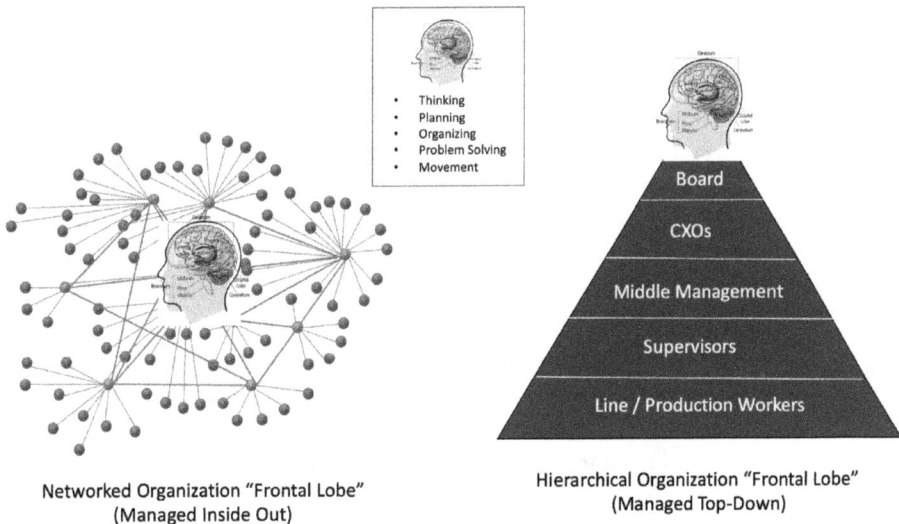

- Thinking
- Planning
- Organizing
- Problem Solving
- Movement

Board

CXOs

Middle Management

Supervisors

Line / Production Workers

Networked Organization "Frontal Lobe"
(Managed Inside Out)

Hierarchical Organization "Frontal Lobe"
(Managed Top-Down)

Brain Image Courtesy of Pixbay, GDT

FIGURE 16.3 Frontal lobes in hierarchical and networked organizations

The day-to-day functioning of the "frontal lobe" (i.e., governance) in a networked organization is usually performed with a softer touch than in more hierarchical organizations. This enables employees to form multidisciplinary teams, often compact in nature, that work in relative autonomy to achieve common goals. Teams are given a "platform" status of some kind (see Chapter 8), say a product or service platform, and are encouraged to "own it" as if they are entrepreneurs. In this model, traditional top-down supervisory mechanisms are less involved on a day-to-day basis than in a vertical organization. The empowered groups are expected to exploit opportunities or manage problems as they occur and without much direct supervision, failing or succeeding based on their own initiative and decisions. When a platform team in a network organization achieves its goals, the company's central coordinating structure can disband it or reorganize it for a new strategic need.

This approach to organizational structure provides one of the greatest boosts to organizational nimbleness, and it is a vital capability for many organizations operating in the metaverse era.

Therefore, most organizations looking to transform themselves into a networked organization capable of succeeding in the metaverse era should expect to build the following attributes into the new structure and business model:

- Create an operating environment and culture that embraces uncertainty as a constant business reality and instills in employees the belief this gives the company a distinct advantage.
- Offset constant uncertainty and turbulence in the competitive environment by organizing in a way that enhances reaction speed through higher levels of flexibility and nimbleness. Examples include use of the internal organizational platform model and empowered governance practices.
- Executives accustomed to avoiding all risks, or who are consumed with mitigating them, will have to change their attitudes and behaviors.
- The networked organization will be more tolerant of mistakes than more hierarchical organizations. They will learn from mistakes, adjust quickly, and move on.
- The central organizing strategy should drive the organization toward a flatter, more networked structure.
- Develop or hire employees who are highly motivated, goal-oriented, team players comfortable with soft supervision and often ambiguous situations.

These employees must be comfortable with frequent and often unexpected reassignments.

- Provide the means (processes, incentives, and resourcing) to empower smaller, multidisciplinary teams capable of dealing with complex challenges, and then actually empower them.
- The critical drivers and sources of nimbleness for the enterprise are documented in the enterprise architecture where they can help guide the evolution of the organization.
- Seek to foster a common culture where everybody understands the new rules of the organization and their roles, and are comfortable with both.

These structural attributes must be documented in a repository that is easily accessible by groups and individuals across the enterprise. If organizational changes do appear to be dictated by changes in the competitive environment, as is likely to be the case in the metaverse, it is especially important that the future-state vision for the enterprise structure be captured in the top layer of the enterprise architecture. This is critical because all else in the enterprise architecture must flow from and support this important statement of organizational direction. If the very structure and nature of an organizational model is going to change, everything else in the enterprise is also a candidate for change.

Finally, if your organization does seek to transition from a hierarchical organization model to a networked one, taking smaller, more easily managed steps is acceptable, at least initially. It is best to experiment, learn, expand the experiment, learn more, and step-by-step, accomplish the goal.

16.3 KEY TAKEAWAYS

- Most, but not all, organizations will need to modify their overall enterprise structures and business models to remain competitive in the metaverse era.
- For those that do need to change, the shift will be toward a flatter, more networked, platform-oriented, empowered, and alliance-oriented structure.
- The primary attributes of this future-state model should be documented at the top layer of the enterprise architecture (see Chapter 18, "Enterprise Architecture.")

REFERENCES

[De Smet et al.21] *Organizing for the future: Nine keys to becoming a future-ready company,* Aaron De Smet, Chris Gagnonis, and Elizabeth Mygatt, McKinsey & Company, 2021 *https://www.mckinsey.com/capabilities/ people-and-organizational-performance/our-insights/organizing-for-the-future-nine-keys-to-becoming-a-future-ready-company*

17

GOVERNANCE FRAMEWORK FOR THE METAVERSE ERA

17.1 INTRODUCTION

For organizations seeking to develop a business model capable of competing in a dynamic and opportunity-rich metaverse environment, the place to start is at the enterprise governance level. Enterprise governance is a framework of accountabilities, processes, and practices by which the leadership of an organization

- maintains the mission definition, structure, and strategic direction for the organization
- keeps an executive-level focus on the horizon and ensures the continuing alignment of overarching enterprise strategic objectives with downstream business and technical operations
- continuously assesses and manages risks
- ensures compliance with regulatory and legal requirements
- fosters a rewarding and productive organizational culture
- makes major decisions for the company, such as lines of business, mergers, and acquisitions
- ensures enterprise resources are used responsibly and efficiently in achieving the organization's strategic and tactical objectives

An effective governance framework helps anchor an organization's strategies and operations in agreed-upon themes, values, and business goals. This framework typically defines the official company image and voice, specifies and formalizes who is authorized to make different classes of decisions at different organizational levels, and designates who has ultimate accountability for these decisions. The governance structure also ensures fairness and transparency in how the organization communicates with its various stakeholders and regulators. Enterprise governance in the metaverse will retain all of these responsibilities, but will perform them in a more agile and responsive manner.

Governance Zones of Responsibility

Governance is frequently divided logically, although not necessarily structurally, into multiple zones of responsibility. The two traditional breakouts are "corporate governance" and "business governance." However, because business processes and digital technologies have become so intertwined and inseparable over the past three decades, a third governance focus area has been established in most organizational governance structures. This focus area is often referred to as "technology governance" (see Figure 17.1)

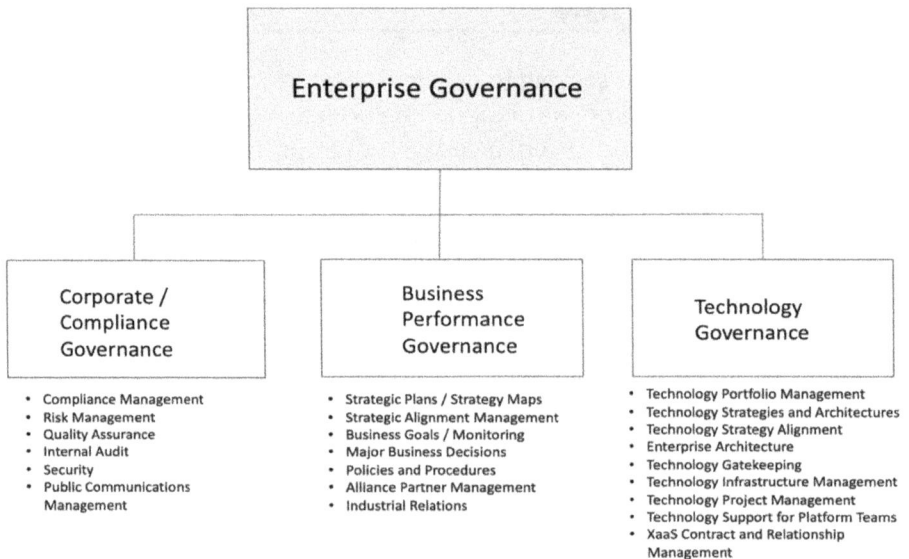

FIGURE 17.1 Logical breakouts of governance frameworks

This chapter discusses overall enterprise governance and the technology governance accountability focus area. The emphasis is specifically on the critical role of enterprise governance in leading a company toward competitive success in the metaverse. Within that area of analysis, the vital role of a new-era enterprise architecture is also highlighted.

17.2 OVERALL ENTERPRISE GOVERNANCE

An overall governance structure capable of operating effectively in the metaverse should have the following attributes:

- a good understanding of the major attributes of the metaverse, especially the critical factors that make it different from the current competitive environment
- a good understanding of the converging technological innovations defining and driving the metaverse (such as AI, VR, AR, and quantum computing)
- a commitment to transform the organization into one agile enough to thrive in the metaverse
- documented Vision and Mission statements that reflect the essential attributes of a company competing in the metaverse era (such as nimble, lean, decentralized, innovative, and business ecosystem-oriented)
- an empowered governance model wherein certain governance functions and accountabilities are delegated to subordinate managers and groups, thereby freeing up executive management to deal more effectively with rapidly changing circumstances
- a commitment to deploying, owning, and using a new kind of enterprise architecture (EA) as a vital tool for steering the enterprise toward successful operations in the metaverse era
- an official governing charter and appropriate policies for EA development, deployment, use, and evolution, including a designated full-time manager for the EA
- an innovative technology platform for the company's EA, one that emphasizes leading-edge technologies, such as AI and augmented reality, to improve accuracy, make the EA user friendly, make updates easier, and maintain tight synchronization among EA layers and components (see Chapters 18 and 19)

Strong Governance in a Nimble, Networked Organization?

At first glance, the situation might seem untenable – a nimble, empowered, and networked organization operating under a strong and disciplined governance structure. How can you have two different things at once, both empowerment enterprise-wide and a strong, disciplined governance structure?

Although managing an extensively networked organization effectively through disciplined governance practices does present its challenges, it can be done and done well. The answer lies in two areas. The first is the effective use of an enterprise architecture to aid in managing the technology governance component. The second is the delegation of certain governance actions and empowerment of employees. Here is a simple example.

Let's say someone has decided to build a house. Unless he is paying cash, he first works with a lender to obtain the necessary resources and then proceeds with his plan. He hires both an architect and a builder. For this small venture, the lending firm is, in effect, his board. The architect is in a staff position supporting his vision, while the builder is in charge of production operations to achieve the vision.

The homeowner is busy with other obligations (work, family, and travel). However, he is completely committed to building a perfect dream home, one with top quality construction and the best value for his money. That is his strategic plan. He communicates this plan to his staff architect and builder. At this point, he also tells them he is not going to have the time to make every decision that has to be made as construction moves forward. Anyone who has ever built a home knows the process is fraught with issues and surprises, from the initial grading of the building site to the installation of the final roll of sod. This homeowner tells his two-person team they will need to handle about 80% of these issues themselves and only bring the challenging, more important issues (about 20%) to him. If, for example, minor changes are needed to the design of the house, his staff architect and construction manager can work them out among themselves. If a major change is required, they can bring that decision to him. If any of the numerous subcontractors cause routine problems, the construction manager should handle them. If a dispute arises over where property lines have been staked out, that issue should come to him.

What we have in this simple example is empowered governance. The strategic vision has been developed by the person building the new home, and that vision has been codified in architectural plans. This master blueprint is maintained by the architect, but it has also been provided to the contractor, and through further delegation to a wide variety of temporary employees, the subcontractors. The new home owner has responsibility for the overall effort but has delegated the primary operational aspects of governance to subordinate managers. These individuals internalize that vision and act on the new homeowner's behalf, making many important decisions among themselves. This has all been enabled by capturing the vison of the homeowner in a master blueprint, which then can be passed on to others for execution, thereby enabling delegation.

The same general principles apply to a decentralized, networked organization operating in a dynamic metaverse economy. The board and the senior executive team are responsible for developing and maintaining the enterprise's basic charter, vision, strategy, and operational goals. These are documented and updated, as needed, in the organization's enterprise architecture. When these plans are executed, a portion of overall enterprise governance accountabilities can be delegated to subordinate managers who have been given authority to make governance-level decisions on behalf of executive management.

Therefore, given their understanding of the competitive dynamics of the metaverse economy, managers of organizations seeking to compete effectively in the metaverse will have created a revised organizational operating model. In this model, at least the next two levels down in the organization (or two levels out in a web-like networked organization) are empowered to act on behalf of executive management and make most local level decisions themselves, including many decisions that previously required executive management approval. These subordinate managers will generally handle 80% or more of the issues and decisions that need to be made, taking only the other 20% to the C-suite for guidance and resolution.

The net result of this empowered approach is a more agile form of governance. Because most of the day-to-day decisions faced in the execution of enterprise strategy are being made by managers closer to the immediate decision context, the organization can be much more responsive to changing events and circumstances. All of this is enabled by current, well organized, and relevant information available in the enterprise architecture. Without immediate access to this information, organizations will find it far more difficult operate with the levels of quickness and agility the metaverse will require. Once again, we see the tight linkages between nimble governance, a robust enterprise architecture, and an empowered organization. For most of today's organizations, developing these attributes are essentially the price of admission to compete in the metaverse.

Summary Notes on General Governance

Before looking in more detail at the "technology governance" component of the overall enterprise governance framework, there are a few points related to general governance that should be reviewed. The general governance framework should ensure that these issues or requirements are addressed properly.

C-Suite Membership

As noted, to become a metaverse-ready organization, the executive suite must be staffed with individuals who understand what the metaverse era means, how these advanced digital, methodological, and organizational innovations could impact their organization both positively and negatively, and the steps their organization must take to be competitive in this new era. All of this must be reflected in the organization's Mission and Vision statements, and these should be documented and kept current in the enterprise architecture.

For most organizations, this will require the infusion of new talent into the executive suite, including carefully chosen alliance partner and consulting relationships. To remain informed and current, C-suite executives must have systematic interactions with individuals and groups who understand the nature of the metaverse and the new economic environment that is accompanying these converging digital technologies. This could involve training programs, consultants, benchmarking entities (such as deep tech ventures), and executive self-development.

Single Manager for EA

While enterprise architecture development, use, and evolution will, of necessity, be highly collaborative and dynamic, there must be a single, accountable operational manager in place for the EA, such as a Chief Enterprise Architect. The senior executive team should ensure such a position is filled with a highly capable individual, and that the roles and responsibilities for this position are spelled out clearly and documented in the organization's enterprise architecture. In smaller organizations, this role might be assumed by someone performing multiple roles, such as IT Manager / Chief Architect.

EA Methodology and Tools

The methodology used to develop and manage the organization's enterprise architecture must be based on a holistic view of the enterprise. As discussed in more detail in Chapters 18 and 19, this view will include the organization's business model strategy (products, services, markets, goals, and priorities), information flows, data collections, applications, and digital technology infrastructure elements (such as computers, networks, special technologies, and the technology components of the cybersecurity infrastructure). Enterprise governance must ensure that this comprehensive perspective permeates all enterprise architecture development and evolution activities. The enterprise architecture is not simply a technology architecture, but much more.

The enterprise architecture methodology must operate on a platform based on leading-edge technologies in order for it to be easily accessible, user friendly in content, viewed as a value-added resource throughout the enterprise, and easily updated in a timely and well-synchronized way. Commercial products and standards-based EA methodologies and products exist, but few offer all of the capabilities needed for maintaining an enterprise architecture capable of supporting nimble business operations in the metaverse era. Some organizations will want to buy a commercial methodology and supporting tools and then modify them to perform at the level required in the new competitive environment. Others might want to build their own platforms. This is an area where enterprise governance will have to insert itself into the process and ensure that a leading-edge tools strategy is being followed in the development of the enterprise architecture. Otherwise, the success of the metaverse transition could be compromised.

The EA Itself

The end product of enterprise architecture planning will be the official central repository of critical enterprise information for use by groups and individuals throughout the organization. The information in this essential repository can take many forms, such as strategies, structures, policies, guidelines, charters, standards, schematics, templates, protocols, conventions, purchasing agreements, forms, and important contacts. The blend of these artifacts and their specific attributes will depend on the nature of the organization, its mission objectives, its competitive environment, and the particular methodology being used.

One goal will be to make adherence to all architectural guidance as easy, natural, and helpful as possible. All stakeholders across the company should view the enterprise architecture as a tool that helps them in many ways – by giving them reliable, sanctioned guidance, by saving them time and money, by improving their ability to communicate and form partnerships (internally and externally), by enabling improved security, and by helping them optimize business, group, and personal performance in their assigned areas of responsibility. The more this goal is realized, the nimbler the organization as a whole will become.

Executives, most notably the Chief Architect, must be wary of simply buying a commercial enterprise architecture planning product or methodology and trying to force it onto their organizations. The design of the product may not match an organization's prevailing philosophy, making a successful implementation highly doubtful.

The general governance structure must act early in the transformation to ensure the realization of these attributes do shape enterprise architecture design and deployment.

17.3 TECHNOLOGY GOVERNANCE

The first part of this chapter focused on the enterprise governance function in general. The focus now shifts to the Technology Governance sub-function shown in Figure 17.1.

All enterprise transformation efforts entail substantial risks to an organization. Therefore, the use of well-established best practices is critical to mitigating these risks. By embracing best practices in technology governance to optimize organizational structures and streamline processes, investments in technology resources are more likely to achieve the organization's overall business strategy and objectives. This is especially important for an organization transforming for the metaverse because of all the new technologies and changing competitive dynamics the organization will encounter.

Sample IT Governance Charter

History has shown most organizations struggle with technology governance. Signs of a failing technology governance process are common and predictable. These include:

- technology investments not aligned with enterprise strategies and priorities
- redundant automated systems for performing the same corporate functions
- persistent problems with technology projects (schedule delays, cost overruns, and user dissatisfaction)

- dead-end systems and applications that cannot communicate with each other
- inconsistent data names
- persistent security issues
- executive mandates without accompanying technology resource allocations
- technology planning taking place on various organizational islands (and even within silos on these islands)
- lack of insistence on business-focused results from investments in technology
- enterprise priorities being ignored while local "pet projects" find resources
- corporate functions often working around, rather than through, the technology governance process

To address these issues, it is helpful to develop, implement, and monitor the systematic use of a strong technology governance charter. This charter should clearly outline the authorities of each relevant executive position, such as the Chief Information Officer (CIO), Chief Technology Officer (CTO), and Chief Architect. Such a document should also establish the structure and purpose of any technology governance steering or review entities that might be needed, articulate the roles and responsibilities of technology governance accountable officials, and offer templates and guidelines for committee processes and decision-making. Of course, all of this information should be readily available from the organization's enterprise architecture. The following section is an example of a generic table of contents for such a charter, designed for a hypothetical enterprise, Genesis Solutions.

TECHNOLOGY GOVERNANCE AT GENESIS SOLUTIONS

Introduction to Technology Governance

- Technology Governance Definition and Objectives
- Key Functions and Accountabilities
- Tools and Processes
- Important Contacts

Role of the Genesis Solutions Enterprise Architecture

- Purpose of the Genesis Enterprise Architecture
- Accessing and Using
- Updating Processes
- Important Contacts

Critical Processes

- Aligning Technology Investments with Business Strategies
- Managing Technology Gatekeeping and Adoption
- Managing the Genesis Solutions Technology Infrastructure
- Investment Portfolio Approval and Prioritization Processes
- Technology Project Management: Tools and Methods

Major Technology Governance Functions and Charters

- Technology Executive Oversight Committee
- Technology Steering Committee
- Chief Architect
- Architectural Design Team
- Project Management Office (PMO)
- Project Management Support

Supporting Governance Documents and Templates

- Technology Investment Proposal Template
- Tutorial: Accessing, Using, and Updating the Genesis Enterprise Architecture

Technology Governance Philosophy – One Size Does Not Fit All

When developing an enterprise technology governance charter, organizational leaders should remember all organizations are different. This is especially true when it comes to the appropriate philosophy and strategy for managing increasingly integrated business and digital technology assets across the enterprise. A university is not like a drug manufacturer. The US Department of Defense is not like a pizza chain. A hospital is not like General Motors. Within this context, organizations can differ in such dimensions as:

- size of the enterprise
- stability of the enterprise (stable or currently in a transformative state?)
- levels of trust and cooperation across the enterprise
- scope, complexity, and strategic importance of external business alliances
- security posture and risks
- mission or industry
- nature of the competitive environment
- culture and morale
- state of existing technology infrastructure and assets within the organization

- management style
- pace of change in the current environment

When defining an appropriate starting point for developing an updated and more agile enterprise technology governance model and supporting charter, understanding the continuum of acceptable technology governance philosophies can be helpful. This continuum ranges from almost complete autonomy in the acquisition, management, and use of business and digital assets to applying heavily centralized control over these assets. Importantly, no location on this continuum is inherently right or wrong. It all depends on an organization's specific situation. Of course, there can certainly be wrong philosophies for specific organizations if their core attributes do not mesh with the philosophy chosen. For example, the US Marine Corps organization would probably not choose a governing philosophy on the far left of the continuum (Complete Freedom – "Let a thousand blossoms bloom"). For a university, however, it might be a different story.

Figure 17.2 relates specifically to the governance of enterprise technology resources, not to overall enterprise governance. As shown in this chart, we can think of this continuum as a "pin chart" where an executive team can place a pin at a number of places depending on the team's current organizing philosophy, mission, culture, values, risk avoidance profile, and competitive environment. As described elsewhere in this book, it is not only possible but likely metaverse organizations can be highly networked and empowered organizations overall, while simultaneously exercising firmer control over its technology infrastructure and enterprise architecture.

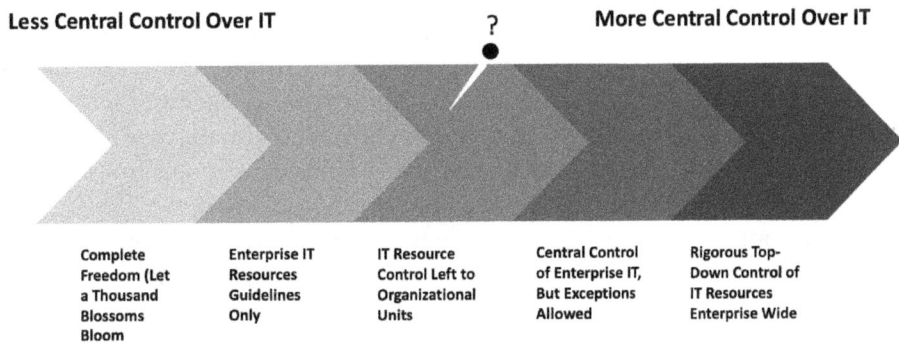

Less Central Control Over IT		?	**More Central Control Over IT**	
Complete Freedom (Let a Thousand Blossoms Bloom	Enterprise IT Resources Guidelines Only	IT Resource Control Left to Organizational Units	Central Control of Enterprise IT, But Exceptions Allowed	Rigorous Top-Down Control of IT Resources Enterprise Wide

FIGURE 17.2 Generic technology governance philosophy pin chart

There are also important considerations with respect to timing. This is because organizations are not static entities. For example, this book focuses on organizations seeking to transform themselves from currently being optimized for operations at the tail end of the digital era to being optimized for the emerging metaverse era (and perhaps the dawning of the quantum era). As companies work their way through these kinds of transformations, they might choose a much more stringent approach to governing the acquisition and use of technology resources, at least until the transformed organization has stabilized. First, they do not want to add to the inventory of legacy technology assets they will have to convert to new-era technologies. Second, the acquisition of new technology resources must enable the new business model that is the central goal of the transformation. It is not unusual to see a tight control philosophy being enforced during a disruptive period for the organization followed by a looser philosophy after a period of stabilization.

Also, if an organization can implement a truly useful enterprise architecture, voluntary compliance with technology architectural standards and preferences can be virtually automatic because that will become the easiest and most effective way for enterprise employees to acquire and use technology resources.

Positioning a company at the appropriate pin location along the continuum is an important first step in preparing to manage its digital technology resources effectively. After this strategic decision has been made, managers can then agree on compatible subordinate issues, such as a technology governing structure and supporting charters and important governing policies and processes.

Managers might struggle when pondering the kind of chart shown in Figure 17.2; they know what they should do but are hesitant to do it. This author has witnessed sustained and intense discussions among members of management teams when deciding where to place the pin for their organizations. This is because some managers know their employees like the freedom of acquiring and using the brands and kinds of technologies they like best. There will likely be grumbling and morale problems if controls and standards are put in place that limit this freedom. To some organizational groups, the idea of imposing an enterprise architecture-based technology strategy managed by a governance structure is simply too bureaucratic and heavy handed. Other managers in the same organization see logic, perhaps even a sense of urgency, in establishing more effective oversight on the acquisition and use of these critical assets.

This is why the pin-positioning task needs to be a group exercise. This helps overcome the self-interest preservation motives of any one particular manager. The mindset should be how best to manage technology assets if an organization is to remain relevant in the metaverse era, not how best to assuage any short-term personal issues and concerns some managers and leaders might have.

That brings us back to the pin chart and a serious organizational philosophy question. Will an executive management team take full ownership and institutionalize the use of a comprehensive enterprise architecture? If the consensus view is "no" or "not sure," the pin will go somewhere on the left side of the chart, the "less control" side. The team is saying the level of executive management control over the planning and use of business technology resources will be light in their organization, and the use of an EA for other purposes will not be an area of emphasis. This is a very soft-touch approach to governing the acquisition and management of technology resources. This perspective will dictate the nature of this company's enterprise architecture policies, charters, and use. This philosophy might work for an organization that has determined the metaverse will have minimal effect on it (like the hypothetical Dalton, Georgia carpet manufacturer mentioned earlier in the book). However, if the team guesses wrong and the metaverse impact is substantial, such an organization might struggle.

However, if another management team says it will both own an enterprise architecture and require its use company-wide, the pin goes somewhere on the right side of the chart, the more control side. This organization will probably be much better prepared to do business in the metaverse.

Requiring the use of an enterprise architecture company-wide is exercising more control within one specific area of overall enterprise governance, the management and use of technology resources. However, this tighter control in one area of the business opens up all of the other areas. That is, an effectively deployed enterprise architecture can be the mechanism that actually enables a highly networked, empowered, platform-intensive organizational model to function.

By requiring an enterprise architecture, executive management is placing an enormously valuable repository of information and guidance right in the center of the networked organization for all employees to use – individuals, departments, functions, and platform teams. Management is telling all employees much of the information and guidance they need to perform their jobs is available in this centralized tool that all employees can use to keep current with what is happening in the organization. This means they do not have to come to executive management routinely for information, guidance, and permissions. Executive management does not have to constantly remind everyone of the organization's strategic and tactical objectives. All of that information is kept up to date in the AI-enabled enterprise architecture. This means individuals, groups, and teams across the enterprise can be empowered to execute their assigned tasks without a lot of management interference or oversight.

With respect to such issues as standards and preferences for specific items of technology used in the company's business (e.g., laptops, smartphones, server capacity, and data capacity) or detailed architectural standards for networks and edge computing, employees will find the easiest, most efficient, pre-approved, and helpful way to obtain these assets or technical guidance is to go directly to the enterprise architecture. This saves them time, money, and frustration in trying to gain answers to their questions and approvals to acquire needed resources. This assumes, of course, the Chief Architect and other entities responsible for working in a collaborative way across the company to maintain the enterprise architecture are doing a good job. Otherwise, the architecture will lose credibility and fall into disuse.

Empowered Technology Governance in Action: An Example

One of the fundamental governance duties of any executive team has always been to review and approve, or not, major capital investment proposals. This is often done using a criteria-driven, stage-gate approach. This means that in order for a proposed investment to be considered for approval, there are number of stages and gates that must be passed first. For example, there is Strategic Fit Gate – how would this investment, if approved, support and advance our strategic objectives? There is always an ROI Gate – what is the expected return, monetary and otherwise, on this investment, and what is the timeline for payback recovery? How will this return on investment be used? There is also typically an Architectural Compliance Gate, a Security Approval Gate, a Legal Approval gate, and so on depending on the organization.

In traditional organizations, most of these proposed investments go through the gate approval process at a lower organizational level through various committees and boards, and the results are then tallied up, summarized, and eventually presented to the C-suite. For a highly networked organization seeking the levels of operational speed and agility required to compete in the metaverse, this process would take far too long. By the time the proposal is approved by corporate, the opportunity for which the proposal was targeted will probably have passed.

What must happen in the metaverse environment of the near future is the decision process must be simplified and decision authority delegated. This is another example of where delegated, empowered governance becomes nimble or agile governance.

For example, this author worked with a company where this exact stage-gate process was used for all information technology investments over a certain threshold amount. When there was a management team turnover, the new CEO decided he did not need to see all of these IT proposals because, for one reason, the proposals all sounded very good and he did not really understand them deeply enough to choose one over the other. So, he asked the company's CIO to form a new, streamlined investment structure and supporting processes for anything related directly to IT. This entailed eliminating a couple of review boards. To ensure he still had his governance hand on this important resource, the CEO capped the total budget for IT at a level 5 percent below what it was the year before. This meant the only IT budget request he wanted to see would be a request and rationale from the CIO to increase the overall IT budget. The CEO said this did not mean he was not interested in IT. To the contrary, he was very much interested and expected regular macro level briefings on where things were headed and why. He and his team did not have time to get wrapped up in the details of choosing one IT investment proposal over another unless some compelling strategic issue was involved.

The CIO did go away and formed a smaller technology and review committee which she chaired. She also streamlined the review process, and from that point on handled all IT budget and investment proposals at that level, relying heavily on the standards and architectural designs maintained in the company's enterprise architecture. The senior executive team still owned the company's overall technology strategy, but delegated an important operational aspect, approving (or not) IT investment proposals that were not highly strategic in nature and therefore require review by executive management. This was an actual example of empowered governance in action.

17.4 KEY TAKEAWAYS

- An enterprise governance structure for organizations operating in the metaverse (and ideally all organizations) should feature a board of directors and C-suite that remain in lock step. This allows them to make quick, informed decisions and initiate prompt action in response to fast-moving threats and opportunities.
- The primary planning and operational tool used by the governing body of a nimble, networked enterprise should be a new breed of enterprise architecture. This new EA should be one that leverages the latest technology innovations to make it easy to use, easy to keep current, and able to change in concert with sudden shifts in strategy, as directed by the governance structure.
- The design of the enterprise architecture and corresponding guidance for its use must align with the dominant enterprise philosophy for the overall enterprise management of technology resources, which can range from an open, free-for-all philosophy at one end of the philosophy spectrum, to a rigid control philosophy at the other end.
- There is no right or wrong position on the spectrum as long as the point chosen does in fact align with the management philosophy of the enterprise.

18

ENTERPRISE ARCHITECTURE (EA)

This chapter discusses the structure and purpose of a representative enterprise architecture (EA), one tuned for the metaverse era, not for prior technology eras. Chapter 19, which follows, takes a deeper dive and provides suggestions for infusing increased nimbleness into each layer and each major component of the architecture, thereby enabling a more agile overall enterprise.

Enterprise architecture-based planning is an ongoing process, coupled with a corresponding information central repository, that organizations employ to organize, develop, deploy, and document basic components of the enterprise, such as charters, business rules, process flows, information flows, data architectures, technology architectures, standards, and preferences. The central goal is to align the items captured and described in the architecture effectively with the strategic goals of the enterprise and sustain that alignment over time.

In their true operational use, traditional EA practices have often been heavily IT-centric (not business-centric) and typically featured complex technological diagrams and related jargon. While this information is useful to a critical subset of the enterprise, most notably to technology infrastructure experts, most members of the enterprise are not frequent users of the EA, even if they are aware one exists.

As organizations transition into the metaverse, an EA better suited to highly networked, fast-paced, and nimble enterprises will be required. This updated version of the EA will be more broadly useful to the enterprise as a whole, not just the technology-focused subset. The EA will have to be more of a master repository of vital enterprise information in easily digestible form than a collection of more arcane technology schematics and diagrams, as useful as these are to their relevant users.

Figure 18.1 shows a simplified, high-level view of a representative EA. When such a structure is populated with appropriate information, it can provide a comprehensive and current model of the entire enterprise. By making each layer of the EA more comprehensible and more immediately usable to a broader array of organizational members, the value of the EA increases markedly. By ensuring timely cross-layer synchronization of adjustments and changes to any layer of the architecture, and by maintaining broadly-based buy-in and support for the EA, the enterprise as a whole becomes nimbler. When used effectively and consistently, few functions, mechanisms, or processes are more important to the long-term success of an organization.

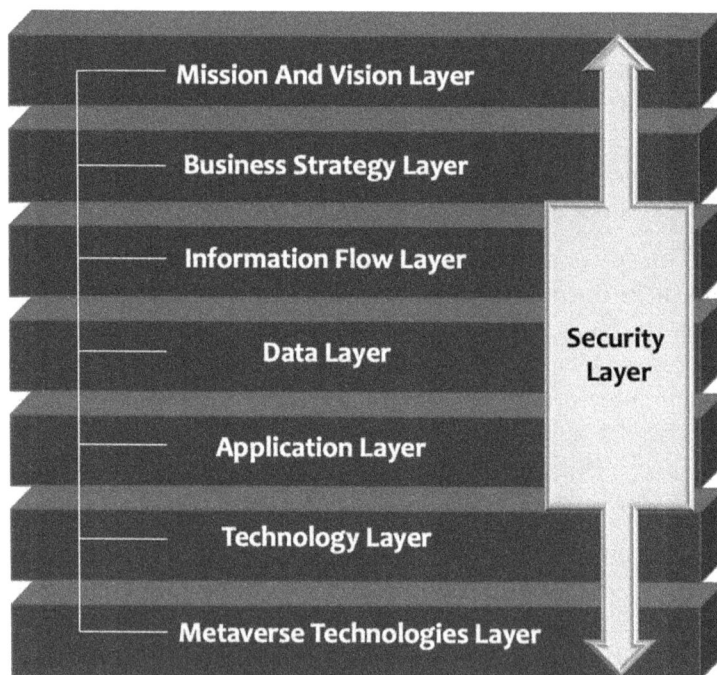

FIGURE 18.1 Representative enterprise architecture model

Generally speaking, a metaverse-ready EA will have the following attributes:

· The current strategic objectives of the enterprise are visible to everyone authorized to see them, as are the assignment of strategic goals, projects, tasks, and priorities to groups and individuals. These are tracked online and updated on a regular basis.

- The entire business model of the enterprise is viewable online to authorized users. This includes not only the current structure of the business and related organizational charts, but governing polices, business rules, major process and information flows, and operational goals for various organizational units. For maximum enterprise agility, the enterprise business model as whole must be an open book available to all authorized users.
- Each layer of the EA shown in Figure 18.1 will have both a detailed technical component, as we find in traditional EAs, and a general use component, which is rarer. For example, the Data Layer will contain traditional data models or maps and a data dictionary, but also contain general-use information, such as contact information for data analytics support and preferred vendors for desktop data management or modeling products.

In addition to traditional EA benefits, such an architecture will offer:

- an advanced query and use capability provided by AI and other metaverse tools and technologies
- a critical tool for use by executive management when steering the enterprise through choppy metaverse waters
- significantly improved visibility enterprise-wide into corporate strategies, priorities, accountabilities, and current progress against strategic and operational objectives
- greatly enhanced agility enterprise-wide due to ready access to current, comprehensible information on virtually any aspect of the enterprise, including information about alliance partners, preferred vendors, position openings, training resources, cloud provisioning agreements and points of contact, and other blanket purchase order agreements
- all of the underlying process models, data models, networking schematics, information flow charts, data maps, and data dictionaries found in traditional EAs

18.1 ENTERPRISE ARCHITECTURE LAYERS ARE INTERDEPENDENT

Criticism of the layered view of an enterprise is based on the unwarranted assumption that each layer will be approached and used in isolation from all other layers. To be clear, all of the layers shown in this model are interdependent, meaning a change in one layer will almost always affect one or more of the other layers, sometimes in multiple ways. This is why a holistic enterprise perspective and the effective synchronization of changes among layers are critical. (Achieving improved synchronization of changes, always a challenging objective, is where advanced digital tools like AI and machine learning can become useful.)

The layer concept is not new in the business world. For example, when an executive team implements an organizational structure to carry out its business functions, it usually implements a strategy analogous to layers, such as a finance layer, a marketing layer, an HR layer, an engineering layer, a production layer, an executive layer, and so on. No one would ever suppose that these "layers" are self-contained entities that operate in complete isolation. To the contrary, they are all highly interdependent components of complex organic entity we call an enterprise. They are simply divided into manageable, interdependent parts because not to do so would be to create an unmanageable, even incomprehensible, mess.

The same holds true for the EA concept. We all know that vision is connected to strategy, and strategy is connected to business models, and business models are connected to information flows, and information flows are connected to data, and databases are connected to applications, and applications are connected to technology infrastructure components. All of these are connected with each other in countless and ever-shifting ways. It can become overwhelmingly complex if we do not abstract this complexity into a more easily comprehensible and usable framework.

This kind of compartmentalization is what an organizational structure does for the management of people in an enterprise, and what an EA does for the management of the myriad guidance tools and other resources used by organizational people – data, information, applications, and various technology infrastructure assets, all tied back to business models and overall enterprise strategies and priorities. Nothing in an organizational structure is viewed as a self-contained organizational entity, and no EA layer is ever viewed as being self-contained. EA layers are simply convenient ways to group like resources and skills for the purposes of planning, analysis, development, refinement, and enterprise support.

The sections that follow provide an overview of each layer of the architecture shown in Figure 18.1. To provide a more complete view, we consider it from the perspective of starting a nimble EA from scratch. In many instances, if not most, a company will already have some kind of EA in place. Management will then have to decide how much of the existing architecture can be used and still have an organization that can compete nimbly and effectively in the metaverse era.

Mission and Vision Layer

Everything in the EA must flow from and support the Mission and Vision of the enterprise. If the leaders of the enterprise are committed to moving the organization to a state optimized for competing successfully in the metaverse era, that strategic guidance must be captured in and flow from this layer. Therefore, it is up to corporate leadership, working with individuals and groups throughout the enterprise, to portray clearly what that future state must be. If the leaders think, for example, they will be competing through various forms of collaboration in 3D virtual spaces, augmented physical places, or a blend of both, they must develop strategic planning scenarios based on that intent. They should then populate the EA with the consensus view of the desired future state of the enterprise as developed through these planning processes. Everyone in the organization needs to understand these intended directions, and they should know they can always find the current version in the organization's easily accessible EA.

The consensus strategy derived from these future-state scenario analyses will drive everything else contained in the lower layers of the EA. This does not mean the approved mission definition and corporate vision cannot be modified through feedback loops involving other organizational components. However, in the final analysis the iron-clad, official, future-state characterization of the enterprise should be maintained in this layer. Anything else is unofficial and not to be trusted.

Business Strategy Layer

With current Mission and Vision definitions in place, broadly communicated and well understood, the organization can proceed. The next step is to translate the mission definition and corporate vision into more detailed and specific operating strategies, structures, and goals. These artifacts might take the form of policies, standards, business rules, process definitions, departmental charters, defined accountabilities, working agreements, alliance strategies, HR strategies, security requirements, financial plans, and marketing strategies.

The sum of these distributed subordinate strategies will comprise the future-state business model or operational blueprint for the company for a particular planning horizon. Of course, some of these more detailed business strategies could come automatically from the installation of enterprise software packages acquired from external vendors. Regardless of the source of input, this business strategy blueprint is what the remaining downstream layers of the EA must enable and support. With this guidance in place, the organization can then begin to ensure the business strategy has the information flows in place to make it work successfully.

Information Flow Layer

To return to the gazelle analogy in Chapter 5, the information flow captured in this layer represents the higher-order sensory capabilities and lifeblood of the enterprise. Information flow must be designed in a way – accurate, secure, timely, well-targeted – that enables the level of enterprise nimbleness necessary to survive and compete in the metaverse. This layer of the EA is especially important because information will be coming and going constantly across the enterprise, in new forms and formats, both structured and unstructured, at an ever-increasing velocity and in unprecedented volumes.

As an enterprise evolves into a nimble player in the metaverse environment, its network of existing information flows will likely have to undergo some degree of change. One of the first steps in the development of the new or revised EA, therefore, will be to validate and document existing information flows. Almost all organizational functions or groups are to some degree both recipients and providers of information. All of this must be documented in an appropriate tool or repository that can be easily updated. Timely updating is critical because information flow patterns are becoming increasingly dynamic for all organizations. Metaverse-era tools, such as AI, can help in developing these complex information flow maps.

The next challenge is to determine how existing information flows need to be modified to support the company's envisioned business model. This future-state information flow analysis can be performed internally based on existing systems and technologies or packaged software can be acquired that imposes certain key information flows. Because of the potential complexity of the to-be information flow architecture, this effort is best addressed in stages, or modules, based on a priority basis. Priorities can be based on a number of considerations, such as critical dependencies (that is, we cannot do A until we do B), priority mission areas, legal requirements, and security concerns.

One decision that could "force" information flow design priorities would be to acquire an enterprise software suite. The insertion of a commercial product into a fully functioning organization presents an information flow condition analogous to a heart transplant wherein numerous arteries must be severed for surgery and then reconnected before the patient can leave the operating room and resume his life. Therefore, these commercial packages must be selected carefully based on well-documented information flow maps.

Data Architecture Layer

Data architecture development and administration practices can either enhance or undermine a company's nimbleness and overall competitive position, especially the company's ability to obtain early-warning intelligence and business value from analytics.

The Data Architecture Layer of the EA helps bring structure, order, understandability, and usability to the diverse structured and unstructured data streams that metaverse organizations will have to capture and process every minute of every day. Data will be coming in from a variety of sources in a myriad of formats. For example, the information flows for some companies will include an endless torrent of data from Internet of Things devices and sensors. This information must be captured, stored, cataloged, managed, analyzed, staged, and made available for use quickly and accurately.

Data management functions for the Data Architecture Layer often involve various aspects of agile methods, data architecture planning, data science, machine learning, data visualization, and other data management and analytics functions. The EA needs to spell these requirements out with good precision, in addition to defining overall data need patterns such as where, when, what, and how many. When designed and executed well, the Data Architecture Layer of the EA can play a vital role in accelerating business performance to the level required to compete nimbly in the metaverse era.

Application Architecture Layer

To return once again to the jungle analogy in Chapter 5, a gazelle constantly senses its surroundings (noises, smells, and sights) to obtain information input for its next steps. Signals of various kinds cause the "applications software" in the gazelle's brain to take immediate action. The gazelle's instant response depends, for example, on whether its software algorithms have perceived "all-safe" vibes or "extreme danger" vibes. If the initial impression is "conditions are safe," subordinate "software modules" begin to work, and the gazelle eats, takes a nap, swats at flies, or does whatever else its brain's "all-safe software application architecture" suggests. However, if the first signal is one of "extreme danger," another of the brain's software modules tells the gazelle to abandon all other thoughts immediately and flee.

The same principle is true for organizations. Information flow execution and data processing functions are all performed by software applications (apps) in a myriad of forms (whether inherited from previous regimes, bought, rented, or developed in-house). Applications capture data, process it, store it, protect it, distribute it throughout the enterprise (and beyond), and automate to some degree virtually every function and process within the enterprise. If there is one critical focal point for performing well and competing with enhanced nimbleness, it lies within an organization's applications architecture. That is why this book devotes a whole chapter to algorithms (see Chapter 9, "Algorithms").

The Application Architecture Layer of the EA includes processes and procedures for designing, building, or acquiring enterprise applications, a relationship map and inventory of existing enterprise applications, and a roadmap for how current and future applications must mesh (via applications programming interface standards, for example) if the organization is to achieve its metaverse transformation objectives.

Therefore, in addition to the organization's production applications themselves being represented in the architecture, a good EA will also provide links to guidance for developing or acquiring future applications. This guidance will describe the tools, protocols, and techniques to be used in designing and building applications. The guidance will also offer a roadmap and best practices to follow when deploying applications for the organization. This helps to ensure the end product is a well-structured application with the right protocols and interfaces to synch up with other appropriate enterprise applications. This development guidance includes standards and guidelines, as well as reusable assets and investments, including standards-compliant reusable software modules that can be used in a variety of application development scenarios.

The applications relationship map and inventory of existing applications helps organizational components plan their local application solutions and other systems in ways that are consistent with the overall applications architecture, both current and future. The goal is to see new application solutions become seamlessly integrated with established ones. This goal applies to newly acquired or developed applications, legacy application enhancements or modifications, and any acquired or rented applications or upgrades.

The Chief Architect must manage the important challenge of ensuring that any changes to the Application Architecture Layer are synchronized with all necessary corresponding changes to all other EA Layers. This will ensure that the Application Architecture Layer evolves in a well-coordinated way with other EA Layers, such as the Data Layer. If slippage ever happens in the synchronization of such changes, the EA will begin to unravel. If further looseness appears, the organization could find itself reverting to the siloed operations of the past and lose its ability to compete in the metaverse. This one reason why the Chief Architect function, already very important, will become vital in the metaverse.

Technology Architecture Layer

When a gazelle's cerebral "software" structure has made the decision to escape imminent danger, its physical "infrastructure" immediately activates (its legs, lungs, heart, muscles, sinews, tendons, and hooves). Because of its nimbleness, a physically healthy gazelle always has a good chance of escaping predators. However, even if a gazelle has a super-fast brain and an incredible nervous system, if it also happens to have a bad leg, it may not escape.

Similarly, when a software application within an organization is triggered, a complex collection of physical technologies is also triggered: servers, edge platforms, operating systems, networks, telecommunications, smart phones, laptops, printers, holographic technologies, and augmented reality technologies. If the organization's technology infrastructure is well designed and well-integrated with other layers of the enterprise, the organization should be able to compete well in the metaverse. However, even if an organization has been superb in defining its business model, has tamed its complex information flows, and maintains stellar data and applications architectures, if it has bad "legs" (i.e., an ineffective and poorly integrated technology infrastructure), it will underperform.

The traditional Technology Layer of the EA is where various models and metamodels of the technology architecture for the overall enterprise are maintained. However, as noted in the introduction to this chapter, the information in this layer has traditionally been highly technical and, at least to non-technical people, quite complex.

Clearly, this level of detail is appropriate and useful for technical experts who use the EA routinely. However, for members of the general enterprise population who seldom use the conventional EA, it would be helpful to provide more general use information. Some of this information could be provided by the service desks or call centers maintained by most larger organizations. However, there are other instances where an enterprise employee or group might not want to go to the trouble of opening up a trouble ticket and waiting for a callback. They would simply want to go to an immediately accessible information repository and get the information they need. Examples of such questions might include:

- Who are our cloud providers?
- How do I initiate a cloud services request for my division?
- Who are our points of contact for developing a hosting strategy for a new augmented reality application?
- Do we have blanket purchase order agreement for this specific cell phone?

As we can see from this small sample, the use of technologies such as AI and machine learning will need to be deployed to make the overall EA, especially the Technology Layer, more conversational and useful to far more people across the enterprise than is presently the case. This capability will become essential as the requirement for enhanced enterprise nimbleness increases in conjunction with the arrival of the metaverse. Early on, many organizations will lack either the will or the expertise to develop such a capability. However, others will, which will force those enterprises that are moving too slowly.

Security Architecture Layer

Most organizations face the challenge of maintaining effective security capabilities, both cyber and physical. As has been true throughout all waves of technological innovation, evil typically accompanies the good. The same is likely to be true for the metaverse era because hackers, thieves, and other miscreants will find ways to use these advanced technologies to serve their own interests.

This challenge will become more difficult when quantum computing arrives and makes today's encryption methods easily breakable. The governance structure of the enterprise will have to factor security into every layer of the EA, carefully considering the threats posed by quantum computing in the hands of hackers. Other emerging security issues in the metaverse could include data security with the increased use of AI and machine learning applications and the authorization issues associated with platforms, edge computing, and the cloud.

Metaverse Technologies Layer

An EA for a metaverse-competitive organization will benefit from, if not require, a special technologies layer. This layer encompasses technologies still in an early stage of adoption, but likely to become important features within one or more layers of the EA, either in the near term or in future EA releases. Examples might include advanced robotics, VR, and holographic technologies. Instead of thinking about how to add nimbleness to this layer, the thought should be about how this layer can add nimbleness to the entire enterprise.

Special Consideration – SaaS

One important consideration when thinking about EA strategies in the metaverse relates to the use of cloud-based applications, or Software as a Service (SaaS). When a company buys or rents a packaged enterprise software solution from a vendor, portions of the EA will be dropped into the company by an external entity (the vendor or vendor contractor). This drop-in might affect one layer of the architecture (like applications), all layers, or somewhere in between (like information flow, data, and applications). This can be good, bad, or neutral, depending on how the EA is developed and managed. At its worst, the acquired package might introduce more data silos and dead-end information flow issues. At its best, the package might help unify and harmonize broad swaths of the architecture. Most deployments will be somewhere in between. Whatever blend of inherited legacy, in-house developed, or externally acquired business and technology resources a company might possess, the nimble EA challenge is basically the same: document, integrate, simplify, and synchronize.

18.2 EXAMPLE OF ENTERPRISE ARCHITECTURE USE BY AN ORGANIZATIONAL UNIT

Let us consider an example. Tracy is VP of Human Resources for a large government contractor, Lunar Haze Technologies (LHT). This company has just launched a potentially lucrative new business line, one that has the potential to significantly increase the company's revenue stream. Executive management is already aware that if the company is to be competitive in this business, LHT is going to have to become faster and nimbler. Already, the company is faced with the need for the rapid acquisition of a significant number of personnel with specific skillsets. Therefore, executive management has established a new performance goal for Tracy and the HR Department: Reduce by 25 percent the average time it currently takes from issuing an interview approval to a candidate to onboarding that candidate as a newly hired employee. Management has documented this new performance goal in the *Business Strategy Layer* of the company's EA, where it will be tracked and progress documented.

Tracy quickly assembles a small team. The first thing the team needs to understand is the company's HR business process flow, focusing on the processes for both the selection of candidates to interview and the onboarding of new employees. Fortunately, LHT has a complete and current EA. The first thing the team does is obtain the process flow chart for the company's HR function. This process map, along with many others, is contained in the *Business Strategy Layer* of the EA. This map allows the team to see the steps in (and the interrelationships among) all of the relevant processes under Tracy's area of responsibility, as well all other processes they interact with in some way, such as certain financial and legal processes.

After carefully investigating the process flow maps, the team identifies certain process steps that can be eliminated and others that can be streamlined. However, the team needs to know more. They then obtain an information flow map for the HR function from the *Information Flow Layer* of the EA. This is a map of all the information streams flowing into and out of the HR Department, as well as internal-only HR information flows. By correlating the maps of process flows with the maps for information flows, the team develops a clearer understanding of the true dynamics of the critical processes they need to focus on. However, they still want to know more.

Next, they obtain the master data architecture for HR, as well for all other functions that affect HR, from the *Data Layer* of the EA. They do this so they can get a better under understanding of how major data items under HR's area of responsibility, such as "Offer Letter," relate to or are impacted by, other data items, such as "Security Clearance." How might these relationships need to be modified? Are new data items needed? How are these to be defined?

Next, the team understands that all of the process and information flows they have been analyzing, and all of the key data elements carried by these information streams, are either partially or fully automated. This means the team cannot change any HR processes unless significant corresponding and enabling changes are made to various software applications. The team must extract the application architecture for the HR function from the EA. They obtain this architecture from the *Applications Layer* portion of the EA information repository. Analysis of this architecture leads to a good understanding of the specific applications that must be modified or replaced to achieve the required reduction in cycle time for new hire onboarding.

After the team has completed its analysis of relevant process flows, information flows, data interrelationships, and the applications architecture, it is ready to define the specific actions that must be taken to meet the objectives set for it by executive management. To accomplish this goal, they need additional help.

The team adds team members from the central IT organization responsible for managing the computer applications that drive all of HR's processes and information flows, as well any other applications that impinge in some way on these applications. The augmented team develops the requirements' specifications that must be met by modifying or extending existing applications or developing or acquiring new applications. Before they can accept the results of this step as a complete set of requirements for meeting their time reduction goal, there are a few more entities that must be involved.

LHT has recently restructured its IT organization so that it now contains a consulting unit comprised of staff with metaverse-era skills in certain priority areas, such as AI, machine learning, and edge computing. Descriptions of these technologies and the main points of contact for each are documented in the *Meta Technologies Layer* of the EA. The team invites some central IT consultants with expertise in all three of these areas to join the team. The task given to these analysts is to analyze the requirements document and explore how the infusion of any one or all of these new technologies can contribute to a reduction in time, improve the affected processes, or both.

The central IT consultants do find opportunities for improving the requirements by using AI technology to expedite the sorting of voluminous resumes to focus only on truly qualified candidates for the open positions. They also identify the benefits of using facial expression analysis technologies to achieve more reliable candidate interviews.

Tracy's team now has an almost complete set of specifications for their needs, but they have another stop to make before presenting their proposal to executive management, including the Chief Architect. They obtain the *Security Layer* of the EA and review the procedures for obtaining a security review and approval for all new system development activities impacting the LHT infrastructure. They engage the appropriate personnel and obtain the necessary approvals.

With security approval in place, the team has its requirements document ready except for one last step. Where in the LHT technology infrastructure will the applications and databases for these revised HR process reside and be operated? Will they operate on in-house, existing servers and networks? Will new computing and networking equipment have to be purchased and installed internally? Or will external cloud resources be more appropriate? A new consultant from central IT is added to the team and, using information from the *Technology Layer* of the EA, the consultant discusses options with the team. After an extensive review of the existing technology environment and the goals of the team, the proposed solution is a hybrid. The team has adopted the strategy of creating a secure HR edge computing platform for processing employment applications, making job offers, coordinating employment development assignments and progress reports, and other related HR functions. A cloud component is included to provide server capacity for other aspects of the proposed HR system upgrade. The applications' modification work will be performed by internal staff, but external consultants will add some of the more advanced technology features, such as the AI-based components.

The proposal is presented to executive management using project submission guidelines and evaluation criteria contained in the *Business Layer* of the EA. The project is approved by management and launched immediately. The project will be managed using the project management guidelines also maintained in *Business Layer* of the EA. One fundamental requirement of the project management guidelines is the LHT Chief Architect will work with the project team to ensure that any changes to any architecture layer (business process, information flows, data, applications, and technology) will be reflected in EA change notices and updates. This way, the EA will remain current and well-synchronized.

The HR modernization project was completed on time and within budget, the required reduction in process times was achieved, and Tracy's team received an outstanding performance award.

Discussion

This hypothetical project demonstrates how a first-rate EA, if maintained properly, can be a tremendous aid to organizational speed and nimbleness. Imagine how much longer it would have taken Tracy's team to develop a feasible requirements solution if it had not had immediate access to all of the various architectures, schematics, the right contact information, and other relevant information provided by this EA. We could most likely triple or quadruple the timeline to completion, and even then, have a less effective end result.

This example is predicated on an ideal environment with an excellent EA in place. Most organizations will never reach this state. However, most organizations can, if they are willing to do so, come much closer to these kinds of capabilities than their present state allows. Organizations expecting to compete in the metaverse will certainly want to come as close as possible to this ideal. For one thing, many of their competitors are likely to come very close to achieving this ideal.

18.3 KEY TAKEAWAYS

- Organizations seeking to develop and maintain both the core competencies and the nimbleness necessary to compete in the metaverse can be aided immeasurably in that quest if they develop and use a nimble, resilient, well-synchronized, and easily accessible EA. The kind of EA required will be feasible only though the use of selected metaverse technologies, such as AI.
- The EA must cover all "layers" of the enterprise, and these must be managed as the interdependent entities they are.
- The EA must be actively owned by enterprise governance, with day-to-day operational oversight provided by a Chief Architect.

CHAPTER 19

INFUSING NIMBLENESS INTO THE ENTERPRISE ARCHITECTURE

The previous chapter discussed the major components (or layers) of a comprehensive, adaptable, and easy-to-use enterprise architecture. This chapter discusses ways to infuse enhanced nimbleness into each component, thereby contributing to enhanced overall enterprise nimbleness.

Ideas for improving organizational nimbleness come from across the enterprise ...

And they are captured in the appropriate layers of the enterprise architecture.

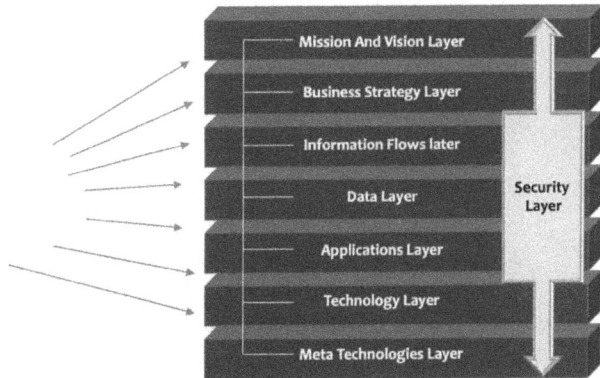

Chart Components Courtesy of Pixbay, Geralt

FIGURE 19.1 Infusing nimbleness into the enterprise architecture

19.1 NIMBLENESS INFUSION AT IMPORTANT ORGANIZATIONAL LAYERS

Before getting into nimbleness infusion at the enterprise architecture layer level, this section provides a preview of how nimbleness can be enhanced at three major *organizational* levels. These organizational levels are the source of much of the drivers for nimbleness that will be captured within each appropriate enterprise architecture layer where they can be formalized, documented, and used across the enterprise.

> **SIDE NOTE:** *When discussing the top, middle, and lower levels of organizations, the frame of reference is not the classic vertical, pyramidic, command-and-control type of organization. That model is becoming increasingly rare, having given way to flatter, more networked, and nimbler organizations. What these terms (top, middle, and low) mean in a networked organization relates more to levels of overall strategic decision-making authority and accountability rather than how an organization might be formally structured.*

Infusing Nimbleness at the Working Level

Many customer-facing employees work in the "lower levels" of an enterprise. As a result, they tend to understand the true business essence of the company, distinctive behaviors of its customers, and day-to-day nuanced shifts in market dynamics. They can often sense subtle swings in customer and other stakeholder behavior and preferences long before executives in higher positions. Because they work within the framework of their company's business model on a daily basis, they understand which organizational policies, processes, procedures, standards, and regulations help the business and which sap the organization's energy, capacity for innovation, and nimbleness.

Because these front-line employees have a deep operational and transactional understanding of the business, they often have good ideas for how to do things better. This is especially true in an organization that emphasizes continuous learning and improvement. Going forward, many new ideas for improvements will be based on the use of metaverse-era technologies or methods. If these ideas can be accessed and used in a systematic way, organizations can improve in a number of areas, not the least of which is improved overall nimbleness – becoming quicker, faster, more innovative, and more responsive to opportunities and threats.

Infusing Nimbleness at the Middle Level

If the good ideas developed by lower-level employees in the organization fail to reach enterprise decision makers and resource allocators they will never be acted on. That is where the middle level of an organization can play a vital role in elevating an organization's nimbleness and capacity for innovation. An effective middle level can serve as an established, open conduit for bringing to executive management's attention suggestions on how to improve organizational performance. (Ideally, in a well-networked organization, these mid-level managers will have the authority to act on many of these ideas without taking them to higher levels for approval.) Importantly, the suggestions do not come from outside consultants. They come from people within the organization who truly understand the business.

Therefore, workers in the middle layer of the organization can enhance nimbleness in two ways. First, as a natural consequence of functioning in their own mid-level organizational roles, they can generate their own ideas for streamlining, speeding up, and improving the business. These new ideas will be based on the kinds of technological innovations currently identified with the metaverse. The second way the middle layer can enhance nimbleness is by serving as an idea conduit and advocate for the people and groups they manage.

Infusing Nimbleness at the Top Level

Finally, we get to the top level – the senior executives, the C-suite, the architects of corporate mission, vision, purpose, values, and strategy. This is the most powerful layer in terms of being able to elevate the organization's nimbleness and capacity for innovation, and it can enhance these attributes in three ways.

First, governance structures are generally populated by bright people who can come up with improvement ideas on their own, in addition to acting on the suggestions working their way up from the middle and lower levels. The C-suite and the board of directors, operating as a unified team, also have direct and immediate control over the financial and business priority levers that can improve overall organizational nimbleness. The challenge they now face is how to channel their innovative thinking toward the opportunities inherent in the metaverse and the enabling technological innovations now converging all around them.

Second, governance executives can respond in a systematic and positive way to the suggestions and proposals emanating from the middle and lower levels. They can, through their actions, let employees know they have been heard and their input is valuable. The governance structure also has the power to act on ideas generated from lower levels in the enterprise. Through timely actions, the governing structure can eliminate bad processes or procedures, and fund and support good ideas, all contributing to enhanced organizational nimbleness.

Third, and perhaps most important, the governance structure is the architect of the overall plan for the enterprise. It can launch an enterprise-wide, metaverse-focused transformation action, or it can flatten the enterprise by reducing the middle layer and bringing lower-level workers in closer functional proximity to senior executives. It can invest heavily in innovative technologies to improve information flows, connectivity, and communications, all of which are critical aspects of nimbleness, or it can enter into business alliances and ecosystems that further enhance the organization's adaptability and nimbleness. Therefore, enhanced organizational nimbleness and capacity for ongoing innovation can be driven in timely, substantial ways by actively engaged senior-level executives.

19.2 INFUSING NIMBLENESS INTO ENTERPRISE ARCHITECTURE LAYERS

To return to the gazelle analogy in Chapter 5, evolution has imbued nimbleness into the gazelle at the cellular level. Infusing nimbleness into an enterprise in a similar fashion is accomplished via the enterprise architecture: layer by layer, policy by policy, component by component, standard by standard, protocol by protocol, information flow by information flow, algorithm by algorithm, and data name by data name. The following sections outline how this can be done within the enterprise architecture. The ideas are simple but obviously challenging in actual practice, especially under turbulent conditions. Before each layer of the architecture is populated with information that will be accessible and used across the enterprise, a number of important questions need to be asked and answered. As noted below, this should be a continuing validation process, not just an annual one.

Mission and Vision Layer

The following are just a few of the areas ripe for nimbleness infusion in the overarching Mission and Vision Layer of the enterprise architecture. Some of the important questions to ask are these:

- *Enterprise Identity* – With respect to our mission and vision statements, has our mission environment changed to the extent it is time for a fresh self-assessment? What or who are we at this moment? What or who do we need to become? If we are not what we need to be, how do we get there? How quickly? Do we need to develop new mission and vision statements that emphasize quickness and agility as signature corporate attributes? Keeping this information current based on evolving events addresses organizational nimbleness.
- *Strategic and Tactical Planning Processes* – How effectively and quickly can we adapt our various strategies and plans based on changing conditions? Are we too rigid and stubborn? Not rigid enough? How can we become more adaptable to unfolding events? How detailed should our various plans be and what time periods should they cover? What hierarchy or taxonomy of plans do we need? Which plans should be developed at the corporate level and which at subordinate levels? How detailed and fixed should our strategic and tactical objectives be?
- *Culture and Values* – Is our culture aligned with and supportive of our nimble enterprise mission and vision? If not, how can we begin to change it in a timely way? What kinds of guidance can we enter into our enterprise architecture that can help us begin to foster the kind of culture we would like to see in this company? What are our core values? What should they be? Do our presently stated values align with our mission and vision statements?
- *Linkage Between Board and C-Suite* – Are we in sync as tandem governing entities? If not, how can we improve? Once there, how can we stay in sync? How can we build this kind of sustained alignment objective into our enterprise architecture so we always keep it front and center for our executive team?

These are not "every-few-years" types of questions. These and other similar questions should be asked on a continuing basis. They cannot be scheduled. An annual review is okay, but events happen when they happen. Therefore, one of the keys to keeping an enterprise architecture relevant and used in the metaverse era is to build enhanced contingency planning into an organization's mission and vision definition processes. Executives cannot assume stable conditions will persist anytime or anywhere in the metaverse environment. This is because the next decade will offer even shorter and more dynamic change cycles than today. Therefore, companies will need to become accustomed to the ground shifting constantly beneath their feet.

For example, a good trial lawyer never steps into a courtroom (typically a dynamic environment) without having first gone through an exhaustive set of "If-this-then-what?" questions for all witnesses. For every witness, the lawyer will know in advance the answers to many, if not most, questions he will ask. However, for other questions, there will be a lack of certainty. The lawyer considers all the potential answers he can think of and then develops contingent strategies. If the witness answers **A**, he will then go down the **A** list of follow-up questions. If the witness answers **B**, he will then go down the **B** list of follow-up questions. This process continues through a complex branching tree of possible responses and reactions to those responses. In the old days, lawyers used yellow legal pads and different colored pens to help navigate the questioning process. Today, more are using PCs, tablet computers, and special software as their primary questioning support tools.

As is true for lawyers in a courtroom, a primary responsibility of C-suite executives is to prevent their companies from being blindsided. For executives, sudden surprises can result from unforeseen shifts in markets, abruptly changing consumer behaviors and tastes, the sudden emergence of new technologies, or surprise global events. These executives must be systematically asking strategic "If-this-then-what?" questions. They should have answers to these questions prepared and ready to act on. Flexibility in adapting mission and vision definitions, as events dictate, adds nimbleness to this layer of the architecture.

The same goes for planning processes. Plans are good, but they must be adaptable to changing circumstances. Building exceptional adaptive capabilities into enterprise planning processes is a basic requirement for enterprise nimbleness.

Finally, symphonies would not sound very appealing if the musicians were trying simultaneously to follow two different conductors operating with two different sheets of music. Board members and C-suite executives must remain in sync as a cohesive team, especially at a time when mission definition and planning processes can be volatile. Otherwise nimbleness will be compromised.

Answers to the kinds of questions outlined above are all an integral part of the enterprise architecture development, deployment, and evergreen processes. The answers are captured and reflected in Mission and Vision Layer of the current version of the enterprise architecture where they set direction and expectations for everything in the layers below it.

Business Strategy Layer

These are a few of the areas were added nimbleness can be infused into this layer:

- *Business Model* – Is our overarching business model – our organizational structure, functional breakouts, key processes, business rules, policies, lines of business, and alliance strategies – in sync with the current mission and vision of the company? If not, how and how quickly can it be modified without adversely affecting ongoing business operations?
- *Business Plans* – Do our current, more detailed business plans support our mission and vision statements? Can they be modified expeditiously as needed? Are they appropriate for current customer and market profiles?
- *Structure* – Are we structured in a way that achieves our strategic and operational objectives, while providing the flexibility to change as needed?
- *Financial* – Are our budgeting processes and business rules flexible enough to shift funds, as needed, based on the sudden emergence of threats or opportunities?
- *Staffing* – Do we have enough flexibility in our HR and staffing strategies to assign manpower as needed in a turbulent competitive environment? Should we have more part-time workers? Do we have contingency plans in place to obtain expensive, critical talent as needed, much like we acquire cloud computing capacity on demand?
- *Alliances* – Have we established a network of alliance partners aligned with our mission, vision, and strategic objectives for the current planning period? Do we have agreements in place where we can augment, or be augmented by, these partners as opportunities ebb and flow?

The Business Strategy Layer of the enterprise architecture is ripe with opportunities for the infusion of nimbleness into the enterprise. This is where an organization's structure is designed, where accountabilities are established, where policies and processes are laid out, where human resource strategies are formulated, where marketing plans are designed, where alliances are formed, and so on. In developing strategies for each of sub-component of the Business Strategy Layer, company officials must ask, "How can we design and manage this function for optimal nimbleness?"

For example, in defining an organizational structure for the enterprise, a flatter, more networked structure is likely to be best for organizations operating in the metaverse era. This structure empowers individuals and groups to act at the very edge of the enterprise, near customers and alliance partners.

If this is the strategy, it affects a broad array of down-architecture decisions (business rules, information flows, data elements, applications design, technology infrastructure decisions, and security strategies).

As another example, when defining human resource strategies, metaverse-era companies might choose a specific blend of permanent employees for those functions best performed in-house and contract employees for areas where more nimbleness in staffing can be maintained. A hybrid strategy might be formulated relative to work-at-home versus in-office work. This decision could have important technology, security, and communications implications that are reflected in the enterprise architecture. Similar thinking should pervade all aspects enterprise business strategy development and implementation.

Information Flow Layer

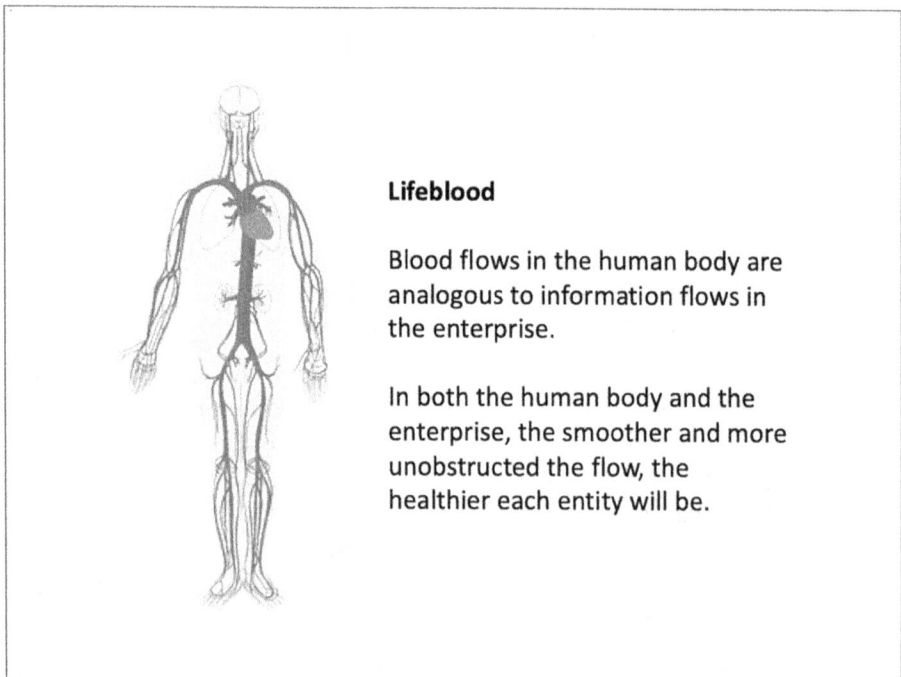

Lifeblood

Blood flows in the human body are analogous to information flows in the enterprise.

In both the human body and the enterprise, the smoother and more unobstructed the flow, the healthier each entity will be.

Image Courtesy of Pixbay, Cliker_Free_Vector_Images

FIGURE 19.2 Information is the lifeblood of any organization

As shown in Figure 19.2, information flow is the lifeblood of the enterprise, the essential connective tissue that keeps the organization living and breathing. However, the Information Flow Layer of the enterprise architecture cannot be optimized without parallel, well-coordinated improvements in the Data, Applications, and Technology layers, all flowing from the Mission/Vision and Business Strategy architectures.

Assuming effective synchronization is taking place, the goal of this layer is to establish an information flow infrastructure that facilitates smooth, enterprise-wide communications and nimbleness.

If a company opts for an enterprise software suite from a vendor, the official information flow, at least for some segments of the enterprise (like finance), automatically comes with the software. However, even the best and most comprehensive SaaS options do not address all of the important enterprise information flows. The better these existing internal flows are defined, and the more effectively they are integrated with each other and with any SaaS options that have been implemented, the more nimble the company will be.

To a large degree, information flows in an enterprise are dictated by, and are a function of, official processes, business rules, and reporting requirements. In other words, an information flow pattern simply mirrors the enterprise itself. In a worse-case scenario, complex and redundant processes, a complicated tangle of business rules, data silos, or different names for different items or data elements will all be reflected in similarly complex, tangled, and slow information flows. The net result is a loss of nimbleness. Conversely, if an organization is streamlined and well-managed in accordance with a well-designed and systematically-used enterprise architecture, it is likely to have smooth and effective information flows and be nimble in its operations.

This all points back to the need for holistic thinking in nimble enterprise architecture planning. Almost everything in an enterprise affects, or is affected by, something else. This is especially true for information flows. Therefore, this layer cannot be addressed in isolation.

Data Architecture Layer

The legacy problem of data silos, islands, and dead-end systems still exists within many conventional organizations. This issue remains a major obstacle to improved organizational nimbleness.

Therefore, for maximum nimbleness, a company must identify ways to better integrate its data through improved data governance, management and analysis practices. This is especially true if the company has a legacy problem of important data being trapped in dead-end or isolated systems. An organization cannot function fluidly and nimbly as a cohesive whole if the databases used to make decisions and operate end-to-end functions are fragmented and dissimilar in their various key attributes (item names and definitions).

Many organizations will find that managing Data Architecture Layer issues will be one of their greatest challenges in achieving a metaverse-era level of competitive performance. At the highest level of thinking, data management issues need to be resolved by joint, "agile-like" approaches to systems development and delivery, involving both business units and IT groups working in unison. Some organizations are addressing the data management challenge through special centers or labs where consensus data models and architectures are developed and deployed via the enterprise architecture.

Application Architecture Layer

A widely-used best practice for developing, maintaining, enhancing, and operationalizing software is called "DevOps." This simply means software developers ("Dev") work closely with IT infrastructure operations personnel ("Ops") to deliver better production solutions faster. Historically, developers and operations personnel often worked in their own silos, with the developers sending software to the operations staff for installation into the technology infrastructure. A DevOps team that includes both developers and IT operations staff working collaboratively throughout the project lifecycle can increase the speed and quality of software deployment, thereby adding nimbleness to the Applications Layer, and thus to the overall enterprise. (Of course, effective DevOps practices add nimbleness to the Technology Layer as well, the systems operations component in particular.)

A further refinement of DevOps has been to add security because too often security issues have been discovered in software too late in the process for easy and timely resolution. This makes resolving the security issues difficult and expensive, in addition to delaying production use of the software. The central premise of DevSecOps is security must be involved in applications development every step of the way.

Another basic requirement for nimbleness in the Applications Layer relates to the effective design and use of "application programming interfaces," or APIs. These interfaces serve as communication translators among different applications, between applications and databases, and between applications and users. When APIs are implemented properly, they allow applications to exchange data and perform their logical functions quickly and securely. APIs allow users to perform complex actions, often involving multiple applications, via one interface.

Consider this example. When we use a map application from Google or some other source, in addition to directional guidance, we might get other information (traffic warnings, points of interest, and speed limits). This is done without the device and application we happen to be using having to penetrate the application software ecosystem of the source providing the information (e.g., Google or Waze). The connection is only at the interface level between the requesting and receiving applications using defined application programming interfaces. This provides a tremendous boost to an application's ease of use, speed, and flexibility.

APIs also allow developers to contract out less critical software development tasks to less expensive sources, confident the applications will be able to communicate and integrate via well-designed interfacing protocols (APIs).

In summary, well-designed APIs can play a vital role in making the Application Layer nimbler. This means the appropriate standards and protocols for developing APIs within an organization should be defined in the Application Layer of the enterprise architecture.

As is true for other architecture layers, nimbleness can sometimes be enhanced by buying applications on a flexible, pay-for-what-you-use basis. This is also true for application analysts and developers as well, adding further nimbleness to the enterprise. However, care must be taken to avoid attempting too much piecing together of pay-for-what-you-use resources in too short a time frame because this might inhibit nimbleness (which occurs because of excessive assimilation complexity).

The Application Layer is also one of the prime areas for the use of proven "agile" methodologies. Agile methods and tools can offer a sharper focus on business priorities, facilitate good collaboration, and increase speed in the design and delivery of applications software. These benefits can also help immensely in maintaining enterprise nimbleness.

Technology Architecture Layer

Similar to the application architecture, one of the most powerful ways to add flexibility to the Technology Layer is to obtain as much as feasible in the way of on-demand (or cloud-based) products, capacity, band-with, and services.

This includes building into purchase or lease agreements the flexibility to scale-up, scale out, increase, or decrease capacity, resources, or services as business needs dictate.

As discussed in the Application Layer section, a mature DevOps approach to the operational implementation of applications can get critically needed software in production faster with less risk of failure than can be achieved with more disjointed, siloed approaches. However, this kind of cooperative approach to software rollout will not happen unless it is institutionalized within the enterprise architecture in the form of documented policies and standards.

Finally, most organizations already use various dashboard-type systems and tools to monitor and manage workloads and resources across the entire technology infrastructure. These tools might be used by internal IT operations personnel, IT outsourcers, tool vendors, cloud vendors, or these and others in some combination. Care should be taken to ensure that the tools being used by the operations staff are not outdated and thus lack the robust capabilities necessary to support a highly nimble enterprise operating in the metaverse era. Today's tools must be able to provide intelligent event management and performance monitoring, use advanced analytics to help detect trends, patterns, and anomalies, and apply multivariate-type analyses to provide predictive modeling, alerting operations staff of potential major incidents before they happen.

Turning once again to the gazelle analogy, all of the high-end, sophisticated sensory capabilities that a gazelle might possess are useless if its physical capabilities are not operating at a commensurate level. The same goes for a modern enterprise: if its technology infrastructure is not itself nimble, the enterprise as a whole will never be nimble.

Security Architecture Layer

The metaverse security challenge will be to provide, wherever possible, effective security solutions in ways that do not unnecessarily hinder organizational nimbleness. If sound security measures can be designed in a way that minimize adverse impacts on all other layers of the enterprise architecture, the organization as whole will be more nimble and, therefore, more competitive.

Metaverse Technologies Layer

As noted in other sections of this book, instead of thinking about how to add nimbleness to this layer of the enterprise architecture, the thought process should center on how this layer can add nimbleness to the entire enterprise.

19.3 KEY TAKEAWAYS

- Enhancing the nimbleness of an enterprise is tied to inserting as much nimbleness as is feasible into every component of every layer of the enterprise architecture used to run the enterprise.
- Just as nimbleness is embedded in the DNA of animals in the wild, nimbleness must be embedded in the organizational DNA equivalent, the enterprise architecture.
- Inserting nimbleness at every enterprise layer is an extremely challenging goal for any enterprise, and many will fail to meet it. Others will meet the nimbleness infusion challenge and become winners in the metaverse era.

20

CENTRAL *IT* AND THE METAVERSE ENTERPRISE

20.1 INTRODUCTION

Throughout this book, we have stressed the importance of modernizing the enterprise governance structure and the need for a modern enterprise architecture in transforming an enterprise to become more metaverse ready. The third component of enterprise transformation to the metaverse involves modernization of the central IT services organization. This area is vital to enterprise transformation in many respects and must, therefore, be transformed itself as a vital and parallel component of the overall transformation.

The venerable "central" IT organization of the sixties and seventies has become less centralized over the past few decades. This came about as changes in technology, such as the personal computer, democratized and distributed IT ownership and management across the enterprise. However, in the metaverse era, most central IT organizations will have to undergo further significant changes. As we move into this new era, central IT will continue to lose much of its remaining centralized image. The function will become more of an evolving, heavily networked, and widely distributed collection of full-time resident staff and on-demand personnel possessing new business and technological skill sets.

This means the central IT of old must continue to evolve into a sharable, technology-intensive knowledge resource, including expertise in metaverse skills appropriate to the needs of the organization. In other words, central IT will no longer be a somewhat "walled off" operational unit comprised primarily of traditional, resident IT skills.

Staffing for the future central technology organization will evolve toward a smaller nucleus of permanent, full-time personnel. These will be augmented, as needed, by temps, consultants, alliance partner personnel, subcontractors, gig workers, and staff provided by on-demand services providers. The expanded use of non-resident, temporary staff will be required for two reasons. First, it will be impractical for organizations to retain permanent employees having all the diverse (and often scarce) metaverse-era technical skills that an organization might need. Many of these specialized skills are needed only sporadically, and many, if not most, will be obtainable on demand.

Second, metaverse-era organizations will want to have as lean an infrastructure as possible, including the staffing component. When the right kinds of resources, including human resources, can be obtained effectively on-demand, that will often be the preferred option. The future challenge for the CIO (or equivalent function), therefore, will be to maintain an optimal blend of permanent and on-demand technical personnel, reshaping it as needed based on the ebb and flow of overall enterprise strategic and operational needs.

A major issued associated with this increased use of temporary or gig workers relates to benefits for these personnel, such as healthcare. There continues to be much discussion and debate in both federal and state governments as to when such a worker should be viewed as an employee as opposed to an independent contractor. Some states have already established criteria in this regard, but most of these are in varying forms of litigation. An organization transferring to the metaverse with the idea of making heavy use of temporary employees should consider their own criteria and be fair minded in the process. For example, an organization might develop a policy that says if a temporary employee is working under its direct supervision and control for a period that extends past a certain number of weeks in a year (these do not have to be consecutive weeks), the person is defined as a part-time employee or consulting employee, not a contract worker, and is therefore entitled to a certain benefits package. It is important to remember that these people will typically be valuable assets to the company who possess special skills and should be treated accordingly.

20.2 BACKGROUND AND CONTEXT – A LOOK BACK

The highly centralized IT services model of the sixties, seventies, and eighties is still used in many organizations today, especially in more traditional enterprise organizational models. Depending on an organization's mission and size, most central IT organizational structures have traditionally been organized along these lines:

- Director of IT (which ultimately evolved into the CIO position)
- Applications Development (sometimes split into business applications and scientific and/or engineering applications)
- Applications Operations and Maintenance (various sub-functions that operate or support production applications, such as set-up personnel, tape librarians, and disk space managers)
- Database Administration
- Networks and Communications
- Computer Operations
- Computer Security (Cyber Security)

The Historic "Toss it Over the Wall" Issue

The individual groups that traditionally comprised the central IT structure tended to operate under a highly rigorous framework of policies and procedures. This process rigor was designed to make every aspect of IT consistent, repeatable, reliable, auditable, and secure.

The primary reasons for this rigor were security and efficiency. However, another important but less obvious reason for these tight controls was the fact that a mistake by any one of the central IT functions shown in the list could cause serious repercussions across the company (a missed payroll, for example). Because few people outside central IT organizations understood the complex inner workings of this function, central IT has always been a convenient scapegoat for whatever business or operational mistake that might occur – "It was caused by a computer error."

The resulting carefulness within central IT led each IT function to "wall itself off" procedurally as a protective measure. This led in turn to the widely-practiced, although not necessarily deliberate, protection strategy known as "silos" (see Figure 20.1).

Central IT Services

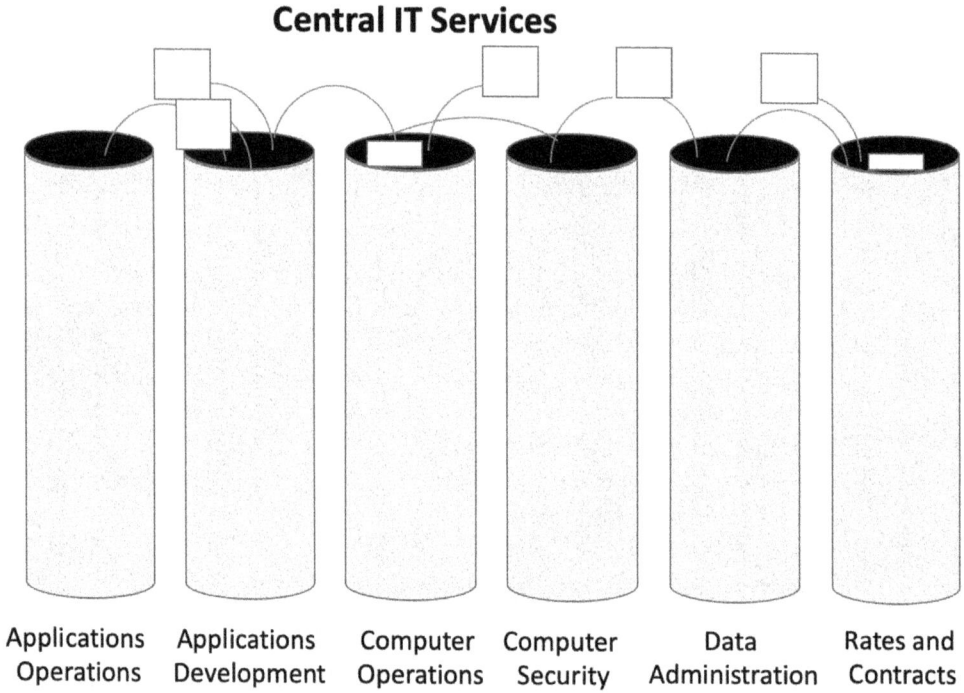

| Applications Operations | Applications Development | Computer Operations | Computer Security | Data Administration | Rates and Contracts |

FIGURE 20.1 A long history of silo-intensive operations

Basically, in the silo method of operation IT, "artifacts" were simply "thrown over the wall" to other silos. For example, Computer Security might work in isolation within its own silo and then send ("throw") new and sometimes onerous security requirements "over the wall" to other groups with little or no advance consultation. Similarly, the Applications team would often "toss" new production software "over the wall" to Computer Operations. Data Administration would sometimes decide to change certain data names or vendor products and toss this information over the wall to an unsuspecting Applications team. This was not conducive to organizational nimbleness.

As we moved into the 2000s, new approaches, like ITIL, Agile Development, DevOps, and DevSecOps began to address the silo problem. An important tenet of all these methodologies was to bring interdependent organizational entities into closer developmental and operational proximity, thereby creating unified, cooperating teams rather than having so many instances of fractured and inefficient siloed operations. However, these unifying approaches were not used universally across the enterprise. Therefore, some aspects of the silo problem have persisted to this day.

Shadow IT and "Departmental Cowboys"

In addition to the silo issue, and to some extent because of it, as we moved through the 1980s and the 1990s, technology advances like departmental computers (e.g., the DEC PDP/11), Ethernet networking, and personal computers led to pockets of "shadow IT" being created all across the enterprise. These often evolved into independent "mini" IT organizations housed tightly within divisions or departments outside of central IT.

For example, throughout the eighties, many corporate engineering divisions obtained their own departmental minicomputers, especially from the DEC VAX line of departmental computers. They would often assign electrical engineers to network these computers with each other, as well as with the personal computers in offices and cubicles. The engineering group would then allow some of its software "cowboys" (basically hobbyists at the time) to write code. For divisions like engineering – finance was another good example – the days of dealing with central IT, with its thorny and frustrating process and procedural barriers, were largely over.

Or, so they thought.

After a couple of years of shadow IT teams appearing across the enterprise, groups and systems began to have trouble communicating with one another. Data names were inconsistent. Arguments over what was official information escalated. Security issues proliferated and worsened. Overall IT costs spiraled out of control (sometimes due to the rampant duplication of applications). New, strategic systems projects often had to be put on hold. Something had to be done.

Gaining Control Over the Problem Created by Shadow IT

Organizations now had a serious problem: rampant shadow IT and software "cowboys," central IT teams "throwing" software "over the walls," strategic system needs not being met, systems not communicating with each other, redundant or incompatible databases, and increasing IT costs. What could executive management do?

One option, driven also by the perceived cost savings potential, was to outsource or offshore the entire central IT operation (the whole thing, people and infrastructure as a package). Sometimes this strategy worked well, sometimes not. Importantly though, it did little to solve the problems associated with distributed or shadow IT. This was because the "miniature IT organizations" that now operated solely within the boundaries of business or staff functions (like engineering and finance) were not typically outsourced.

Another option for gaining control was to buy pre-built commercial software packages to support major business functions, such as finance, procurement, CRM, and HR. This approach solved some problems, but not all. In some instances, the acquired software introduced new problems. For example, one major problem was that acquired systems were often unable to sync well, or even communicate with, legacy systems and databases.

Another solution for achieving improved management of enterprise IT resources was to adopt an enterprise-wide, architecture-based approach to IT and business systems planning and management. As discussed in earlier chapters, these efforts often failed for a variety of reasons, and the problems associated with traditional approaches to central IT services quickly resurfaced.

However, if the guidance offered in this book is followed, an architecture-based approach to enterprise management coupled with sound governance practices does have a good chance of succeeding. This strategy alone could help an enterprise move successfully into the metaverse era. However, will the central IT organization still have important roles to play in such a game plan?

Yes, even in the fast-paced metaverse where decentralized and networked organizational forms will have become the norm, certain centralized IT functions will still be required. However, the fundamental nature of the centralized IT model will have to change. In other words, central IT must itself be transformed simultaneously as an integral component of the overall enterprise transformation strategy, and with similar overriding goals – enhanced nimbleness, quickness, capacity for innovation, and competitiveness. Helping organizations achieve that outcome is the focus of the remainder of this chapter.

Why the General Concept of Central IT Should Not Be Abandoned

Information technology and business functions have become intricately interwoven so that one cannot exist without the other. All companies are now more or less software companies. This intertwining means that having IT organized into its own centralized function can become more of an obstacle than an aid. Therefore, the trend toward embedding IT staff in non-IT business functions and units will likely accelerate. This will be accomplished by making central IT a network of resources, including metaverse-related technical skills, that can be used by business units as needed. Because there are so many exciting and disruptive digital technology developments now unfolding, a dedicated, but transformed, central information technology function will become critical if an enterprise is to make intelligent and effective use of these developments.

Therefore, the transformation of central IT must proceed in parallel, and correlate with, the transformation of the overall enterprise. This is because a new central IT will have to provide essential, ongoing technical support for the overall transformation of the enterprise, as defined in the enterprise architecture. Of course, the reality is that sustaining ongoing business operations during the transformation will require the availability of many current skills. Therefore, the transformation of central IT will have to carefully sequenced and synchronized with ongoing operations and transformation needs so that both areas of need can be optimized to the extent possible.

These new realities mean the areas that will be viewed as centralized IT functions in the future will in many ways be different from those we see in conventional IT organizations. This is because transformed IT departments will have to be organized around a new suite of technologies, skills, and service models.

New Roles for Central IT

IT services functions in the metaverse era will not only require a different organizational approach than we have seen historically, they will have to take on new roles in a new kind of operating environment. For example, metaverse era organizations will place a heavy emphasis on continuing business innovations as an essential requirement to remain competitive. This will in turn require IT services to place an added focus on creating and operating testing and development labs, demonstration centers, and innovation factories to provide the technology and software solutions that can enable and support business innovations.

We have discussed the requirement for metaverse era organizations to participate in complex business ecosystems involving disparate alliance partners, vendors, and even customers. Members of these business ecosystems will be integrated operationally by a diverse blend of technologies, data streams, and processes, all of which must be resilient, secure, and scalable. The IT services functions of the various business ecosystem members will have to work together to maintain a technology infrastructure capable of sustaining these strategic operational objectives. This will typically be a daunting challenge. How well this challenge is met will be a vital factor in the success of individual businesses as well as the entire business ecosystem.

In addition to these functions, central IT will have a vital role to play in the management and use of the new kind of nimble enterprise architecture required for competitive performance in the metaverse. An enterprise architecture should be owned by the enterprise governance function, with both strategic and operational accountability being the responsibility of a Chief Architect. However, much of the day-to-day design, implementation, and execution support for the architecture will still fall under the umbrella of the central IT organization (or whatever new name it might receive).

Moving Central IT Services into the Metaverse Era

Figure 20.2 offers a representative view of how central IT could look in the metaverse era. Those of us accustomed to neat, box-and-line organizational charts might be discomforted by the sight of a networked, nimble, loosely organized, and sometimes amorphous collection of central IT professionals, all tasked with responding, on an on-demand basis, to user groups across the enterprise. This more "organic" look is much more likely to prevail in the metaverse than a structured, static diagram, one that looks stable and neat on paper, but does not reflect real organizational life in the metaverse.

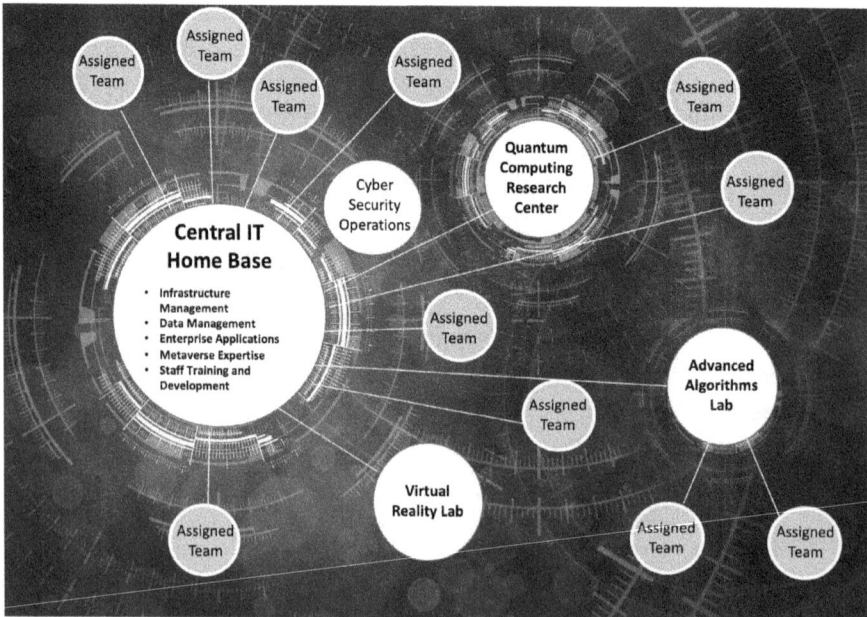

Photo Background Courtesy of Pixabay, xresch, artist

FIGURE 20.2 A distributed, networked organization model for central IT

Figure 20.2 shows there is a "Home Base" for central IT that serves as the operations, development, and project assignment center for central IT personnel, both permanent and temporary. When enterprise business units need help for a particular project, an individual or team is assigned from the home base. Permanent IT personnel who are not currently on assignment will typically be participating in training and development modules to which they have been assigned, depending on their chosen skill set and job preferences. In light of the fast moving technological innovations these professionals will have to master, continuing education is vital. Part of this training will be accomplished by working within the labs, innovation factories, or centers of excellence represented by the larger white circles in Figure 20.2. Non-permanent IT (or other technical) personnel not on assignment will, according to appropriate contractual agreements, be released until needed at some later date.

There will also be within the central IT home base certain elements of more traditional internal functions dealing with enterprise technology, applications, and data infrastructure operations. The home base also contains an office that manages contracts with external individuals or service providers, such as cloud resource providers.

The smaller circles shown in Figure 20.2 show dispersed central IT individuals or teams supporting various enterprise business components. Central IT staff assignments to support these diverse business units might range from a couple of hours of consulting to multi-year embedding within a business unit to support larger, longer-term projects.

This kind of on-demand expertise will be critically important for a nimble enterprise operating in the metaverse era. Business and functional groups will often need to make quick, autonomous decisions on various system, platform, or technology selections. New-era IT organizations can help these business units make decisions quickly, while simultaneously ensuring the technology choices they make are compliant with the enterprise architecture, meet security requirements, and can interface with other relevant systems and databases.

Finally, central IT in its transformed state will play two vital roles in the design, implementation, and use of a nimble enterprise architecture. First, central IT will be tasked with outfitting the enterprise architecture skeletal framework selected by the governance function (such as the TOGAF or Zachman frameworks) with appropriate leading-edge technologies and methods (e.g., AI, ML, algorithms, visualization aids, synchronization tools, and application programming interfaces). The goal of this role is to make the architecture framework much easier to use and maintain, both during development and after it is deployed. The IT organization will also work with the governance structure and the user community to build modularity into the enterprise architecture to help reduce complexity, enhance adaptability and resilience, ensure effective synchronization among architecture components, and support a priority-based based approach to building and evolving the architecture.

Second, once the new or revised enterprise architecture is operational, central IT will play an important role in keeping the architecture updated with evolving technologies, methodologies, and shifting enterprise business strategies. All this will be done under the direction of the Chief Architect.

In summary, "central IT" in the metaverse will serve as a company-wide distributed network of easily accessible knowledge-transfer and mission-support personnel highly skilled in the use of metaverse technologies and methods. Some will be permanent employees, while many others will be temporary. In the new and highly dynamic competitive era of the metaverse, non-IT enterprise personnel working in business, staff, and functional roles will have enough trouble keeping up to date with the core business or technical areas that define their areas of responsibility. Therefore, they will want quick and convenient access to top-notch technical support to help them on an as-needed basis. Business units might need advice, for example, in such areas as sophisticated algorithms, solution platforms, edge computing, or virtual or augmented reality applications. When this happens, staff from the networked IT organization can be tapped quickly to consult and otherwise assist as needed.

20.3 KEY TAKEAWAYS

- The success of any organization seeking to transform itself into a nimbler entity capable of competing in the metaverse era depends on having ready access to people highly skilled in emerging metaverse era technologies.
- At the same time, these organizations must be lean and efficient, which means every component of the business cannot be staffed with these kinds of experts.
- The best approach, therefore, is to concentrate these experts into one organization for administrative and personnel development purposes, but view them as an enterprise asset that can be used, as needed, on an on-demand basis.

- This organization has the responsibility for operating the organization's in-house IT infrastructure (those resources defined in the data, applications, and technology layers of the enterprise architecture). This role, while more focused and smaller in scale today, is similar to what conventional IT organizations have always done.
- This hybrid model represents the central IT organization of the future.

CHAPTER 21

CONCLUSION AND PATH FORWARD

21.1 INTRODUCTION

The central premise of this book has been the strong likelihood that organizations across all industries have entered, or will soon be entering, a new competitive era, one being driven by a broad array of converging digital innovations, such as AI, machine learning, and quantum computing. For global organizations, this new era places a premium on nimbleness, innovation, and creativity. There are abundant business opportunities in this era, but only for organizations prepared to take advantage of them. There are also serious risks for organizations that fall too far behind in responding to the metaverse.

As discussed throughout this book, the effective transformations of three closely related organizational functions are among the initial keys to success in this new environment. The following sections discuss in more detail how these transformation objectives can be achieved.

The first function is a unified and agile enterprise governance structure, one where its members maintain a good understanding of the evolving metaverse phenomenon and its likely implications. A metaverse gatekeeping and educational program should be in place to ensure this continued awareness happens. The board of directors and the executive management team must be able to respond as one in the face of the turbulent competitive conditions their organization is likely experience in the near future.

Within the organization, enterprise leadership must establish an empowered form of governance. This is a strategy wherein subordinate managers are authorized to internalize certain key aspects of overall enterprise and technology governance functions and execute them as if they are fully in charge. Only by decentralizing and sharing the governance workload in this manner can an enterprise maintain the speed and nimbleness necessary to compete effectively in the fast-paced metaverse era.

The second function to be transformed (or developed if one does not exist) is a comprehensive, modern, easy-to-use enterprise architecture. This is the essential tool used to support effective and nimble enterprise governance, as well as guide and enable the enterprise metaverse transformation. For most organizations, this will be a new kind of architecture, one that makes use of advanced technologies, such as AI, in its development and use. These technologies will make the enterprise architecture easier to use, more relevant to all organizational members, and capable of being kept current and well-synchronized among its various components.

The third function to be transformed early in the process is a more distributed, networked, and nimble structure and operating model for central IT functions.

A general path forward for achieving these goals contains seven crucial steps. These steps are summarized in this section and discussed in more detail in following sections:

- Step 1: *Obtain Internal C-suite Agreement on the Possible Need to Transform the Organization.* Educate the C-suite on the reality of the metaverse phenomenon and its likely implications for the organization. Seek to obtain agreement among C-suite members for the company to perform the necessary due diligence, and then go forward with an enterprise transformation program if the due diligence warrants such action.
- Step 2: *Obtain Backing from the Board of Directors.* Make sure the board of directors is well informed about the metaverse and its implications. Explain to the board why the company is in the process of evaluating the need to launch a transformation program. Ensure that the board understands fully the rationale for the transformation and is solidly behind such a transformation strategy should one be launched.
- Step 3: *Perform Due Diligence and Make the Decision.* Perform a due diligence deep dive into the likely implications of the arrival of the metaverse era for the company. Assess how other organizations are responding to and preparing for these implications. If the due diligence confirms the need to transform, commit to launching an appropriately-phased transformation effort. Be as aggressive and comprehensive in your planning as your

circumstances will allow. Decide to "own" the metaverse disruption rather letting the disruption "own" you.

• Step 4: *Establish Transformation Phase One Strategies and Goals.* The executive team must define (in detail) the elements of Phase One of the transformation, including critical priority business areas for transformation actions, goals, and objectives. In the Phase One definition, address how to keep ongoing business operations under control as the transformation moves forward simultaneously, a tough balancing act. Also address how to sustain the gains made in Phase One after the transformation has moved forward and initial objectives have been achieved. Ensure that Phase One contains a blend of tough challenges, like enterprise architecture development, and relatively simple actions to gain experience, confidence, and buy-in.

• Step 5: *Assign a Stellar Team.* Assign a well-respected, capable team to manage the transformation on a day-today basis.

• Step 6: *Launch.* Formally launch the transformation.

• Step 7: *Persevere to Full Transformation:* Continue the effort through Phases 2 and 3.

21.2 PHASING THE TRANSFORMATION

With respect to phasing the transformation, this can be viewed as a three-phase effort, as shown in Figure 21.1. For most organizations, a two-year transformation period is a reasonable estimate, with the understanding that the organization will continue to evolve after this period. In summary, the three phases are:

• *Phase One:* Launch the transformation and complete the most critical initiatives that will contribute to increased agility and metaverse readiness.

• *Phase Two:* Launch and complete the second-priority wave of tasks that will contribute to increased agility and metaverse readiness. Continue to complete and refine the Phase One initiatives.

• *Phase Three:* Launch and complete the third-priority wave of tasks that will contribute to increased agility and metaverse readiness. Continue to complete and refine Phase One and Phase Two initiatives.

The transformation, if successful, will be a continuous, lasting effort with no defined end. This is because highly adaptive and resilient organizations go through various degrees of transformation endlessly as conditions around them change.

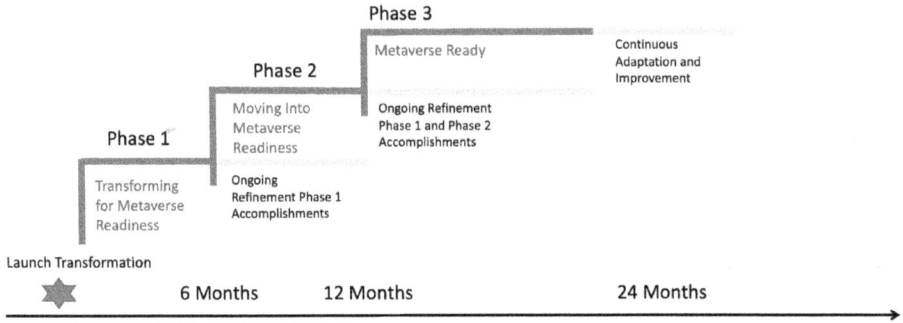

FIGURE 21.1 Phases in the journey to organizational nimbleness and metaverse readiness

Breaking the transformation into three phases will help the organization better manage tasking and goals. Actions to make substantial progress in achieving enterprise decentralization and enhanced agility are launched in Phase One. They are then refined and augmented as needed indefinitely thereafter. The next set of priority initiatives is launched about six months later. These initiatives will be refined and augmented indefinitely thereafter, building on the Phase One accomplishments. The same goes for Phase 3. In roughly two years or less, depending on the organization, its competitive environment, and the quality and intensity of the effort, the organization should have achieved a reasonable state of metaverse readiness. This would signal the end of the formal metaverse transformation project, and the organization would assume a normal continuous improvement posture, but it would do so as a new kind of organization, one that is more agile and adaptable than before.

In a dynamic metaverse environment, organizations will have to transform themselves repeatedly, but typically on a much smaller scale than the initial transformation, at least until the next major technological disruption occurs. These ongoing adaptive changes might affect only one or a few components of the organization. Viewing the transformation as consisting as three phases makes it seem more comprehensible, manageable, and doable than one massive program described as having no end.

The following sections provide more details about the seven steps in Phase One of a representative transformation plan.

Step 1 – Infuse Knowledge of the Metaverse at the Highest Enterprise Levels to Gain Support for Possible Transformation.

When entering a new technological era like the metaverse, it is risky to react in a routine, business-as-usual way. Organizational leaders must be focused sharply on assessing the likely implications of these major disruptions and take aggressive ownership of them before the organization falls behind. Approach these disruptions with the confidence that comes from being a prescient early mover. Be committed to establishing the organizational nimbleness that will help your organization meet the metaverse disruption to your advantage. Respond in ways that will differentiate your company and help you stay ahead of the competition. For this to happen, the organization must develop a good understanding of what the metaverse is all about.

Therefore, it they have not already done so, executive teams should be taking steps immediately to infuse increased knowledge about the metaverse into the organization. Depending on the size of the organization, the prevailing sense of urgency, and budgetary realities, they should to take some combination of these actions:

- Bring in qualified consultants, hire new employees already having this expertise, or identify existing employees who can develop this expertise rapidly.
- Form a small team comprised of personnel suited to this kind of investigative work. Have them drill down and perform due diligence on the metaverse and related technologies and assess how some of the more relevant technologies, based on the judgment of the team, might apply to your organization.
- Arrange presentations of the investigative results to C-suite executives.
- Develop a strategy for ongoing knowledge enhancement related to metaverse developments.

This is not a one-time initiative. The knowledge enhancement process must be continuous, with a core group of metaverse-savvy personnel serving as your gatekeepers. At a minimum, ensure you have competitive level expertise in:

- The overall metaverse phenomenon
- Platforms
- AI and machine learning
- Holography
- Quantum computing
- Algorithms

- Deep tech
- Blockchain
- Immersive technologies (VR, AR, and MR)
- Edge computing
- Robotics
- Central IT support strategies and structures for the metaverse era

Step 2 – Obtain Backing from the Board of Directors.

A topic raised often in this book is that to succeed in the metaverse era, the board of directors and senior executive management of an organization must be in complete agreement on the enterprise mission and vision. If there is tension or lack of agreement on these fundamental directional statements, efforts to improve organizational nimbleness will slow down, if not cease altogether. Therefore, enterprise leaders should take the time to educate (then re-educate, as needed) the company's board of directors. They should explain to the board that pending further due diligence, the company is about to launch a major enterprise transformation action to become more agile and better equipped to compete in the metaverse era. They should work with the board until they have their full backing to proceed, if further due diligence warrants such action.

Step 3 – Perform Due Diligence and Make the Decision.

As you perform deeper due diligence on the reality and implications of the metaverse, be prepared for a flood of information, a good portion of which will be conflicting. Do not be overly concerned with such labels as "the metaverse" or "deep tech." They might not last. Also, do not let any negative views or what seems to be excessive positive hype associated with these labels deter you from taking their underlying realities seriously. The convergence of important new technological developments and current-era technology and methods are creating novel solution models and value streams for many organizations. This ongoing synthesis will change the competitive environments of most organizations, both public and private. As a consequence of these developments, there is a high probability that your organization is going to have to become nimbler to remain competitive, maybe even survive. An organizational transformation is your path to a state of organizational nimbleness that is metaverse ready.

However, you have to be sure you want to launch such a transformation. A halting, half effort is probably worse than just standing pat for a while. Being sure requires that you have a good sense of the scope and difficulty of such an effort. Work with one or more subject matter expert consultants and your metaverse gatekeeping team. Assess how other organizations are responding to and preparing for metaverse implications. In particular, investigate one or more deep tech startups. Do not make a final decision until you have evaluated lessons learned from others that have successfully executed such transformations. If the information you gather and your analysis of it so indicates, make the decision to go forward with the transformation and proceed to Step 4.

Step 4 – Establish Transformation Phase One Strategies and Goals.

Your due diligence analysis has been completed and you have decided to initiate action on the transformation. You can begin by setting up a dedicated area where, over a several week period, you will create a definitive Phase One strategy for your metaverse transformation. Among the many initial actions you will need to take include sharpening the focus of the effort on top priorities and opportunities, identifying ways to ensure sustained alignment throughout the transformation, identifying a blend of easy "wins" and tougher challenges, and defining how to build long-term sustainability into the transformation plan.

Focus Initially on the Top Priorities

If the executive team has done a good job with its metaverse general awareness educational program, and if it has evaluated its benchmarking of companies successful in similar transformations, the next area of focus is identifying the initial priorities for the transformation. These priorities should provide the focus and energy that will drive Phase One forward.

We know from other chapters in this book that three of the initial priority objectives should be (1) ensuring alignment between the board of directors and the C-suite on the critical need for the metaverse transformation (which will have been done at this stage), (2) beginning work immediately on a new enterprise architecture framework (which will be populated with essential information as the transformation unfolds), and (3) launching the process of transforming the central IT services function so the new skills needed as the transformation moves forward will be available when needed.

With these three precursor steps identified as Phase One priorities, executive management must now focus in on defining the other critical business areas to be addressed as part of the Phase One migration. These include establishing the core capabilities needed to compete in projected metaverse markets (e.g., enhanced agility). Ensure you have a good mix of pilot learning projects involving targeted metaverse technologies (such as augmented reality, machine learning, and edge computing). These learning pilots, which can be small and simple, are valuable for insights into how these technologies might be used later. Of course, the metaverse technologies selected for pilot efforts should have strategic significance to your organization and not simply be detached learning exercises.

Agreeing on a critical few priorities is always a difficult challenge. Too often, organizations run into such problems as:

- *"Let's do them all."* Everything seems so critical nothing is taken off the list of candidate priorities, and the default strategy is to invest in all of them. This means the organization has not actually identified its priorities, and the effort will likely slow down at some point without having achieved its strategic objectives.
- *"My way or the highway."* The loudest or highest ranking manager often wins. Given the pressures involved in a transformation of this scope and importance, senior managers often make use of their position and populate the priority list with the projects or investments they think are the most important ones. This is in lieu of a more systematic and cooperative effort among managers with different ideas and perspectives. Being autocratic is a very risky approach.
- *"We worked so hard to get to where we are."* As discussed elsewhere in this book, many organizations find it extremely difficult to uncouple from a previous technological disruption to which they have finally adapted and to some degree mastered. This means that even though a "real" top priority might be to abandon a way of doing business that has suddenly become obsolete, there can be great reluctance to make the necessary changes.
- *"Each organizational unit gets a strategic priority."* Many organizations still operate through the existence of various islands or silos, which often operate as walled-off entities that seek to optimize their own operations, not those of the enterprise as a whole. This can lead to each of these entities landing one or two local priorities on the initial transformation priority list. Local appeasement is certainly not the kind of disciplined, enterprise-wide transformation planning focus emphasized throughout this book, and such an approach is likely to jeopardize most such efforts.

However, simply identifying and listing these critical few areas will not be sufficient. Business or functional processes in organizations are typically more complex and interrelated than one might imagine. Clear explanations of the larger context surrounding the realization of projected business value from these priority areas of the strategy is vital to downstream employees. Therefore, these priorities must be given careful thought. Executive-level rationales for these value propositions should have enough situational context to fully inform affected down-organization stakeholders and help them adjust their ongoing operations as best as they can to remain aligned with the new strategies being implemented.

Without divulging competitive secrets and other sensitive information, offer informative descriptions of how the functions or processes that are currently in place will be performed more effectively after Phase One of the transformation is complete. These benefits can be expressed in terms of creating new competitive discriminators, internal operational improvements, substantial economic returns, or a leveraging role in enabling even larger improvements in other areas of the enterprise.

If this more comprehensive explanation pattern is repeated effectively each time a strategic priority is chosen or a strategic objective altered, downstream buy-in for the transformation will be much more likely. Equally important, downstream buy-in will be valuable in sustaining the transformation in the longer term. However, if the transformation is handled in a more secretive way, achieving enterprise-wide buy-in when the "big plan" is finally unveiled will be much more difficult.

As noted earlier, throughout this communication process, sound judgment must be applied to ensure that critical proprietary information, sensitive planning information, or evolving trade secrets are not communicated enterprise wide as part of the process. Enough general information about broad strategic directions, first priorities, and their rationales can be provided internally without disclosing highly sensitive information.

Sustain Alignment Throughout the Transformation

In any major transformation effort, the inner operational workings of the organization will, to some degree, be jolted. Assuming key strategies are going to be changing at the top of the enterprise, how can leaders ensure downstream business processes and goals of the organization can remain in alignment?

If an organization has been effective in its management practices in the past, its overarching enterprise strategies will have been kept reasonably well aligned with downstream business operations and performance goals. The trick is to retain this alignment as the organizational jolting takes place. The kinds of areas that need to be keep in alignment include IT and other technology strategies and architectures, product and line of business strategies, marketing strategies, investment decisions, resource allocations, and group and individual performance plans. If these downstream business dynamics cannot remain in alignment with changes to enterprise-level strategies, excessive harm could come to the business, at least until alignment can be restored.

One way to avoid this problem lies in the effective and timely communication about changes in strategic plans. This communication should be accompanied by the corresponding translation of revised strategic objectives into implications for downstream operations. This can be accomplished more effectively if revised enterprise strategies are discussed early and directly with business managers throughout the organization. Of course, executive managers busy managing a complex transformation cannot be expected to break down the implications of new strategic directions for every aspect of lower level operations. However, most of these lower level managers have a keen understanding of how the present business operates, how value streams are created and delivered, and how business value is captured. These unit level managers are highly resilient individuals who can, when challenged, react well to changing circumstances. Therefore, if executive management is effective in keeping the entire enterprise fully informed as to what is happening at the most strategic levels of the enterprise and why, the organization as a whole will likely prove itself very adept at meeting executive management half way and keeping ongoing business operations in reasonable alignment with changing strategic directions.

This dynamic can work in reverse, as well. As transformation implementation progress moves forward, management can assess the extent which the organization as a whole is adapting to the changes and sustaining alignment. This awareness can help management adjust the pace and scope of the transformation. This might mean increasing the time needed to meet one or more transformation milestones.

Therefore, one of the first key considerations in formulating a transformation plan is how to ensure effective channels are in place to inform key managers throughout the enterprise about ongoing changes in enterprise strategies and the general implications of these changes. This communications process must be continuous.

Build Sustainability into The Transformation Plan

As the transformation moves forward, there will be disruptions and a general unsettling of the entire enterprise. Even if executive management has done well in keeping everyone informed about the rollout of strategic changes, and even if the down-organization groups have done well in their efforts to adjust and keep everything aligned, there will still be general discomfort among personnel throughout the enterprise. This condition could, if not addressed, undermine the sustainability of all that has been accomplished during the transformation.

One way to address this issue longer term gets to the heart of this book – transforming the organization so that, as a matter of course, it becomes more adaptive, agile, and resilient in the face of constant change. Through constant messaging and the celebration of transformation progress, the mindset of the overall enterprise employee population should evolve gradually into a new one. Whether this occurs after Phase One or sometime during or after Phase Three depends on the organization. When it does occur, the new culture will view the company as having evolved into a perpetual state of evolution, a new normal. The new, metaverse-capable organization will view constantly changing competitive conditions as a desirable condition because swift adaptability will have become a core competency and a primary discriminator. "We thrive on change," will have become the new motto.

Of course, not all employees will have bought into this new culture and could find life in the fast-paced, nimble organizational style uncomfortable and stressful. Being able to think on your feet and shift directions quickly, often with little or no guidance, can represent a whole new world for some employees. However, with effort on the part of both the company and employees, this angst can be mitigated on a variety of ways. Here are a few:

- *Ensure an adequate overall staffing level.* One of the key transformation questions that must be answered by management is, "Are we properly staffed for the pace at which we want to operate and the demands we will be placing on employees to be agile and comfortable with frequent changes in assignments?" There is no good way to know this until the transformation starts and the organization accelerates its operational pace. At the earliest signs of widespread burnout, stress, poor morale, or good employees quitting, executive management should consider the likelihood of an understaffing problem. One immediate action that can be taken is the use of "burst staffing," or "just-in-time staffing." This entails making quick hires from a staffing agency for temporary tasking assignments and support for critical project-based initiatives. This helps alleviate some of the stress on permanent employees and buys time for management to study the staffing level problem in more detail to develop a long-term solution, one that brings staffing levels and the preferred method of operation into better alignment.

- *Get the right employees in the right work environments.* All employees have different strengths and weaknesses. Managers and direct supervisors can usually tell which employees perform better under unstructured, dynamic conditions and which perform better under more structured conditions and less frequent rotation from task to task. With this knowledge, managers can help alleviate some of burnout problem by trying to ensure employees are slotted into situations that align better with their capabilities.

- *Adjust training capabilities and strategies.* Sometimes the angst being felt by employees asked to perform under a new method of organizational operation is simply a lack of training. An employee might be a first rate, expert worker in one tasking area and struggle to understand what is expected or how to perform well in other areas. This places an obligation on both the organization and the employee to map out the likely tasking profile for the employee and then ensure that the employee is properly trained for the various possible tasking assignments in that profile.

- *Allow employees time to re-center and re-set.* When any of us are working at a frenetic pace throughout the day every day, we have to find ways pause and get mentally refreshed and re-centered. Otherwise, we become increasingly less effective. This comes back to an effective dialogue between supervisor and employee about ways to optimize employee performance (both quantity and quality) by building into work schedules periods of time when the employee can take a break and recharge. This should be employee-specific. Some might like to take walks around the office or campus. Others might like to read. Others might like to listen to music with their headphones. Some might even like to take a brief nap. In a truly fast-paced environment, this should be allowed (within reason, of course), and be scheduled so it does not slow down a project or otherwise adversely impact important work to which the employee is an important contributor.

The second factor in effective sustainability will be the state-of-the-art enterprise architecture that will inform and help enable the enterprise to retain exceptional communications and adaptability capabilities going forward.

A third important factor that will support the sustainability of Phase One progress will be the empowered governance strategy instituted during Phase One. By empowering downstream managers to make governance decisions on behalf of executive management at the point where the need for the decision arises, the organization will become much more adaptable and resilient. Enhanced organizational nimbleness was, of course, a central objective of the transformation initiative to begin with.

Step 5 – Assign a Respected, Credible Team.

In any kind of major, enterprise-wide initiative, the quality and credibility of the program's leader and team members will determine the outcome, for better or worse. Therefore, a critical first step in launching such a transformation is to assign a highly capable and credible team. In this kind of major transformation you are, to some extent, gambling with the future of the company. Therefore, you must assemble the best team possible to increase the odds in your favor. In particular, the face of the transformation effort, the team leader, should command respect and have credibility throughout the enterprise. These kinds of people exist in small numbers in all organizations, and they are easy to identify. They are natural leaders with a distinctive charisma. They have typically rotated among various leadership positions across the enterprise over several years. With such a person playing the public facing lead role, the transformation will have a significant head start in terms of enterprise-wide buy-in.

Another critical member of the team should the organization's CTO or Chief Enterprise Architect. This is the individual who will be responsible for developing and maintaining the organization's enterprise architecture. Because of the vital role the enterprise architecture will play in enabling the critical capabilities that will define the transformed enterprise (i.e., nimble, quick, adaptable, and metaverse-savvy), he must remain in lockstep with the transformation every step of the way.

Membership should also include at least one highly credible outside consultant who is well versed in these kinds of transformations and metaverse-related issues. Not only will you be relying on the knowledge of this consultant, but the consultant can access the resources from his company to provide you any additional relevant expertise necessary.

One other key member should come from the metaverse gatekeeping team identified in Step 1. This is the team that performed due diligence on the metaverse phenomenon and helped educate both the C-suite and the board on the opportunities and threats they discovered during their investigations. This team will continue its metaverse advisory and educational gatekeeping role. Having a member on the transformation team helps ensure good linkage between the two teams.

The remainder of the team should include well-respected, highly competent members drawn from various lines of business or functions from across the enterprise. These individuals should have magnetic personalities and be viewed as pragmatic employees who can build coalitions and offer common sense solutions to problems. This is because these team members will have two roles to play. First, they will work directly within the transformation effort to perform tasks assigned by the team leader. They will also work informally outside the transformation program itself to build collations to support strategies emanating from the transformation team, to solve problems, to extend and amplify communications efforts by the executive team, and to help stop emerging pockets of resistance before they can gain momentum.

Step 6 – Launch the Transformation.

With all of the necessary groundwork done, it is time to get down to business. Executive management should launch the effort in a highly visible way (such as through video presentations and group gatherings). Give the transformation effort a reasonable, descriptive name (nothing cute). The tone of the rollout announcements should be a blend of good-spirited "we are going to have fun becoming a world-class metaverse organization" messaging, but also somber and serious "we cannot and will not fail" messaging. Ensure that all employees are comfortable in their belief they will be kept in the communications loop every step of the way. This kind of transformation will be difficult to accomplish and will alarm employees throughout the organization, so plan on celebrating enterprise victories along the way with periodic events like "pizza days" or milestone award ceremonies.

Step 7 – Continue the Effort Through Phases 2 and 3.

Transfer seamlessly into Phase 2 and from there into Phase 3. Do not lose momentum after Phase One objectives have been met. Continue to refine those that were not fully completed.

21.3 IMPORTANCE OF "IN THE ZONE" LEADERSHIP FOR TRANSFORMATION

The major technological disruption faced by today's CEOs will require for the entire executive team a level of ongoing preparation, focus, and mastery of the overall challenge that most will never have experienced. For a couple of years perhaps, the management team, and especially the CEO, will have to remain in the enterprise transformation "management zone" if the transformation is to succeed. So, what does that mean?

Stephen Curry once made an NBA record 13 three-pointers in one game. When asked about it later, he said he had been "in the zone" that night: the game seemed to have slowed down, the basket had looked bigger, and he knew every shot was going in automatically.

This book emphasizes in a variety of ways the importance of nimble enterprise governance and strong leadership for companies seeking to operate effectively in the metaverse. The C-suite and the board of directors must remain in lockstep and manage their enterprise as a unified team (never an easy goal to accomplish). However, these terms and phrases do not in themselves convey the full measure of the kind of keenly focused leadership that will be required to lead a company successfully through a transformation to the metaverse. These terms, while valid, can be glossed over easily and, in many instances, ignored.

However, these terms and phrases about strong leadership are critically important within the context of this book. When a CEO is trying to move an organization from its current state to one that is fully capable of thriving in the metaverse era, perhaps even the quantum era, he is in for a serious fight. This transformation effort could easily become a fight for the very life of his organization. He will have to battle strong, entrenched forces within his organization, as well as powerful forces outside the organization. He will have to overcome confusion, acrimony, resistance, competitors, naysayers, inertia, constant changes in his competitive environment, mistakes, blind alleys, technology changes, Black Swans, badgering Wall Street analysts, and even himself, with periodic doubts about what he and his team are trying to do.

To win all of these battles, and ultimately win the enterprise transformation war, an executive team is going to have to be "in the leadership zone" a good deal of the time.

When you are concentrating, focused, and well-prepared, time can appear to slow down. Issues become clearer. You seem to know what is going to happen before it happens. Your actions seem effortless. Your confidence is supreme. You are aware of what is happening, but you do not have to think through your immediate next move; you act instinctively and do not feel as if you are pressing. Your precisely correct actions in critical decision moments take place spontaneously. You own the game and your opponent knows it. Many of you have probably experienced this sensation, even if only briefly, in some endeavor in your own lives.

We would not, of course, expect any management team to be in the zone continuously, or maybe ever at the Curry level. However, we can say this with complete confidence: the winners in the race to become strong competitors in the metaverse era will have management teams that come closer to being "in the zone" far more often than their competitors.

How will they do this?

They will do this through the deep-rooted confidence that comes from exceptional preparation. They will do this through consistent board and C-suite cohesion, with both entities acting seamlessly as one mind with one voice. They will do this through superior knowledge – knowledge of what such a transformation entails, knowledge of what the metaverse is all about, detailed knowledge about what it takes to become a transformed organization, knowledge of how to use advanced technologies for organizational nimbleness enhancement, and the confidence that comes from having at your fingertips instant access to critical decision information available from your state-of-the-art enterprise architecture.

These nimble leaders will have internalized all of this information to the point where the path forward becomes sharply clear and unambiguous, where the next action to be taken at any point in the transformation journey is obvious, and where the decision outcome is predictable and favorable.

Stephen Curry was able to make 13 three-pointers in an NBA game because of intense preparation. He had made thousands of three-pointers before: in the NBA, college, and high school games, during formal and informal practices, and even as a child playing in the driveway. He was meticulously prepared and extremely confident. That made being "in the zone" from time to time a natural state for him.

Consequently, in any contest between organizations, the winner most often will be the unified team that through meticulous preparation finds itself consistently in the management "zone." These teams will win more often because their leaders are supremely confident and because that confidence is grounded in hard work and superb preparation.

Therefore, whenever this book uses such terms as "leadership," "nimble governance," "agile management," or "a unified team acting as one," it is in reference to transforming an enterprise into one that is metaverse ready. This is a challenge that requires the management team to be in or very near the "management zone" as often as possible. The purpose of this book is to help readers become better prepared and more confident in the face of metaverse transformation challenges.

21.4 KEY TAKEAWAYS

- A CEO preparing his organization to possibly launch a metaverse transformation should lead in a hands-on way the execution of the following high-level action steps:
  - Step 1: Obtain internal C-suite agreement on the possible need to transform the organization.
  - Step 2: Obtain backing from the Board of Directors.
  - Step 3: Perform due diligence and make an informed decision.
  - Step 4: Establish Phase One strategies and goals.
  - Step 5: Assign a respected, credible team.
  - Step 6: Formally launch the transformation.
  - Step 7: Continue the effort through Phases 2 and 3.
- The execution of these steps over a two-year period will require a level of executive team preparation and sustained focus few team members have ever experienced.
- See the following chapter for a detailed case study on what these actions might look like.

CHAPTER 22

Case Study in Transforming to the Metaverse

22.1 INTRODUCTION

This chapter brings together the metaverse transformation guidance provided throughout this book and presents it in the form of a hypothetical case study. This is the story of how a company mired in competitive mediocrity and low-margin technology services transformed itself to a state of metaverse readiness and a new beginning. All organizations are different, of course, and each one will have to shape its metaverse transformation plan according to its specific situation. However, this template provides a useful starting point and general model for developing metaverse transformation strategies.

22.2 THE METAVERSE TRANSFORMATION OF GENESIS STAR TECHNOLOGIES

Company Profile

Anne Jones is the CEO of Genesis Star Technologies (GST), a $10 billion government contractor. The company is engaged heavily in the IT outsourcing business, with a focus on federal government contracts, but it performs significant private industry work as well. GST is heavily invested in expensive infrastructure, with six regional data centers to support its IT outsourcing and managed services contracts. Keeping these centers updated with the latest technology, including on-demand resourcing for hardware and software, is an ongoing challenge for the company. GST also provides various lines of general enterprise IT services work, such as systems development, cloud consulting brokerage services, and cyber security consulting and solutions. GST's business performance profile is mediocre due to intense competition in an increasingly commoditized market. The company has a decent backlog of contracts, but almost all of it is low-margin work. Because of its heavy reliance on government contracts, GTS is heavily influenced by changes in federal budgets. Overall, the business outlook for GST is lackluster, and its stock price has been stagnant for the past few years. The 10-member Board of Directors for GST has expressed serious concerns in recent board meetings about the performance of GST and its prospects for the future.

Realizing a Change in Direction is Essential

Anne, who has been CEO for only two years, knows her team needs to develop a plan that will make a real difference in a timely way. One member of her executive team, Joe Smith, Chief Technology Officer (CTO), has been stressing to her for over a year the importance of impending technological and business environment changes resulting from the emergence of what many people are calling "the metaverse." He arranges a small demonstration of one metaverse technology, an AI-based chatbot. Anne is intrigued by the possibilities.

Between Joe talking about the metaverse and the pressure she faces to develop a plan to improve the company's future, Anne hires a consultant from a large management consulting firm to educate her and her team on the metaverse. With the entire executive suite in attendance, the consultant lays out the complete metaverse landscape over a two-day, highly participative offsite meeting. The consultant explains the need to pay less attention to the term "metaverse" and focus instead on the large constellation of converging technology advances and innovations that have given rise to the term.

As a result of the offsite meeting, Anne is convinced that GST must transform to compete effectively in the metaverse. She knows some of the members of the C-suite still do not share that view. To find out what everyone in leadership believes, she decides to bring the transformation issue to a vote. Should GST consider a major transformational effort to compete effectively in the metaverse era? The result of the vote is five in favor of exploring such a transformation and four against. One of the four against thought GST had too many near-term crises facing them to divert attention to something this speculative. (Maybe wait a year and revisit the issue.) Two remained unconvinced the metaverse was defined well enough to take it seriously at this point. The fourth thought GST was one the verge of winning not one *but two* major government IT outsourcing contracts worth a total of more than $350 million. The company should not jeopardize its chances with these large contracts. (Maybe explore the metaverse next year.)

Anne thinks waiting is too risky. She is ready for the company to change directions and wants consensus. She has two options: replace the executives who are not interested in the metaverse transformation or persuade them to change their minds and support the transformation. She chooses the latter course and begins an aggressive educational program for the skeptics. The program includes a variety of components, including the input of additional expert consultants and benchmarking visits to two companies suggested by the consultants as being deeply and effectively into the use of metaverse technologies. Over the course of a few weeks, the accumulating evidence eventually becomes compelling, even to the initial skeptics. Anne takes another vote. The results are nine for serious consideration of an appropriate metaverse transformation strategy, zero against it.

Now, she must convince her board of directors.

Gaining Support from the Board of Directors

Anne's plan to convince the board of the possible need for enterprise transformation takes shape over the following few weeks. The plan she will present, after much debate with her executive team members, is to acknowledge the fact that the company has no real discriminators in a heavily commoditized industry, one where contracts are almost always awarded on low-margin, lowest-cost bids. To change the outlook for GST, her plan is to transform the company into a "metaverse-strong" entity, one that is more streamlined, more agile, more resilient, and able to tout some true discriminators.

Now, it is time to talk to the board.

Anne begins with a private, informal talk with the board chairman. She is pleased to find he is well informed about metaverse issues in general. She relates to him the peril GST faces due to the changes that are about to take place in the company's industry. The chairman understands, but knows he has nine other strong-willed board members to convince. He knows some board members are very conservative and could be dismissive of a term like "the metaverse." Anne shares with the chairman the approach she used to inform and reach consensus with her own executives.

The chairman knows his board members cannot spend as much time as GST's C-suite members spent learning about the metaverse. So he asks Anne to identify the two most compelling sources of information and influence she used to win over her executives. He tells her he will arrange a special board meeting to have these two sources make their cases. In addition, he will present the metaverse challenge to board members as a concern that has been troubling him personally for some time. Employing a little "reverse psychology," he explains to Anne how he will tell the board after the special metaverse educational meeting that he would like for them to agree to invite the GST CEO in and question her on what she is doing in this area. He thinks this strategy will appeal to the inherent nature of the board, which is to give advice and urge action rather than have the CEO come in and tell them what she plans to do without receiving their input first. (Taking the latter approach might get some of them into a defensive posture, which the chairman wants to avoid.)

The metaverse expert briefings do a good job of educating board members. However, the chairman is still not sure everyone is in agreement. He then takes a cue from Anne's approach and posits a statement of strategy for the board to vote on, not for action but simply to get a sense of the group's metaverse opinion. The chairman asks the board members to give their opinions about the following statement: "Genesis Star Technologies is nearing a crossroads wherein it either transforms itself into a metaverse-capable company or it runs the risk of business failure." To the chairman's surprise, the board members are unanimous in accepting the statement as being true. The chairman then agrees to ask Anne Jones to attend an emergency board meeting. The main topic of the meeting is: "What are you doing to prepare Genesis Star Technologies for the risks and opportunities that might arise from the arrival of the metaverse?"

A week later Anne shows up at the meeting as requested. She politely answers questions from board members. As she does, she demonstrates to them, somewhat surprisingly to some, that she is well informed on metaverse issues. She then describes to the board the ongoing metaverse educational sessions she has been having with her team. She agrees with board members that the metaverse is an extremely important topic, one the company has been investigating in depth. She thanks them for their insights and concerns. She then agrees to come back to the next meeting of the board and present her plan for adapting GST to metaverse-era challenges, should further due diligence support such an action.

Anne does come back a few weeks later with a fully developed plan to launch an initiative that could result in a bold transformation action to convert GST into a strong, metaverse-capable, highly competitive organization. Anne takes this opportunity to implore the board to support her in this endeavor because it is going to be a daunting challenge. Moreover, she warns that if her team does go forward with her plan, as she thinks they will, there will be many actions and decisions that will have very short reaction times. The leadership will all need to work together in what promises to be a turbulent, risky period for the company.

After Anne's presentation to the group, three board members make critical points. The first board member tells Anne that if the transformation effort does go forward, there is no way she can develop internally and in a timely way the skills, services, and offerings necessary to begin competing in the metaverse. She is going to have to rely initially on a strong mix of strategic alliances, acquisitions, and the recruitment of a nucleus of personnel experienced in metaverse technologies. Choosing the desired mix of these resources and then closing the deals on the right ones will an extremely complex challenge. Therefore, she needs to bring in an external firm skilled in this kind of match-making and help them quickly understand her preliminary vision. She should do this even before a final decision is made. Anne agrees strongly with the suggestion and promises to make that happen.

The second board member interjects at that point and tells Anne he wants to piggyback on the previous point. He tells her she will soon have two critically important and simultaneous missions. These will be to transform the fundamental nature of the organization while simultaneously running existing, legacy business operations profitably. These two missions will be in constant conflict, which means the metaverse transformation plan could easily jeopardize the future of both. His advice is twofold. As just discussed, pay special attention early on to the metaverse capabilities acquisition process – entering into alliances having the right skills. If this step fails, the overall effort is likely to fail. The second point is to try to keep most of the initial organizational transformation actions relatively simple and with manageable risks. Anne will need to have an early string of successes to establish momentum and enhance confidence, while also maintaining high employee morale and keeping current operations running smoothly. Anne agrees on this point as well.

The third board member asks to be heard. She offers her view that the current GST organization is too bureaucratic and manual in its operations and too process and procedure-driven to succeed in the metaverse. This is the result of the company having built a process-intensive business model around the goal wringing all of the costs and risks possible out of their contract bids in a commoditized market. To succeed with the new plan, she explains, Anne is going to have to focus the initial phase of the transformation on making the company less bureaucratic. It needs to become leaner and more software-driven, with AI-based solutions doing some of the internal work now done by middle management personnel who manage through complex spreadsheets and spend too much time on energy wasters like complicated stage-gate review processes. If AI and algorithms can help with the routine administrative tasks, she advised, the company's human creativity resources can begin to shift to the edge of the enterprise. This would help GST act swiftly and decisively to rapidly moving events and new business opportunities.

Anne thanks all three board members for their insightful and extremely helpful observations. She will ensure all three points become critical considerations when shaping the overall transformation strategy,

With all major board member concerns having been addressed, there is agreement on Anne's proposed plan, and the board pledges its full support. For the time being at least, the board and the GST management team are in sync. They are acting as one. The board's endorsement supports what is likely to become a major GST transformation effort, depending on the outcome of further due diligence.

Reviewing Progress

A few weeks later, Anne reviews her accomplishments so far. She has already informed the C-suite on the metaverse and its implications for GST. She helped the chairman of the board educate board members on the metaverse challenge, and she solidified the board's support for a fundamental change in strategic direction – the transformation of the GST enterprise to become "metaverse-strong." She hired an external firm with skills in acquisitions and alliances. The company has developed a database containing detailed profiles of significant companies operating in the metaverse environment. This Acquisitions and Alliances Team (the A/A Team) is already actively engaged. Finally, Anne and her team have just completed a comprehensive and detailed due diligence exercise and concluded the enterprise transformation is truly needed. They will meet the metaverse disruption head-on rather than allowing it to sideline them. They are ready to begin.

Initial Transformation Launch Plan (Phase One)

After an extensive work session with the executive team, Anne comes back to the team for a presentation and final review of the consolidated and agreed-upon six-point initial launch (Phase One) plan. This is what she presents to the team,

> *[**Note:** This section is from Anne's point of view. She is speaking directly to her team in the following plan presentation, all the way through the "Timeline" section.]*

Anne: Before I go over the details of the plan, I want the team to know we have formulated this plan within the constraints of budget and cash flow realities. We have taken on some additional debt to help fund the transformation, and we are in discussions to sell one more of our data centers, depending on how our current business operations perform during the transformation and how many outsourcing contracts we win. We would like to get out of those low-margin contracts, but we need the cash flow. Of course, if we had more money and other resources we could go faster with our transformation effort. But this plan, as outlined, will have adequate funding.

Second, we are about to face the unprecedented challenge of keeping current operations running as smoothly as possible while simultaneously beginning the process of transforming to the metaverse. As I will discuss in more detail in the empowered governance step of our plan, this will place more responsibility for ongoing operations on our business unit leaders and department heads. I will take the lead in informing each one of them about this new challenge, and I am sure they will respond positively.

Now, let me go over the plan item by item.

1. <u>Assemble a Stellar Team</u>: Working together as an executive team, we have assembled the following ten-person Metaverse Transformation Team.

   - *Team Lead:* Our team leader will be Sylvia Edmonds, currently VP, Contracts for GTS. Silvia is a 20-year employee who is widely-respected and well-liked across GTS. She has held other senior positions in GTS, and is known as a gregarious, pleasant person grounded in deep technical and management expertise and capabilities. Sylvia is known for her ability to take on new and complex assignments and execute them flawlessly. She is a natural leader and an obvious choice.

- *Lead Consultant:* We have brought on board a well-respected consultant from the Boston Consulting Group. He has current expertise in metaverse trends and issues, as well as a solid background in organizational design trends and enterprise transformations. He has assured me his company has deep expertise in metaverse-related developments and trends, and he can access those resources as needed. This consultant will also work closely with the A/A Team to help analyze any alliance or acquisition opportunities the team might propose.
- *CTO:* As an integral part of the overall Phase One effort, our CTO will launch a project to create Phase One functional and technical requirements for a new enterprise architecture. Working with our newly appointed GTS Chief Architect, he will launch and manage the enterprise architecture development effort in parallel with the overall transformation initiative.
- *Metaverse Gatekeeping Team Liaison:* The small metaverse gatekeeping team we formed at the beginning of the educational and due diligence phases of this process will continue in an advisory capacity to the transformation team. The current leader of that team will serve directly on the transformation team to maintain linkage with the gatekeeping team.
- *At-Large Members:* To round out the team, we have chosen five people with impressive records of accomplishments and desirable personality traits for the team. These five include a software design expert from one of our business units who is well-known both inside and outside the company, and is familiar with deep tech ventures; the GTS VP for Marketing and Business Development; the Group Manager for all Department of Defense IT services contracts; and the VP of Human Resources. The deputy managers for the Marketing and HR organizations will fill in for the VPs during Phase One of this project, maybe longer. We also brought back a retired former employee and former Naval Admiral, Mike Evans, who was very popular and widely admired when he was with the company. He still does consulting work. Mike has deep expertise in a wide variety of digital technologies and important trends, and understands how they are being used in enterprises. He also has an extensive network of contacts that could be quite useful to the company downstream in this transformation.

2. <u>Establish Phase One Strategies and Goals</u>. As you know, our entire executive team has been working hard to develop an initial list of strategic objectives and business priorities to be addressed beginning with the launch of this initiative. This list will be given to Sylvia and the Metaverse Enterprise Transition Team for execution and management oversight. The team will report on progress and issues to the Executive Council each Friday morning in person at a 10:00 a.m. stand-up meeting. Significant problems or issues will be reported to me or to our COO as they occur. The out-of-the-gate list of strategic priorities include the following:

- *Launch Work on New GST Offerings and Capabilities Portfolio:* Our COO will form and lead a new GST core business offerings team comprised of GST group leaders, strategic planners, business development staff, and the A/A Team. The charter of this critical initiative is to develop the first phase of a new portfolio of metaverse-focused skills, solutions, products, and service offerings. These are products and services we must develop to become metaverse-capable and extract our company from the commodity trap we are presently in. For example, AI, machine learning, and augmented reality-based solutions and services will be among the initial priorities. The deliverable from this team will be a high-level mock-up of a new, metaverse-focused solutions and services portfolio, along with major win themes, solution models, examples, catch phrases, and other marketing material. From this deliverable, the most attractive options will be selected for the immediate investment of development resources and possible strategic alliances.
- *Pilot Our Empowered Governance Strategy:* I will schedule a series of meetings with senior group and division managers across GST to go over our new empowered governance strategy. In this meeting, I will explain expectations for these managers in terms of exerting leadership and making decisions locally that would typically be made either by me or other senior staff members in the current organizational model. This will be the first major step toward a more empowered, decentralized, and networked organizational structure.
- *Develop a Plan For Employee Morale.* We are committed to doing all we can to keep employee morale high as the transformation is launched and moves forward. Our HR Manager will assemble a team to outline a plan for achieving this goal. Our employees need to know the next

two years will be stressful and we understand that. We will explain to them they will have challenging but not overwhelming work assignments, that we will be tolerant of mistakes, and that our managers and supervisors will be available to them at all times to discuss any work-related issues or concerns they might have. During the first year, we will do our best to launch initiatives and projects that have a high probability of success and reasonable risk profiles.

- *Launch Central IT Services Transformation:* Our CIO will initiate immediate action to begin to transform our central IT services organization into a new structure, one better designed to support our more networked and less bureaucratic GST organization. As this moves forward, the CIO will add at least six new employees skilled in metaverse-era technologies and methods. He will attempt to get a good cross section of skills, including advanced algorithms, AR/VR, edge computing, AI/machine learning, 3D reconstruction, and blockchain. These areas were selected after coordinating with the team working on the updated portfolio of product and service lines for GST.

- *Identify Powerful Metaverse-Related Use Cases:* Our COO will work with division managers across GTS to identify two internal and two customer-based use case opportunities where metaverse-era technologies, especially AI, might be applied effectively to improve existing operations or enhance proposed solution designs. These initiatives will hopefully be so impressive in the results delivered others will want to follow suit.

- *Develop Edge Computing Pilot:* Our CIO will select an appropriate system or technology deployment, either existing or planned, that will be a good candidate for a model edge computing-based solution. The goal is to develop a solution that can be used as a guide for future edge computing opportunities. We expect this to be a small, relatively simple pilot so we can be pretty sure of success and gain some goodwill and buy-in as a result. In addition to benefiting our organization internally, edge computing consulting and services is likely to become a business offering for us.

- *Identify Platform Pilots:* Our COO will work with group and division managers across GST to select two programs or projects that can be converted to a platform-based organizational and management approach. Under this approach, the teams assigned to these platform-based initiatives will be given unprecedented authority to make decisions, design and deliver solutions, and invest resources as they see fit. They will be rewarded based on delivered results and project success, not the processes or methods used. We expect the platform-based approach, coupled with the empowered governance action item, will accelerate us toward a more networked, nimble, quick-learning organization.

3. <u>Continuation of the Metaverse Advisory Team (MAT)</u>: This small team, with rotating membership, was designated initially as our metaverse "eyes and ears." It will continue, reporting to the Transformation Team Leader. This team will continue to provide regular updates on important metaverse developments and trends. In addition to internet research, the team will visit with consultants, vendors, universities, alliance partners, and even willing competitors to gather information and exchange ideas on metaverse trends and implications.

4. <u>Stage Setting and Communications</u>: To set the stage for official Phase One launch, we will modify our mission and vision statements to reflect our fundamental change in direction. Eventually, when Phase One of the new enterprise architecture system is in place, these two vitally important statements will be documented in this central repository for maximum visibility, along with explanatory context. Also, we are creating an enterprise-wide communications plan that will include informational videos, video conferences, large group meetings for all employees, and Q&A sessions with division and other senior managers. Both myself and the COO will attend as many of these meetings as possible. At least one of us will be at every meeting. The communications process will be continuous, offering detailed explanations to downstream managers on evolving strategies and their implications for relevant components and company business operations. For message impact, we will work with a contractor to have me appear at the largest initial central group meeting as a hologram. Over the top? Maybe. But the management team thinks it will be effective.

5. <u>Launch</u>: Phase One of our transformation initiative launch officially using the communications channels I just mentioned on the morning of October 23, 2023. A schedule of all information sessions will be provided on that date.

6. <u>Press On with Phases Two and Three</u>: Based on what I know will be successful execution of Phase One, we will then transition seamlessly into Phase two and later to Phase 3."

The Timeline

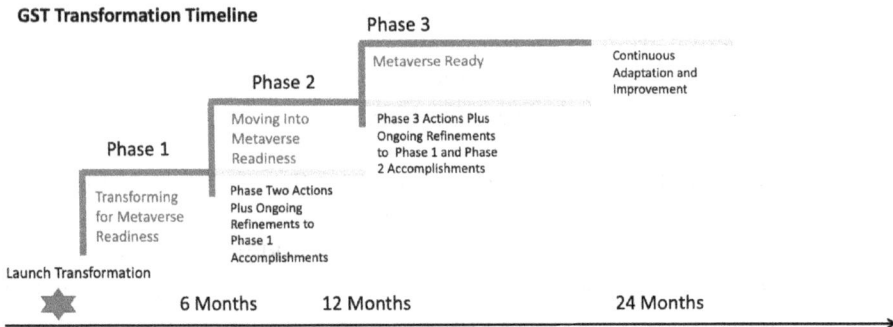

GST Transformation Timeline

Phase 3

Metaverse Ready

Continuous Adaptation and Improvement

Phase 2

Moving Into Metaverse Readiness

Phase 3 Actions Plus Ongoing Refinements to Phase 1 and Phase 2 Accomplishments

Phase 1

Transforming for Metaverse Readiness

Phase Two Actions Plus Ongoing Refinements to Phase 1 Accomplishments

Launch Transformation

6 Months   12 Months   24 Months

FIGURE 22.1 Multi-phased timeline for GTS metaverse transformation

As this timeline chart shows, Phase One projects will be new, high priority initiatives, while Phases 2 and 3 will involve a blend of new projects and ongoing refinements and extensions to previously launched projects, as needed. After Phase 3 has been formally completed, GTS will have become a highly adaptive enterprise and able to adjust perpetually, as needed, to ongoing changes in its competitive environment.

Results After Six Months

All of the initial plan actions were to have had their major milestones met within a six-month period. As of that date, this much had been accomplished:

- *Alliances and Acquisitions:* Using advanced AI and data analytics methods, the A/A Team had developed a very useful database of metaverse-capable firms of all sizes that could become alliance or acquisition candidates for GST. Among the attributes collected for each firm were size, primary products or offerings, a composite index of success attributes (such as profitability), likely fit with the GST evolving mission definition (such as target market sectors), and the likelihood of being amenable to a deal. Discussions are underway with multiple companies and numerous promising opportunities have already been identified.
- *Directional Statements.* GST now has new mission and vision statements, as well as supporting context and planned actions. These were communicated to the entire organization using a variety of communication channels. They were also captured in the first operable version of the solution framework being established for a new enterprise architecture.

- *Communications.* The initial round of enterprise-wide communications was completed outlining the strategic initiatives underway, and a new round is to follow the closeout of the first six-month (Phase One) period just concluded. This new round will also preview the imminent launch of Phase Two. The CEO's entrance as a hologram in the initial kick-off meeting for Phase One was a success. Two of the completed Phase One projects will be demonstrated at the kickoff sessions for Phase Two. There will also be a multimedia update on the new GST enterprise architecture.
- *Central IT Transformation.* The CIO has developed a new structure for central IT services, one better designed to support the new GST organization. The new structure will be more widely distributed across the GTS user community and well-networked for efficiency and speed. New employees with important metaverse skills have been hired and a "Metaverse Innovations Lab" has been created. This will be an open lab for use by internal and external entities to conduct experiments and do pilot projects. Additional actions are underway to expand implementation of this strategy. This includes communications with vendors who might be interested in showcasing their products in the lab.
- *Enterprise Architecture.* The CTO worked with the Chief Architect to develop first-cut functional and technical requirements for a new enterprise architecture. A project team was formed and work continues on the architecture. A Phase One beta version was rolled out and used to showcase the new GST Mission and Vison statements, along with relevant context information. The team feels good about being able to integrate AI into the access mechanisms for the architecture to help users navigate it more quickly to find the precise information desired. A few powerful, AI-based conversational products are being analyzed with the help of a systems integrator partner, who will help with the design of the EA framework.
- *Use Cases.* Two internal and two customer-based use-case opportunities were selected as potential proof-of-concept projects where metaverse-era technologies might be effectively applied. Work is underway on all four initiatives.
- *Empowered Governance.* Anne did hold a series of meetings with senior group and division manager across GST where she explained her new Empowered Governance strategy. She also detailed her expectations for these managers to assume responsibility for exerting leadership and making decisions locally that would typically be made by the CEO and her staff in the prior organizational model. Their prompt acceptance of this new approach will be vital to keeping current operations running while

the transformation effort continues. This was the first major step toward a more empowered, decentralized, and networked organizational structure. The change was well received by the subordinate managers.

- *Edge Computing Pilot.* The CIO did select an appropriate planned project for an edge-computing-based solution. Work on that project is underway.
- *Platform Pilots.* The two projects selected by the COO for conversion to a platform-based approach have been converted and appear to be making excellent progress. The executive team is receiving positive feedback about this approach and more platform-based projects and programs are under active development.
- *Metaverse Gatekeeping Team.* The metaverse "eyes and ears" team for GTS is functioning very well and producing valuable results. The team is now linked to the new Metaverse Innovations Lab in an advisory capacity.
- *New Offerings Portfolio.* Working with the A/A Team, the initial mock-up of the slate of metaverse skills, solutions, and services that GST seeks to develop as major lines of business has been completed. The marketing materials are impressive, but the board member who had forewarned of this challenge had been right; GTS is going to have to rely even more heavily than initially planned on alliance partners, consultants, and new hires to create and deliver these products and services. Two new offerings were selected as priorities and work is underway to make them a reality.

Phase 2 Launch

After a review of all accomplishments during this initial six-month start-up phase, the CEO launched Phase Two. In this phase, each of the initiatives outlined in the original five-point plan will continue to make progress. However, the transformation still has a long way to go and there are vital areas that must addressed if progress is to be maintained and schedules met. With that in mind, the Metaverse Leadership Team coordinated with the executive team to work out budgets and secure resource allocations. With that process completed, the Transformation Manager launched new initiatives in the following focus areas:

- *Conduct in-depth benchmarking reviews of selected deep tech companies.* Some of these more specialized and (to some degree) unique companies or ventures will be evaluated simply for educational purposes. Anne wants to know how they are organized, how they operate, and what makes them successful. Anne is convinced that emulating companies that are already operating successfully in a metaverse-like environment is a good way to for

GST to navigate its own metaverse transformation. In addition, Anne and her team might choose one or two of these companies to invest in. The idea is not only to share in some of the financial gains these companies might make if they are successful, but to learn from them faster and more effectively by actually working with them.

- *Review ways to address staffing issues as the transformation continues.* The CEO and the VP for Human Resources are aware of a looming problems in staffing. Some existing skills are going to be no longer needed, while many new skills must be acquired. Under the leadership of the HR Deputy Director, now filling in for the HR VP who is temporarily serving on the Transformation Team, HR will develop a master strategy to (1) minimize the effect of changes on existing staff through retraining or cross-training opportunities, and (2) minimize the addition of new permanent staff when acquiring new skills. The goal is to achieve Objective 2 by using on-demand staffing firms, temporary employees, consulting employees, and other options.
- *Plan the initial company-wide rollout of Version 1 of the new enterprise architecture, featuring an AI-based conversational use capability.* This will be Version One of what will eventually become a full-fledged, completely populated, current, accurate, and easily accessible planning tool and information repository for the entire enterprise. The initial release is to get everyone accustomed to its look and feel. There will be enough information in the initial phase to motivate employees to try it out. That way, they can grow along with the EA as it evolves and be completely comfortable using it as it evolves into a mature product.
- *Plan the first celebration event.* Anne and her team are delighted by the amount of progress made during Phase One of the transformation. To celebrate this progress, the company will hold a celebratory "pizza day" event for all offices and campuses. During the event, to be broadcast live via video hookups, Anne will present Outstanding Performance awards to the edge computing team, one of the platform teams, and the Chief Architect for a superior job in getting Phase One of the new enterprise architecture up and running in time to demonstrate it to employees across the company and to the board. She will also thank GST employees for keeping ongoing operations running smoothly and in alignment with critical strategic and business objectives as the first phase of the transformation ran its course. This is an important action because all GST employees need to know good progress is being made, both in keeping ongoing operations running and achieving initial transformation goals. Finally, as a show of appreciation for

the hard work performed enterprise-wide during Phase One, every GST full-time employee receives a two thousand dollar bonus.

• *Create a Quantum Computing Demonstration Center.* The Metaverse Innovations Lab is already proving to be a popular attraction for employees, potential customers, and potential alliance partners. GST is being credited for its forward thinking in this area and hopes to leverage this positive image to create constructive relationships with other organizations having a special interest in metaverse technologies, including a major university. The creation of a new quantum computing demonstration center is expected to yield similar benefits.

Results After Two Years

Over the next 18 months, the GST executive team continued to make progress in the transformation effort, solidifying gains from Phase One and adding new tasks and goals for Phases Two and Three.

Now, two years after initial launch, GST has been substantially transformed and the leadership team considers the company metaverse ready. The company is already competing for contracts using four of its newly-added metaverse-related or enhanced offerings, while simultaneously honoring legacy contracts and continuing to compete for select contracts in legacy markets to add to its cash flow. Three of the new offerings were the result of new alliance relationships. One was developed through the acquisition of a startup that had a capability in the federal government's use of blockchain-based solutions. However, the management team knows it is going to have to quicken the pace of hiring people with the right blend of metaverse skills. The supply is thin and competition for valued skills is intense.

Staff training and redevelopment programs are underway and working well. Employee morale has been high throughout the transformation process. The new culture (embracing change) is not completely where it needs to be yet, but culture change always takes time.

The investments the company had previously made in its large managed services centers around the country are still producing returns because of the lengthy periods of several legacy IT outsourcing contracts. However, active discussions are underway to sell three of the six centers to conventional IT outsourcing companies.

Progress toward a more decentralized, networked, and nimble organization has been given a boost through a combination of the growing use of platform models, the impact of the empowered governance strategy, and a completely transformed IT services organization.

Alliances with two deep tech companies are working well, especially with respect to knowledge transfer. The feedback from across the company has been very positive. The new enterprise architecture is a resounding success. GST has patented the EA's AI-enabled conversational technology framework and is in negotiations with multiple companies to jointly license and offer the framework and related consulting services as an integrated product offering. GTS will have other market discriminators in place soon, and Anne feels it is fully capable of competing with anyone in its market space. The board of directors is impressed and pleased by the rate of progress and more favorable outlook for the future.

A Moment of Reflection

In a quiet moment of reflection, Anne Jones thinks back over two years to how fortunate she was to have had one person, CTO Joe Smith, finally convince her to think more seriously about the metaverse. This coincided with the board applying pressure to do something different to get GST out of the low-margin, commoditized IT services business environment it had become mired in. Had those two forces not happened simultaneously and at the right time, GST would most likely have lost extremely valuable time in transforming itself for a more successful future. Now, Anne feels GST is far ahead of her former competitors, most of whom are now just beginning the process to transition into metaverse-ready enterprises.

Anne snaps out of here reverie. She realizes she has an important meeting scheduled with the CEO of a large, deep-pockets company interested in touring the newly completed Quantum Computing Demonstration Center. The CEO of this company is seriously considering a quantum computing-based joint venture with GTS, one that could substantially accelerate the growth of both companies.

22.3 CONCLUDING THOUGHTS ON THE CASE STUDY

This case study provides a realistic example of how an organization can prepare for and execute a successful transformation to the metaverse. Genesis Star Technologies was in a difficult competitive position. Business performance was lackluster and its future outlook was not promising. In addition, the board of directors was placing increasing pressure on the CEO to do something to improve both short-term performance and the future outlook for the company. The strategic challenge Anne and GST faced at the beginning of this case study was how to compete more effectively in its commoditized, low-margin, legacy business. That strategic focus was about to change. The arrival of the metaverse was the catalyst for that change in direction.

The company was fortunate to have one employee, the CTO, who understood the value of the metaverse. He believed, based on his lengthy experience and expertise in digital technologies, that this development was important. He was persistent in communicating this to his CEO, which was a part of his job as the lead technology gatekeeper for the company.

GST was also fortunate to have a CEO who, after repeated appeals from the CTO to take a closer look at the metaverse, was able to sense something important was in the air. Her instincts told her the CTO was right, that the metaverse was real and presented a mix of threats and opportunities she could not ignore. After all, who could ignore the continued global fascination with all those AI-driven chatbots? The risk of inaction was simply too high to accept, and she would not be reluctant to make major changes, especially if doing so might save the company.

The first big metaverse transformation hurdle for GST had been overcome. At the most senior level of the company, there was acceptance of the fact that the metaverse was real, important, and required serious, high priority attention.

The GST CEO knew that significant movement away from the company's status quo could not be achieved if the overall governance structure was not supportive. She worked the governance alignment issue diligently until the Board of Directors and all C-suite executives were in complete agreement. They would support such a strategy if further due diligence indicated it was the best path forward.

Making the Right Moves

After performing a comprehensive due diligence assessment of the likely implications of the metaverse for GST, the decision was made to launch the transformation. From that point forward, the CEO and her team made all the right moves and executed a successful transformation. They were particularly successful in the following areas.

- They assigned a well-respected team to lead the effort, with support from carefully selected outside entities having metaverse and enterprise transformation expertise and contacts.
- They broke the transformation down into manageable phases. They knew Phase One had to address priority business needs, but it also needed to include some easy wins to help build momentum. They achieved this mix.
- They knew the central overriding goal of the transformation had to be a more streamlined, networked, and nimble organization, attributes they captured in new vision and mission statements for GST. They then took several actions to begin to move in this strategic direction.
- For example, to help move in the direction of a more networked and nimble organization, they implemented a delegated governance strategy, wherein lower level managers would make many decisions formerly made only at the C-suite level.
- To further advance toward a more networked, nimble organization, they began the process of using empowered, fast-acting platform teams, as opposed to permanent organizational structures, for various projects.
- They knew that the development of a state-of-the-art enterprise architecture had to be among the initial priorities. The EA would be the critical central repository of information that would support and help guide the transformation through some very complex challenges, then support sustained performance post-transformation. Because they went back to the drawing board and built the new EA on such advanced technologies as AI and machine learning, they were able ultimately to license their EA platform, along with related consulting services, and add the package to their business offerings portfolio.
- They knew that the current central IT organization lacked the skills, structure, and methods of operation to support the target organizational model. They began immediately the complex process of transforming central IT with the understanding that the IT organization had to continue to support ongoing, current business operations while simultaneously transforming to a new structure and service model.
- They knew personnel issues would be complex and difficult, and they formed a team under the HR VP to make sure to address this challenge head-on and keep working it throughout the transformation, which they did.
- They knew that when adopting selected metaverse technologies for internal use, targeting powerful use cases could make an enormous difference in fostering enterprise-wide buy-in for the transformation. Therefore, that became an early focus in metaverse technology adoption and assimilation.

- GST executives knew they had to work continuously to keep current business operations running smoothly enterprise-wide while simultaneously transforming the overall company. They never allowed one responsibility get too far ahead of the other.
- They knew they lacked the skills and experience to succeed in the metaverse during the early phases of the transformation, so they placed an emphasis on forming alliances, hiring staff, and carefully acquiring metaverse-strong resources.
- They knew the powerful public relations and credibility impact such factors as the ability to see and try out metaverse technologies could have. Therefore, they created a metaverse innovations lab or factory, and began work on a quantum computing demonstration center.
- They knew they needed to celebrate wins all along the way, including Phases Two and Three, which they did in a variety of ways to keep the celebrations interesting and relevant, such as giving team awards both for outstanding transformation contributions and excellence in ongoing business operations, as well as giving all employees three rounds of bonuses.

22.4 A FAIR QUESTION

A fair question for the reader to ask at this point is as follows:

GST was in a difficult, low-margin industry with mediocre prospects for the future when it decided to implement a major transformation strategy. But what about a company that is already performing well with excellent prospects for the future? Why would they want to risk a good thing by undergoing a difficult and unpredictable transformation to the metaverse?

This question can be answered with another question: Is it better for a company performing at a mediocre level to be blindsided by a technological revolution than a company doing well? Being late to recognize and respond to this major disruption would hurt either company, but the company doing well would have potentially much more to lose. It is understandable the company doing well would be more hesitant to change, at least in the near term. Both companies could be impacted in similar ways by the metaverse disruption, depending on their markets and industries. Therefore, it is a prudent and appropriate action even for companies performing well in the current market to take precautionary actions now. Their entire competitive environment could easily be changed in the near future.

For example, few companies know more about the metaverse than the company formerly known as Facebook and now known as Meta. The CEO of that company, which was doing quite well at the time, was not reluctant to change strategic directions, investing billions and changing the company's vision and name in the process. This was done in response to what he believed to be a fast-moving major technological revolution, the metaverse. This instance shows highly successful companies are already deciding to engage in organizational transformations to be better prepared to optimize metaverse opportunities and minimize metaverse threats.

The Risks of Doing Nothing

We can see how the actions taken by GST might seem intimidating or unnecessary to many managers. True, some organizations in certain industries might not require such a comprehensive approach, at least not in the near term. (Remember the carpet manufacturer in Dalton, Georgia?) However, for most organizations, an approach similar to the one reflected in this case study should be considered, and soon.

Doing nothing in the face of the converging array of technological innovations making headlines and gaining more acceptance every day is a risky posture. At the very minimum, an organization should form a small team dedicated to monitoring and assessing the metaverse phenomenon on a continuing basis and providing high-quality, regular briefings to the executive team, much like the GST CTO provided to his CEO. The information gathering and analysis by this small team should be thorough and include

- visits to deep tech ventures, vendors, and universities
- inviting qualified and reputable consultants
- reading and suggesting books on this topic
- staying current with relevant articles on the metaverse by highly credible sources, such as the major business consulting firms and recognized industry analysis groups.

To go beyond doing this minimum, most organizations could benefit from additional modest steps, such as the following, based on the situational context of a particular organization:

- Pilot selected metaverse technologies, most notably AI, machine learning, and augmented reality, targeting these pilots to powerful use cases within the organization.

- Pilot the use of the organizational platform approach to resourcing and managing a project or a major customer support structure.
- Pilot an edge computing solution.
- Consider testing an empowered governance approach in a selected business area.
- Take a serious look at advanced enterprise architecture concepts and best practices and consider ways to begin to address this critical need (even if you do not plan to go down the transformation path right away).
- Consider hiring consultants to develop a more conversational familiarity with metaverse concepts and realities.

Don't Get Blindsided

As mentioned often in this book, no one should let the name "metaverse" get in the way of understanding the more critical point. There is an impressive constellation of digital and quantum innovations, such as AI and quantum algorithms, converging synergistically with each other and important current technologies, such as cloud computing. This convergence has the power to change entire industries in a very short time. In fact, this is already happening in ways that are affecting many sectors of the global economy. These changes will continue to happen in ways and at speeds that will surprise most of us, most likely blindsiding countless organizations in the process. This same pattern has happened with previous technology-driven disruptions, such as the Internet and the smart phone, and will probably happen this time. The hope of this author is that readers of this book will not be blindsided and will prosper in the metaverse.

Index

www.ingramcontent.com/pod-product-compliance
Lightning Source LLC
Chambersburg PA
CBHW061338210326
41598CB00035B/5819